Understanding Old Age

Understanding Old Age

critical and global perspectives

Gail Wilson

SAGE Publications

London • Thousand Oaks • New Delhi

First published 2000

SAGE Publications Ltd
6 Bonhill Street
London EC2A 4PU

SAGE Publications Inc
2455 Teller Road
Thousand Oaks, California 91320

SAGE Publications India Pvt Ltd
32, M-Block Market
Greater Kailash – I
New Delhi 110 048

British Library Cataloguing in Publication Data

A catalogue record for this book is available from the British Library

ISBN 0 7619 6011 2
ISBN 0 7619 6012 0 (pbk)

Library of Congress catalog card number available

Typeset by Keystroke, Jacaranda Lodge, Wolverhampton
Printed in Great Britain by Biddles Ltd, Guildford, Surrey

To the memory of Rachel Richardson and James Richardson, my grandparents, Denise Shaw and Betty Beard.

CONTENTS

LIST OF FIGURES AND TABLES

ACKNOWLEDGEMENTS

Many people have contributed to this book and first of all I would like to thank all those older men and women who gave their time in interviews and informal encounters over the last ten years, particularly in Brent and Barnet (London), Montaigu-de-Quercy (France), Reykjavik (Iceland) and the travelling Gujarati elders en route between India and the USA. In terms of content, the book would have been impossible to write without the outstanding collections in the British Library of Political and Economic Science, and my thanks go to Rupert Wood, Social Policy liaison representative, and all his colleagues who have been so consistently helpful.

In Australia, more thanks to Joan Vipond and Graham Andrews for their hospitality and intellectual contributions, to Penny Hebbard and the bush walkers in Canberra for doing ageing differently, and to Michael Fine, Peter Saunders, Diane Gibson and colleagues at the Social Policy Research Centre, University of New South Wales and the Australian Institute of Health and Welfare, Canberra.

So many colleagues, relatives and friends have given support, made suggestions, taken part in discussions, found literature and processed data. To those who are not named my apologies and thanks. At the London School of Economics I owe many debts to current and former colleagues and students: Claire Collyer, Helen Cylwik, Tanvi Desai, Yasmin Gunaratnam, Sun Woo Hong, Kumiko Iwai, Junichi Izumi, Dagmar Lorenz-Meyer, Junko Otani, David Piachaud, Sally Sainsbury, Marion Williams and Jane Pugh who drew the figures. In other countries I would like to thank Yukiko Yukawa and Natsuko Masuda for inspiration over the years, Pierre Verry, Harikrishna Majmumdar and Premlata Majmumdar for wisdom on ageing, Matthias Haldorsson for hospitality and enlightenment and Lydia Potts and Angela Grotheer for being inspiring colleagues and wonderful hosts.

CHAPTER 1

AN AGEING WORLD

One of the great successes of modern times is that in worldwide terms, more people are living longer, there are fewer early deaths and there is greater prosperity. Social security systems have allowed millions of older men and women to add a new life stage ('life after work' or post retirement) to the old model of youth, work and decay. In developing countries, longer lives mean older men and women go on working and contributing to economic and social development in ever growing numbers. If jobs are available, output is higher and there is the possibility of greater life-time productivity. This is especially true if the unpaid work done by older people is also taken into account. At present, only paid work is counted in world economic totals; however, reforms are on the way and soon many countries will have statistics for unpaid work as well as paid work (Murgatroyd and Neuburger, 1997). In most parts of the world the numbers of people of working age are increasing. They are usually better educated and healthier than in the past and their productivity may be higher. The population over pension age is growing (see Chapter 3), but the labour force is growing faster and there are no demographic reasons for an ageing crisis for many years to come. Democracy, which has often accompanied population ageing, raises the chances that wealth will be more widely shared.

Fear and rationality

Any such up-beat message about ageing will seem hollow to many people. Why be positive about more old people? Even the positive aspects of living longer are sometimes questioned, if living longer means being old for longer. This is not surprising because the fear of old age is part of our heritage and pervades our societies and our policies, as well as many aspects of our personal relationships with elders – or the lack of them. On the other hand, as inheritors of the Enlightenment, most Europeans and North Americans subscribe to ideals of equality, the rights of man (which theoretically now includes woman), freedom, and self-determination for all. Our ethical position is that elders (however we define them) have the same rights to a good quality of life as other adults. (Children still have fewer rights, though their position is changing.) In practice we know that equal rights for all are hard to come by. We live with the knowledge that most elders are disadvantaged in some way, and we (and they), take this as normal or even 'natural'.

Hopefully, readers of this book will already be convinced that the solution to old age is not to say, as one student announced in class, 'I think you should just line them up and shoot them'. Of course, he said he was joking, but was he? He was certainly expressing his own alienation from older people and the very deep fear of death and ageing that most of us feel. Given that ageing is an emotive subject for most Westerners, avoidance is one response. In America more and more people are involved in 'looking after' old people – in keeping them out of the way:

> According to this perspective, those performing society's 'dirty work' with respect to the elderly would include legislators, social workers, Social Security administrators, nursing home entrepreneurs, psychiatrists and interpreters of pension guidelines to name just a few categories. These specialists in elderly care are akin to undertakers who protect Americans from their dead, only in this case the 'loved one' is conscious. (Williamson et al., 1982: 236)

The urge to help, sanitize or control those we fear, or who inspire disgust or loathing, has long been identified as one aspect of care. Carroll Estes (1979) has called us 'the aging enterprise' – we who research, write about or provide services for older people. How is it, she asks, that we make a living from 'helping' people who have probably not asked to be helped, and who may have no way of opposing our well meaning attentions. This is a fair question once we recognize that even the best intentions can have harmful outcomes: for example, care can always be interpreted as surveillance or labelling; and calling people 'old' when they are merely retired from paid work stigmatizes them unnecessarily.

There is also another ageing enterprise which is not there to help elders at all. The aim is rather to help the young fight off the 'burden' of the 'unproductive' old. Authors writing for this enterprise with titles like *Born to Pay: The New Politics of Aging in America* (Longman, 1987) or 'Why the Graying of the Welfare State Threatens to Flatten the American Dream – or Worse' (Howe, 1997) specialize in doom and gloom predictions of rising tides of crinklies and crumblies overwhelming social security systems (see Health Advisory Service, 1983) and dragging down national ability to innovate and compete. Perhaps even more pernicious, there are authors such as Callahan (1995) who present carefully reasoned philosophical arguments why money should not be spent on prolonging 'natural' lifespan. They represent the intellectual face of common-sense ageism which devalues older men and women and their place in society.

> For policy purposes, the group characteristics of the elderly are as important as their individual variations. Those characteristics legitimate age based entitlements and welfare programs as well as social policies designed to

help the elderly maintain social respect. They could also be used to sanction a limit on those entitlements. (Callahan, 1995: 24)

And so to deny lifesaving, or even life enhancing, treatment to older men and women on the basis of age.

It is therefore fair to ask where this book stands. If writing about old age can itself run the risk of being ageist and may intensify the disadvantages of older people by labelling them as different from other adults, what can be the ethical justification of the book? And if ageing is contested, what is ageing and who are the old? There can be no definitive answers to these questions. There is bound to be dispute in a controversial and emotive area of understanding and knowledge. However, this book aims to improve knowledge of ageing and older people and so is a contribution to the first ageing enterprise. The following chapters oppose ideas that older people have 'had a good innings', or reached the end of their 'natural' lifespan, or that they are unproductive. I have assumed that later life is worth studying for its own sake, even though there are times when it is vital to assert a common humanity across all age groups. I also assume a value position that policies and practice should work towards giving old and young full citizenship rights and the 'capabilities they need to flourish' in Sen's terminology (Sen, 1993). Manifestly, there are few societies in the world where the majority of older women and men are flourishing and where old age is a time to look forward to, but this is no reason to assume that the disadvantages of later life are 'natural' or fixed. A decline in strength and a changing physical appearance may be inevitable in old age, but the degree and meaning of change are very variable. The actual impact of physiological changes depends on whether the environment is hostile to disabilities or supportive, as the disability lobby has so clearly shown (Morris, 1993). The cross-cultural approach to the study of ageing shows that most of the attributes of old age are culturally determined. For example, it is not 'natural' for older men or women to live in poverty, or to take care of grandchildren, or to spend time in religious contemplation, but it is easy to believe it is if we are locked into one culture only.

A principled stand against manifestations of ageism (Bytheway, 1995; Palmore, 1990) or the socially manufactured aspects of disadvantage is not the same as the certainty that the values of Western social gerontology are the only moral position. Katz (1996), for example, implies that all Western gerontologists are attempting to impose their own ways of seeing older people across the world. He quotes Cohen:

> Both the 'universal' old person claimed by gerontology and the Western-derived agenda cited to solve her or his problem maintain a utopian stance, demanding state patronage incompatible with local economies and legitimating the state's shrugging of its shoulders. (Cohen, 1992 quoted in Katz, 1996: 3)

But there is no universal old person (see Chapter 2) and although collective action of some sort is essential for late life support, collectivities differ and countries are short of good policies.

The fact that this book is about old age does not mean that old age exists in any fixed or generalizable form. In a globalizing world, the meaning of old age is changing across cultures and within countries and families. Changes in all aspects of old age have been so great that Bourdelais, for example, says that popular understanding has lagged far behind (Hardy, 1997; Riley and Riley, 1994). We might even say the 'notion of aging has definitely had its day' (Bourdelais, 1998: 129). Certainly identities are becoming more fluid and less fixed as elders lose status in some cultures and gain a whole new life style in others. We can start with some basic assumptions that underpin the arguments presented in the following chapters. Readers who are not interested in theory may like to skip to p. 13 for an outline of the book.

Language and meaning

Words like 'old' or 'old age' or 'pensioner' carry many meanings which are often implicit or even deliberately hidden. Does old age exist, and who for? For example, here we have to ask whether older people feel old and define themselves as old, or whether young people see them as separate and 'old'. What are the boundaries (if any) of old age? What is the nature of the boundaries (multiple, fixed, moveable, administrative, personal)? What are the experiences of being old? These words can be taken as unproblematic. For example old age is defined as beginning at 65 in many contexts, but that is to oversimplify and to obscure differences of meaning, power and culture. Many writers are happy to leave these stones unturned, and since much of what is said in the following chapters is based on the work of other authors, there are times when the complexities of meaning and power relations seem to disappear. At these times I would ask the reader not to lose sight of the many simplifications and hidden power relations that are involved. The aim must be to achieve a use of words which is 'good enough' for the aspect under discussion (Cohen, 1998) but which very possibly over simplifies or homogenizes complex or diverse ideas or categories. This means that we should be aware that our terms and definitions are working tools which hide a vast range of taken-for-granted meanings and power relations.

Those who campaign as and for older people are aware of the problems of language. For example, 'old' is not a polite word for people in Western societies. In the English language we move from 'the old' to the hopefully more polite 'the elderly'. Both terms express the depersonalization and objectification that comes from defining people by a single characteristic and lumping them together in one category, such as 'the' young, 'the' disabled. Next the static and homogenized 'old/elderly' can be compared with the less definitive and more personalized 'older people' or 'elder'. In France the shift has been from *'vieillard'* a masculine term used collectively to include women, to *'personne agée'*. In America senior (citizen) is thought to be more polite. When the European survey organization Eurobarometer asked a sample of European elders what they liked to be called, 'senior citizen' came out top overall, but the label is rarely used in the UK, where 'older people' is more popular (Walker, 1993). These collective terms ignore differences in sex, class, ethnicity and age. In some cases they will be 'good enough': we may want to ignore differences or we may want to express the alienation and separation of older people from the rest of society, and so calling them 'the old' will be accurate.

Everyday language in Western cultures commonly confuses words that mark differences in *seniority* and terms which imply *disability*. The use of pension age to define 'older people' implies a seniority that is administratively defined. The healthy majority of pensioners in countries where the social security system delivers a 'retirement wage' (Myles, 1991) rarely think of themselves as old when they retire. The same is true in societies where a person is not old until they are disabled (Keith, 1994a). The status of 'clan elder' or older woman (mother-in-law or grandmother, for example) implies seniority not disability.

Seniority may also be associated with physiological changes. Balding or grey hair are traditionally associated with ageing and sometimes with wisdom. The menopause is a personal rather than a public change in the West, but in cultures where it is public, it can mark a time of new freedom and well-being for older women. These boundaries are markers of change but it would be hard to argue that they define 'old age'.

As with terms for ageing, simple approximations of words are often not 'good enough' for comparing social policies. Families, for example, are a mainstay of support in later life, but when policy makers speak of 'the family' (see Chapter 9) they may have very different activities and policy outcomes in mind. Governments range from believing that the family (and maybe a few Non Governmental Organizations – NGOs) will do everything needed to support an ageing population (parts of Africa), to providing a very high level of support to independent elders and caring family members (Denmark). And the 'family' may mean only spouse, children and grandchildren/great-grandchildren, or it may include a range of cousins, aunts and adoptive children (see Chapter 2). Gender relations and interpersonal expectations, standards of living, types of housing and daily activities, will all differ, and structure the basic idea of who family members are and what they should do for each other. A policy discussion that assumes uniformity will greatly oversimplify the issues.

In campaigning terms, there is a constant tension between the idea of older men and women as 'just like everyone else' and the idea of age-related difference. The concepts of universal human rights and the intrinsic worth of the individual are important when campaigning for equal rights or equal citizenship for older men and women. Some gerontologists and campaigners for better treatment for older people have therefore argued that the old are no different from other adults and that it is ageist to categorize older people as different (Bourdelais, 1998). A related argument is that older men and women who are frail or suffering from a disability should be treated first and foremost as disabled or frail rather than as 'old'. They should then have access to the same benefits as younger disabled men and women. Such discourses are useful when the aim is equality. Also, if 'the old' are not to be treated as 'the other', alien and, by implication, lower forms of life than the young, it becomes important to emphasize continuities over the life course and to blur the boundary between midlife and old age.

However, even in campaigning terms there are problems with approaches to ageing which deny difference. For example, differences in the position of men and women in society mean that policies that appear to be the same for both sexes act in different ways and have different gender outcomes. Outcomes will also differ *within* genders, by income, class, culture or health status, to consider just a few causes of difference (Gibson, 1996). In the same way, existing inequalities between young and old are only intensified by assuming equality across the adult life course in societies where age discrimination is part of the social structure. For example, as Townsend and others have pointed out (Estes, 1979; Phillipson, 1982; Townsend, 1981; Walker, 1980), enforced retirement ages, low pensions and prejudice against hiring older workers mean that incomes fall in later life for nearly everyone. It follows that structural change and/or positive discrimination in favour of older men and women are needed to increase equality in ageist societies. Legislation to outlaw age discrimination, and to ensure better work opportunities and better pensions is essential in nearly all countries. Just as few feminists would now rely wholly on a universalist approach to citizenship rights, with no distinction between men and women, so elders and their pressure groups need reforms that are specifically targeted at older men and women as well as universal reforms aimed at equality for all.

Social construction

The above approach to the language of ageing assumes that old age is socially and culturally constructed, as well as being manifested in bodily changes. The physiological and the social are often confused. They can even be combined, as when chronological age is used to define old age and frailty as the same thing. The problem is compounded because in gerontology, unlike feminism, we have no equivalent of sex and gender to distinguish between biological and social ageing. Sex is a biological term, but gender is used in social science to mean the socially constructed characteristics of masculinity and femininity in different societies or periods of history (see Chapter 2). This lack of a word for the socially constructed characteristics of later life leaves a gap in the language of conceptualization that makes it very easy to think of biological and social ageing as the same thing. Just as sex used to be seen as a scientific measure of the 'natural' and 'wholly objective' differences between men and women, so biological characteristics of old age (physical ageing – wear and tear, slow-down of metabolic processes, etc.) are still widely seen as equally natural and incontrovertible. As Rubinstein says when criticizing this approach, '"biology" is our significant folk construct of aging but perceptions of aging are cultural so biology must be a cultural perception' (Rubinstein, 1990: 110). It then follows that the various socially imposed disabilities associated with old age in different societies can be seen as every bit as 'natural' as declining strength or slower metabolism. Since physiological decline is very variable, we may even come to think that social disadvantages are more 'inevitable' than biological ageing processes. Only death is indisputable but even here, the meaning of death and the emotions it arouses differ across age groups and cultures and between individuals.

Identity and 'the other'

For some people there is no boundary to be crossed into old age. They continue to think of themselves as the same as they have always been – but a little older. For others there are boundaries which are personal, and boundaries which relate to society. They may be chosen or imposed, and the chances are that they will rarely coincide. For example, a very long lived senior chief in a traditional African society may be quite happy to call himself old, he may be seen as old by others and he may belong to a group which would normally be defined and define itself, as old. There is no such agreement in ageist societies and we expect to contest or accept different aspects of ageing in different ways. 'I am old', 'You are old' and 'They are old' will have very different meanings depending on who is speaking, who to, or who they are talking about. Experiences of ageing can be disabling (we, who are old, cannot do this because we are old) or enabling (we, who are old, have experience and know better). Keith (1982) for example, records how residents in an old people's home translated being old into being collectively much more experienced than the young home manager. On the other hand, 'They are old' is a distancing mechanism. They are different or, in the language of Wilkinson and Kitzinger (1996), they can be constructed as 'the other' (see also Titley and Chasey, 1996). The characteristics of the other are first, that they are not like us, second that they are not as varied as us and we do not have to take account of their individuality in the same way, and third, in the worst cases, they are not quite as human as us. It follows that separating older people from younger can depersonalize them and help to identify them as a weaker group and so increase their weakness.

The social construction of old age can be linked to changing ideas of identity in later life. The idea of a single, often stable, identity has now given way to the understanding that men and women can *sometimes* construct or choose a range of identities. Some of these identities will be imposed by others and some will be constructed by older people themselves. To take a concrete example, a young 60-year-old pensioner may join a pensioners' campaign group, or she may refuse on the grounds that she is not old and only old people belong to pensioners' groups (much more likely in the UK). Instead she may become a volunteer at a day centre, 'helping old people'. In these aspects of her life she is making her own choices about identity and its boundaries and contesting the definition that she is 'old'. In other spheres the choices are made for her. Family or friends may regard her as young or old, largely it seems, depending on her appearance and vitality and their own age or family position. To her grandchildren she will surely be 'old'. Her children may think she is 'still young', something that is not quite the same as 'young', and her older friends and relatives may genuinely see her as young. Whatever she and her friends think, the state will have identified her as a pensioner. In the UK in 2000 she will either draw her pension or be required to write in saying she is deferring it. At 75, however fit she is, her GP will attempt to check up on her health.

In the above example, the boundaries of later life are being defined differently by different individuals and social structures. They are being accepted or contested in different ways, and within the boundaries the meaning of old age differs, so being a pensioner is one thing, and being a volunteer helper is another. The example also shows that at 60 or 65 in prosperous Western countries it has become very easy for large numbers of people to contest the boundary of old age, but at 80 it can be much more difficult. As one woman said: 'I didn't feel old until I had my 80th birthday. Then I thought, well 80 is old isn't it. It has changed my attitude a bit' (author's interview).

Social policy

When social policy is considered from the point of view of older people it is hard to subscribe to the prevailing market-led orthodoxy. Competition in a market economy leads to poor outcomes for those who lack economic resources – most notably older men and women, but also any other individuals or groups who cannot find paid work. Economic policies are often presented as rational and inevitable but, given the power structure of society, these so-called inevitable choices usually end up protecting younger age groups and resulting in unpleasant outcomes for those in later life (cuts in pensions or charges for health care). The 'facts of life' about ageing populations are the stuff of media reports. Wherever we are, it is easy to believe that all societies, but particularly our own, are facing a rising tide of elders whose care is going to be too great for the changing family (i.e. women) to cope with, and whose pensions cannot be paid. The fact that hard evidence for these myths is either nonexistent or inconclusive appears to have had no effect on public perceptions, and barely impinged on the minds of policy makers. Until research is done on why this should be so, we can only conclude that it is the result of an emotional fear of ageing and the ease of scapegoating a weak group. It certainly prevents a more informed approach to policy-making.

Discussion of social policy in gerontology usually moves into a doom and gloom exposition of demography at this point. A look at the figures suggests that something more is needed. As Figure 1.1 shows that there is very little relation between the increase in the population of pension age and the share of national income devoted to state pensions. In 1980 the over 65s were 15 per cent of the population in the UK and state pensions cost 6 per cent of GNP. These percentages had risen massively since 1908 when the first state pensions were paid in the midst of predictions of imminent bankruptcy. The welfare state has not only failed to collapse under the burden, but has expanded massively. In France in 1980 much the same proportion of people were over 65 (14 per cent), but pensions were 10 per cent of GNP. In both countries there were scares about the unsustainability of pensions. However, the French system was already paying out more in 1980 than was projected for the UK in 2025. In the USA the figures were 11 per cent over 65 and with pensions of 6 per cent of GNP. Looking forward and taking the International Monetary Fund's highest projections for 2025, the increases shown in Figure 1.1 do not appear unsustainable in any country, despite the continuing variety in numbers of elders and amount of pension paid. UK pensions were projected to rise to 9 per cent of GNP (an increase of 3 per cent in GNP share over 45 years). In France and the USA the bill was projected to rise to 16 per cent and 8 per cent of GNP respectively (with populations over 65 rising to 19 per cent and 23 per cent). Although the projections indicated that the cost of pensions in the USA would be only half as much in GNP share as in France, the so-called pensions crisis has received more attention in the USA than in France. It is clear from these figures that a change in the number of elders can always be used to create a moral panic and as justification for retrenchments in welfare spending.

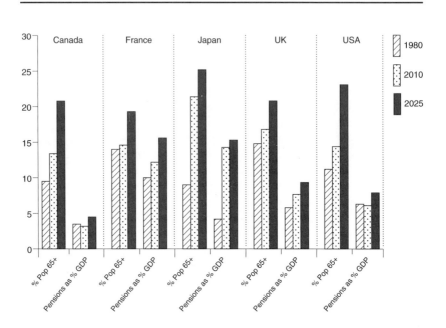

Figure 1.1 Projections for population over 65 and per cent GDP spent
on public pensions, selected countries
Source: Calculated from Heller et al. (1986).

It is also clear that the actual figures for the number of older people or
the cost of their pensions vary so widely that rational policy-making
appears to be non-existent. Fear or political expediency rules, not
rationality.

Theorizing ageing

The theoretical approach underpinning this book is that age is socially
constructed and one aim is to deconstruct superficial and biased
knowledge of ageing. Another is to analyse the problems of later life and
the ways that the 'old', however defined, are constructed as alien or
'other'. Most theories of ageing take a more straightforward view of later
life. Over large parts of the world the 'golden age' theory of ageing
prevails – once elders were respected, looked up to and cared for by
their families in traditional, stable societies. Now things are not so good.
In times past older people were believed to be nearer to God or the
Gods than the young, and their behaviour and place in society was meant
to reflect this. Wisdom, spirituality and magic powers were seen as
attributes of long experience or nearness to death. Now the spread of
materialism, industrialization, urbanization and Westernization have

led to the breakdown of religious authority and family solidarity and the devaluation of the wisdom of the old.

This modernization theory (Cowgill and Holmes, 1972) is immediately attractive in common-sense terms. When older men, and sometimes women, controlled resources, the young had to respect them if they wanted land or a house, or a husband or a wife. There might be disharmony and resistance but in the last resort the elders had the economic and ritual power. Now, if the young can take paid work outside the community, or go to town and surf the Internet, why should they listen to backward and ignorant elders? And, more to the point, why should they live in a stressful extended family or support their parents or in-laws when they are old? Researchers quickly attacked modernization theory for being too simple. The old were not always supported in traditional societies (and they are widely supported today in modernized societies). The poor, the weak, the childless and widows could have a bad old age in unmodernized societies. However, modernization theory can be attractive to politicians and policy-makers. It enables them to point to national or cultural traditions that should be preserved because they are morally superior to the materialistic and decadent West. Families care for their own, elders are not institutionalized and special policies for old age are not needed. Such attitudes/myths are widely supported by elders themselves and by younger men and women.

In the West, the development of gerontological theory on ageing can be seen as a journey from the personal and individual, through structured dependency theory, to identity and beyond (see Victor, 1987 for a good summary). This journey is certainly not over. One problem is that theories have been produced by scholars in mid-life and they have largely viewed old age negatively. Another is that people who have been ageist all their lives do not change when they become 'old'. All field researchers have met the 80-year-olds who 'don't feel old' themselves and don't want to mix with old people. It follows that theories are likely to be negative whether they start from the view point of mid-life professionals or take account of the views of older people. Cumming and Henry (1961) are usually charged with a highly functionalist view of ageing which saw disengagement from society as good for the old and good for society. Despite its many strong points, disengagement theory rapidly became unfashionable and was contested by theories of active ageing (Atcherly, 1987). Aspects of both these theories can be supported by research. There are discourses that see old age as a time of well-earned rest (these are usually men's discourses) and there are discourses on the importance of keeping mind and body active. In the same way old people in many cultures think that a dignified disengagement from mid-life activities is appropriate in advanced old age, even though they also think that they should keep in touch with the rest of society as far as they possibly can. Theories may conflict logically but they often make sense to individual elders as representations of different aspects of their lives.

The next step was to move from individually based theories, which can be used to blame older people for their own problems if they do not conform, to an understanding of the effects of social structures. Estes (1979) in the USA, and Phillipson (1982), Townsend (1981) and Walker (1980; 1981) in the UK presented a more progressive view in structured dependency theory. Their argument was that society is structured in ways that make older people dependent. They are forced out of the labour market by ageist employers and by welfare state pensions. As 'non-working' (i.e. not in paid work) dependants, they are not respected, and if they should become frail they are forced into residential or nursing homes where all ability to direct their own lives is denied. Large areas of our daily lives, from public transport through housing to socially devaluing stereotypes of elders presented on TV, make it almost impossible for older people to function as normal adults (Evans and Williamson, 1984). There is obviously a great deal of truth in this version of ageing theory. Much more could be done by society to facilitate the participation, citizenship rights and self-respect of elders. However, the theory presents older people as victims and many do not see themselves as such.

As social science has been influenced by postmodern ways of thinking, the idea that any one theory is going to be a useful guide to understanding the immense variety of later life begins to look optimistic. In the first place, a theory that could accommodate the diverse views of elders themselves would have the edge over a theory that simply told them what they were from an academic perspective. For this we move to the idea of identity in later life (without claiming that it is the full answer). It is helpful to have a theoretical framework which allows analysis of the ways in which people see themselves and their groups, and also the way they are defined by other people or by social structures. This consideration leads us to the idea that any theory of ageing must include a life course perspective (Riley, 1996). Men and women are not just 'old', they are ageing people with pasts and futures. Their pasts may be personal and include all sorts of experiences that made them what they are, or stopped them living as they would have liked. Also, as members of an age group born at a specific time (a cohort), say before or after the Great Depression, they have a common historical experience, even though the impact of that experience is likely to depend on socially structured characteristics like nationality, class, gender or ethnicity. Men who grew up in the 1930s in England were often pushed into secure jobs by their families, whether they liked the work or not and regardless of class. They then spent their working lives in jobs they did not enjoy and never would have chosen for themselves. They were, of course, lucky to have work at all. In contrast, the Babyboomers, that large cohort born between 1945 and 1959, even have their own association in America and are proud to have inaugurated new lifestyles at each stage of their lives. Since one of the changes was to have fewer children, they now worry about their pensions and have banded together to form a political pressure group (the Association of Baby Boomers).

Identity is not necessarily the same as individuality. While the individual who constructs his or her life course (usually his) exists, especially in prosperous Western countries (Giddens, 1991), it is more common on a world scale for older men and women to construct their identities in relational rather than individual terms (see Chapter 2). They do not necessarily see themselves primarily as separate individuals but more as members of a family or lineage, defined by their relationship to other family members (son of . . . or mother of . . .) or as a member of a community (someone who is known as fulfilling a certain role). Such an approach is more common in non-Western societies and among women. In small communities with face-to-face contacts, the question of who you are as an individual may be much less important than where you fit in with the pattern of family and power relations. Older people in such communities are less likely to feel devalued because they have a clear and established identity, but globalization brings individualization and threatens the social cohesion which supports older people

The book

The social lag between the growth of market individualism and collective structures to support those with reduced market power is enormous (Riley and Riley, 1994). And power in society is not simply a matter of distribution of resources – emotional and material. Power also relates to the structure of knowledge. Our knowledge of elders is an aspect of the way power is distributed in our societies – the way elders are seen as a burden on the young, the solutions put forward, the research which is financed and the representations of older men and women in the media (see Chapter 12). It goes without saying that misrepresentations of elders, as of other subordinated groups, are endemic in Western societies (Lorenz-Meyer, 1996; Stearns, 1977). For example, we are likely to be familiar with images of the rising tide of demented elders overwhelming our health services (Health Advisory Service, 1983), with the ever-growing burden of sick and idle pensioners battening on the young as they struggle to make a living for themselves and their young families, and with the impossibility of employing unadaptable, out-of-date older workers in today's rapidly changing economy. Such knowledge is, of course, deeply biased. It makes it difficult to consider the future of our societies in constructive ways. This book therefore aims to look more critically at knowledge of old age and to consciously correct some of the biases which inform current discourses on ageing.

The message of this book is that we are moving into the unknown and that better and less biased knowledge will be helpful. One way to achieve this is to consider later life in a cross-cultural context; another is to look critically at some of the dominant themes in the policy debate on ageing. Chapter 2 therefore starts with attitudes to ageing in different cultures. The boundaries of old age, if there are any, and the experiences of being old vary across cultures. So do attitudes to individualism and families and these inform policy. Chapter 3 takes a critical look at demography as applied to older people. The dominant values which underpin demographic knowledge are shown to be culturally constrained rather than universal. Demographic definitions of the number of old people, dependency ratios and demographic transitions are all open to conflicting interpretations and bias, but their main contribution, that the worldwide population of older people is increasing faster than ever before, is uncontested. The chapter identifies five versions of the demographic transition (the shift from high birth rates and high death rates to low birth and death rates). Each has different implications for population ageing and so for policy.

Low birth rates feed through to small cohorts of younger voters in Western democracies, where population ageing has been going on for some time (Chapter 4). The result is an ageing electorate with very large numbers of potential voters who are over 50. Theory and facts on older voters are both lacking. Older voters have been shown to vote more often and more consistently than the young. We do not yet know if this is something specific to the groups of people who first voted in the early part of the 20th century, or whether it will persist. The questions are: to what degree do elders form a politically conscious interest group, and how far are they likely to be motivated by self-interest rather than collective ideals in the future?

As with population ageing, the forces of globalization appear to be unstoppable but the economic changes currently associated with the dominance of free-market ideologies could, and I would argue should, be contested (Chapter 5). The dominance of free-market economics following the collapse of the former Soviet Union and Eastern Europe is undisputed. A less obvious side effect is that it has decimated opposition to the economic orthodoxies of the World Bank, the World Trade Organization and the IMF and endangered most social programmes that support older people. Given that the world economy is now more closely integrated and possibly more easily destabilized, the balance between greater fragility and better world regulators of market disaster is likely to determine outcomes for many people, and even many countries. This is especially true in developing countries with small, weak economies, where the threat of collapse does not mobilize the same concern on the part of super-powers as, for example, the threatened bankruptcy of Mexico in 1989 or Russia in 1998.

Another aspect of globalization and economic change is the movement of older men and women across countries and continents. A shrinking world in terms of communications and travel has changed the lives of older migrants. Chapter 6 presents a discussion of different forms of migration in later life as a challenge to dominant discourses of elders as conservative, passive and unadaptable.

Pensions, which loom so large in Western debates on the ageing populations, are rare in the rest of the world. Most elders must work to support themselves and many also work to support succeeding generations of their families. Pensions, even if very small, can be helpful in supporting or bargaining with other family members, but the full benefits of longer life can be most easily seen where pensions are high enough to allow choice in lifestyles. In Chapter 7 they are shown to be far from universal, but to be a highly successful collective phenomenon which has transformed the life of many. Current problems have not been adequately solved but are usually presented as much more serious than they are (International Social Security Association, 1996).

Elders themselves frequently see health as the main determinant of the quality of their lives. Chapter 8 presents some of the reasons why this should be so and challenges the belief that the rising costs of health care for the ageing population are unsustainable. Health and adequate material and emotional support are very closely linked. If paid work becomes impossible to find and pensions are inadequate, as is common in large parts of the world, informal work and reliance on the family take their place. Such reliance is very rarely one way and the positive role of elders in development and in social and family life has been seriously underestimated (Chapter 9). Attitudes to family caregivers (mostly women) vary greatly across the world, but support for caregiving is problematic in all countries. The next two chapters (10 and 11) discuss services for old people and forms of institutional care. Chapter 10 is not confined to a discussion of services that support frail elders and their caregivers but also considers older men and women as consumers and providers of services. Care outside the family presents special problems in developing countries and Newly Industrializing Countries (NICs), where governments often resist the need for policies to support caregiving and institutionalization on ideological grounds. In advanced welfare states there is a lack of technical knowledge on how to manage good quality services for vulnerable groups of people and this, combined with long traditions of using the poor quality of services as a deterrent rationing device, causes problems.

Any one of these topics could form a book on its own and most already have. It has been hard to choose what to put in, and even harder to leave out so much. The aim is to raise issues rather than provide a comprehensive view of any aspect of ageing. The final chapter therefore looks critically at the dominant discourses that are available and suggests directions where a different theoretical framework or paradigm could be useful.

CHAPTER 2

AGEING ACROSS CULTURES

This chapter considers aspects of ageing as they relate to differences in culture. It is concerned with the questions: when does old age begin? and what is it like to be old?

> Older people are highly visible in Hong Kong, especially in the early morning hours when they congregate on hill slopes to absorb the good morning air and carry out their exercises . . . at 6.30 . . . nearly every park and playground in Hong Kong at any time of the year is occupied by older people who following their work outs, gather in groups of two or three for leisurely discussion of matters of mutual interest. . . . Later in the morning, old women, some with a grandchild strapped to their back, go off to the street market to buy fresh vegetables and live chickens and fish for the day's meals while old men congregate in teahouses reading the paper and discussing current events, including the results of the previous day's horse races. (Keith, 1994a: 90)

> Mrs N., aged 60 plus. Lives with 10-year old grandchild in isolated hut made out of 'rawly chopped wood, twigs and leaves.' Husband deserted her 10 years ago. Daughter died when the child was two. Son-in-law went away and has never been seen since. She has very little food for the boy who has grown wild and runs away often into the forest. Other children will not mix with the boy because they say he is a devil. The village chief says that everybody is poor so they cannot help the woman. He thinks they have nothing but forest leaves to eat. (Tout, 1989: 120)

These two very different examples show that older people pass through the years of later life within different frameworks of social beliefs and values (cultures). The first quotation is a general account and describes a relatively pleasant and well-structured life, different for men and women, and definitely problematic if a woman becomes frail and finds housework a struggle. The other focuses on a casualty in a traditional society where old age is respected and, in theory, collectively provided for. It reminds us that there are very large areas of the world where a functioning family is essential and an individual is unlikely to survive for long alone (see Chapter 9). The cultures within which older people live help to determine when (or if) they are seen as 'old', and what being old means. Beliefs and attitudes that are dominant in one society usually exist in a muted form in others and practices that seem exotic when described in some pre-literate culture are almost certainly present in our own societies. In Hong Kong Keith (1994a) goes on to say that old age is popularly meant to be a time of well-earned rest. Men may achieve this but for most women the reality is continuing hard work. Elders with more money can pay for servants to do the housework and can spend time travelling to visit their children and playing mah-jong with their friends. In most societies the ageing experience differs according to gender and social class.

Culture also influences the way we think about old age as well as the way elders live. In Western societies there is a dominant perception that they (others/foreigners) have culture but we, the heirs of the Enlightenment, have culture-free, scientific approaches to understanding the world and making policies for the problems we identify (see Chapter 12). The scientific approach tells us that we all get old and ageing is a matter of biological wear and tear. Such scientific or modernist knowledge belongs largely to biology, medicine and psychology but spills over into other disciplines and popular thought. Science has shown that tissues age over the life course and some mental processes also change. The ageing body has characteristics that can be identified in any part of the world. This does not mean that all ageing bodies are alike or that they manifest the same changes at similar chronological ages, or that physiological 'old age' will be the same in different cultures. It does, however, offer an approach to ageing which is firmly embedded in modern Western culture and which passes as dispassionate and 'scientific'. However, Western attitudes to ageing are far from dispassionate (Chapter 1).

The outstanding characteristic of the 'scientific' approach is that it assumes that the basic framework for understanding old age is in place. The only task is to fill in the data that will enable interpretations to be made. At its worst, this approach produces very biased knowledge, as when a 65-year-old white American professional man is counted as an older person in the same table or set of definitions as a 65-year-old farmer in one of the more unhealthy areas of Africa (see Chapter 3). They have in common sex and a birth year, certain for the American and possible for the African, but that is about all. Such knowledge has a place but there are other approaches to knowledge which aim to ask questions about different ways of understanding aspects of human life. For example, age in terms of years may have very little to do with the ageing body. Time and biology are not necessarily synchronized. Even within the same culture, one 70-year-old may be going jogging every day while another can barely get out of the house.

A social constructionist perspective (see Chapter 1, also Vincent, 1995) starts by looking at different cultural values and beliefs about old age, and the ways they relate to our own taken-for-granted understanding of ageing. As Keith says, 'Work with older people in another culture should be the basis for clearer understanding of ageing' (Keith, 1982: 3). This is true, but culture is a problematic term. It refers to sets of beliefs, practices and values that change over time. It therefore seems likely that young and old have always held slightly different sets of beliefs within any one culture. The difference today is that globalization has brought such widespread and rapid changes that older cohorts are now likely to belong to cultures which differ on many points from younger cohorts in their own countries or communities.

'The other'

A culture, a shared set of beliefs and practices, implies that there are others who do not share these beliefs. Often the boundaries of the in-group are even more important than the content of their beliefs – it may be easier to identify outsiders than to agree on what the insiders have in common. The concept of 'the other' is useful in thinking about those who are 'outside' any group of insiders. At the crudest, we have two stereotypes of ageing: 'they put all their old people in homes' and 'families look after the old'. These widespread beliefs about the care of frail old people are one way of defining a cultural heritage, and part of the process of defining outsiders as the 'other'. When migrants age it is widely believed in the dominant culture that they will be looked after by their families (see Chapter 6). This appears to be a belief that is strong in any country where there are ageing migrants, but it can also apply to any group seen as the 'other'. For example, Cohen (1998) found in northern India, Hindus assumed that Muslims looked after their parents better and so Muslim elders were less likely to become demented. Such simplistic views are contested and greater familiarity with the condition of migrant communities may bring acceptance that the family will not provide everything. The NHS and Community Care Act 1990 in the UK, for example, called for culturally appropriate services for older migrants.

The opposite stereotype – that all elders are institutionalized in Western countries – is possibly even stronger and is an example of a myth that lives on despite very low levels of actual institutionalization of the older population (see Chapter 11). Even within widely varying definitions of what constitutes an institution, it is hard to define as much as 10 per cent of the populations over 65 as institutionalized in Western countries (see p. 147). In other words, at least 90 per cent of elders live on their own, as couples, or with their families (a minority) in Western countries. The big difference between developed countries and the rest of the world lies in the proportion of older people who live in multi-generation households. On the other hand, if we take the small but growing numbers of over 85-year-olds, virtually all live with families in the developing world and the NICs, but 20–30 per cent are commonly in some form of residential care in the West (see Table 11.1).

Ageing in different cultures

In the past there were fewer older people than there are today, and it appears that social structures gave most of those who survived some means of support. By definition those who did not survive did not need support, but we do not know how many were unsupported and so died. Meade Cain (1986b) for example, found that villages in Bangladesh contained very few older widows without adult sons, although statistically they should have been present. He concluded that without the support of an adult son, an older widow would find it almost impossible to survive in the local village culture. Brothers-in-law felt no obligation to a widow and even expected to take her land if she had any. It is safe to say that support for elders cannot be assumed in any culture and that even where support is widely assumed to exist there will be individuals and groups who will not be supported.

However, before we consider support it is worth asking whether old age was, or is, a recognized life stage or status. In many societies this is doubtful. As noted earlier, the Western certainty that categories such as old age can be standardized across the world leads researchers and policy-makers to fit other cultural beliefs into their own framework. So, for example, adult men in age-graded societies in Africa may have passed through age stages from childhood to the status of elder, but being an elder does not mean that a man is old. His chronological age correlates only loosely with his age grade and his grade indicates that he has attained a certain seniority. He may be able to enjoy the fruits of an accumulation of wealth and power but he is not necessarily old in years or in any way decrepit. Such wealth and power may be expressed in the number of wives and children. Young wives will look after him if he needs attention, that is, if he becomes old in a Western sense (Rwezaura, 1989). The traditional Hindu life course (Basham, 1954; Cohen, 1998) can also be expressed as stages that do not include being old. According to the model, men move from youth to marriage and householder status, through active life, to withdrawal and religious contemplation. Withdrawal can only begin once sons are old enough to take over the support of the family. In such a model some men will begin to become contemplatives at around the age of 50, while others may wait very much longer. Being a hermit or a holy man is a matter of life stage, but not of old age. If they decide to forgo the last life stage and stay on in their own households, men or women may indeed become 'old'. Cohen notes two processes:

> . . . *the loss of authority and the loss of usefulness* (original emphasis). Both were gradual and contested processes, but each marked, fitfully, a shift in how an old person was heard. The first, the loss of authority over household decisions and resources was associated with anger and a hot *dimag* [brain,

mind]. The second, the loss of usefulness, that is, of any significant interpersonal role within the household, was associated with emerging criticisms
of the old person babbling meaninglessly. (1998: 241)

So as he says, bad-tempered and mentally frail elders were widely
identified within a culture that respected old age. Such a duality is
mirrored in Western cultures where elders are widely *dis*respected but
may still be respected either as individuals or because they conform to
certain expectations of successful ageing.

A key question is whether seniority is desirable and how one becomes
a senior? It appears unthinkable in most Western cultures to want to
become 'old'. However, when old age is defined as seniority it may well
be a very desirable state. Respect, and the chance to direct the work of
others rather than actually working oneself, is something to look forward
to and enjoy when it comes, but is it old age? As with the holy man or
woman contemplative in India, these are life stages associated with later
chronological life, but they need not be reserved for the old. More
important in these cultures, an older man or woman who has reached
an honoured life stage is primarily an honoured person. They may, in
passing, be old but that is not their main identity. In such cases the
boundary to old age may not be contested. Even in Western societies
many people are very glad to retire from paid work and in personal terms
do not contest that boundary.

Types of boundary

Boundaries can be defined bureaucratically, by life stage and social
transition, or they may be physiological (incapacity, menopause, greying
hair and wrinkles). Different cultures may have their own markers and
there will almost certainly be differences between men and women. Such
boundaries may well mark changes and differences in the distribution
of resources and social status (see Foner, 1984; 1994).

Chronological ageing and bureaucracy

The importance of chronological age as a boundary manifests itself in
various forms of bureaucracy and has come to dominate administrative
systems the world over. Retirement age is the most common boundary
in countries with pension systems. The relevant age can vary from
50 to 67 (in Iceland for example). Documentary evidence of age has
become essential for foreign travel (elders who wish to visit their migrant
children) and entitlement to age-related benefits, such as tax breaks,
lower fares, free medicines, cheap theatre tickets, cheap hairdressing,

special hours access to the Internet (to take one example from a municipal library in Australia). When large numbers of older people are uncertain about their ages, special procedures have to be set up to find out if they really are 'old'.

Some will see age-related benefits as markers of a dependent status and ageism. Noiriel (1992), for example, has argued that the problem of ageing migrants arises directly from the development of the French welfare state. The fact that older migrants qualify for a pension and for other forms of assistance at one end of the life course, and that racialized migrant youth is the object of expensive programmes of control at the other, results in the formulation of age as a social problem. Longman presents a similar view from an American perspective:

> But over the past half-century passing from one's sixty-fourth to one's sixty-fifth year has become without question the most significant milestone in American life, carrying with it an entitlement to benefits and social services that are denied even at the cost of life to younger citizens. (Longman, 1987: 109–10)

Such institutionalization of the threshold of old age presents a boundary that is clearly drawn.

Life stage

Life stages as markers of different parts of the life course have produced a very large academic literature. Most cultures give some importance to life stage as distinct from chronological age. For example, a girl becomes a woman when she marries, her status improves when she becomes a mother (preferably of sons), and she can reach old age or seniority in a variety of ways depending on the culture – by marrying off a daughter, by becoming a grandmother or by reaching the menopause. Men's transitions may also relate to marriage and parenthood. The view that old age is related to life stage can be seen in the common Western fear of becoming a grandparent at the age of 40 or 50. Women in particular, faced with constant exhortation to remain young and attractive, can find it difficult to come to terms with publicly being called 'Nan' or 'Granny' when they still see themselves as 'young'.

Incapacity

In other societies there is no such category as a *healthy* old age. Men and women are not seen as old until they can no longer support themselves. This view of old age appears to have been common in hunter-gatherer societies where most activities were directed towards survival, but it is not limited to them. Elements of it form a major strand in Western ageism: if a person is old (aged 60 plus, using a chronological boundary) they are assumed to be weak in mind and body. In contrast, Keith, (1994a) describes an Irish town where the old, defined as pensioners, were indistinguishable from men of working age in dress and in means of support – part-time seasonal work and unemployment benefit or pension. When asked to name people who were old, the inhabitants mentioned only those who were disabled. Even when challenged about various 80-year-olds, they denied that such people were old as long as they were active. Old age only set in when they became dependent.

Such a view is widespread in England among pensioners who may characterize their contemporaries as 'old' but see themselves as 'not old' as long as they can remain independent of assistance (Sainsbury, 1993). Here is an example from a focus group of sheltered housing tenants. As the group discussed the difficulties of keeping their active communal life going, one man said:

> 'Yes our coach trips are falling off. They're too disabled', but then he quickly corrected himself: 'They're not disabled but they can't walk anywhere when the coach stops. They just have to get out and sit in the bus shelter and then get back on when its time to go home, so there's no point them going'. (author's focus group)

These men and women in their 80s were determined to maintain their image of themselves and their housing scheme as for active, sociable people who were 'not old' and 'not disabled'. The arrival of a man in an electric wheelchair was frequently mentioned in connection with the new frailer intake of tenants, but each time it was immediately pointed out that he was 'very active'. Hazan (1980) identified a similar process at work in a Jewish day centre where he interpreted the interactions of the older people as the need to make time stand still.

Being old

Ideal ways of being old vary across and within cultures. If we start with the traditional Hindu view of ageing – that being old means being more saintly, gaining greater respect and possibly achieving a better position in the next life – there are obvious compensations for reaching old age. Being nearer death may still be unpleasant, though that should not be automatically assumed. In the West the idea of a daily prayer for death to come soon does not fit well with active ageing, but in many cultures it is the correct and satisfying thing to do. Women in India may also become contemplatives in later life but they may instead choose to retain their connection with their families and organize the lives of their daughters-in-law, especially if they are not widowed.

There are other countries where the status of being old is still desirable – but almost certainly only if an adequate standard of living is possible. Interviews with Ghanaian elders reported by Nana Apt (1996) show graphically the disappointments that come from status that is not supported by adequate material resources. To be head of a lineage but at the same time resented by the younger generation, treated with disrespect and left in poverty, is contrasted with the satisfactions of old age when resources are adequate.

A major issue for older men and women in any society is whether their position changes simply because they are old, that is, age automatically brings a higher or lower status (always with certain exceptions). For example, an older holy man is more revered than a young one, or a grandmother may be treated with more respect and able to choose more freely how to spend her time than a young wife. Working in the other direction, retirement has been described as throwing older workers on the scrap heap and as a major input to the structured dependency of older people in Western countries, making the retired automatically lower status than those in work. The difference for women is that it is normal in most parts of the world where women have low status when they are young for the power and status of women to increase over the life course (Chaney, 1989). In the Indian subcontinent among other places, traditional society favoured older women very strongly as against younger women. Age and motherhood enabled a women to gain status and influence, especially over her sons and their wives, so that in later life a woman could expect to have power over her daughters-in-law and be able to control many aspects of her daily life (Jeffery and Jeffery, 1996). However, such a process of successful ageing might be interrupted if she became a widow and could not control her son. Women's power is usually over other women. Their power over men may be confined to 'influence' or it may be overt and respected by men. Older women's horizons expand with age but, if as in India, their power is mainly over young women, and at their expense, conflicts are likely when the traditional system weakens and younger women assert themselves.

The alternative to cultures where age automatically confers higher or lower status is that social structures are a framework that enables older men and women to move up or down in status or well-being by their own efforts. Societies, traditional or otherwise, allow women or men with talent and ambition (and also luck since the presence of sons may be an essential) to become powerful. Such frameworks may be more or less ageist. Merely being post-menopausal can enable a woman to dispense with many disempowering constraints, but what she actually makes of later life may depend more on her own abilities than on the enabling or constraining power of the social structures she operates within. In Western societies it can be hard to think of ways that elders who do not already have some form of power or resources before they retire can accumulate them in old age. As the theorists of structural dependency have shown, social structures in the West disempower the old rather than empower them (Estes, 1979; Phillipson, 1982; Townsend, 1981; Walker, 1980). The exceptions may be older widows who find themselves not only provided for by their late husband's pension but also able to control their funds as never before. Elders may also look on the bright side and be glad of the freedom and unconventionality that is allowed them.

Religion and art

Spiritual resources have traditionally been an important province of elders and still remain so in some cultures, even if they have been down-graded in Western societies, and may be less valued elsewhere. In traditional cultures power may depend on controlling access to knowledge or ritual. This is very common in age-grade societies where older men control important rituals. In societies that see themselves as continuous with their ancestors, men and women get closer to the ancestors as they age, and must be respected accordingly. An old man may approach a godlike status as he reaches the end of his life and is about to continue it another way as an ancestor (see p. 45).

In terms of artistic or other cultural resources, some art forms are dominated by the young but others may be practised into late old age. Even when no longer able to practise, elders may become great teachers or communicators. Such older teachers and artists appear to be much more common in countries where elders are traditionally revered, for example Japan, China or India, than in the West. It is possible to think of certain Western music teachers who continue into late life and Picasso, among painters, but these are exceptions rather than the rule. The clearest manifestation of the importance of older people in national culture is perhaps the Japanese practice of designating older artists or other celebrities as 'national treasures'. This has now been adopted by the United Nations and Australia where Dawn Frazer, the former Olympic swimmer, is a national treasure.

Resistance or acceptance

There are cultural prescriptions for being old. Is old age to be accepted or contested in personal terms? In the West the answer is fairly clear and resistance is the culturally approved norm. This is not surprising given the importance of independence and reciprocity. Jerrome said of her study of older women who joined groups:

> ... the ideal response to old age is resistance and struggle.... The preoccupation with health and fitness , with activity and resistance to the encroachments of age, achieves collective expression in formal meetings and individual expression in informal talk and activities. (Jerrome, 1992: 190)

Many other authors and poets have expressed similar emotions. Myerhoff (1992), for example, dramatically portrays the determination of older Jewish Day Centre members to resist the marginalization of old age. In other cultures a dignified acceptance of all that life can bring, including ageing and death, is the prescribed stance. Within both there are individuals who do not conform.

Social policy

The content of cultural difference can have a direct effect on policy. As a broad generalization, Islamic and Asian countries have very strong religious or philosophical bases for respect for older parents. This does not of course mean that all elders in these communities are well cared for and feel happy in their old age. There are structural and individual constraints on caring capacities. For one thing, widespread poverty can make it difficult to fulfil ideals, for another, not everyone has a family and, further, not all families are dutiful, let alone harmonious (see Chapter 9). However, in such cultures it has been politically acceptable for governments to base policy on the assumption that the family provides for old age. In more extreme forms this ideological stance also assumes that it would weaken the moral or religious foundations of the nation if government were to intervene with generalized support for elders. In other cultures, mostly in Africa, religion is oriented towards the lineage rather than the narrower definition of the family and, in theory at least, the basis for support may be wider still (Rwezaura, 1989). In both, the presence of children or descendants is absolutely vital for feelings of well-being or respect in old age.

    These examples emphasize the importance of authority. Those without authority in later life are unlikely to have command over resources unless there are special collective provisions made for them, as there are in welfare states. Authority may be underpinned by accumulated power and wealth, or backed by religious or other social sanctions. The difference may be important in terms of the way that social policy develops. If support in later life is dependent on the accumulation of power within a traditional social system, the breakdown of that system greatly weakens the claims of older people. On the other hand, if support is a matter of religious duty, it may well be incorporated into law or otherwise become part of the policy of a modern state.

Conclusions

Old age can be socially defined as a time of fulfilment or a time of denigration and marginalization. Is to be old to be genuinely respected as a senior citizen, or is this just a polite way of saying people are 'past it'? There is enough anthropological evidence to make it entirely clear that there is no 'natural' view of ageing and that old age is constructed differently in different societies. There may be no clearly defined transition to old age, only a gradual development which at some point can be said to have occurred. (The transition rites in age grade societies are an exception.) Cultural boundaries are drawn differently in different societies – they may be unclear and fuzzy but can still be identified and have effects on people's lives.

In Western culture the dominant discourse on ageing is 'scientific' and deemed to be culture free. In reality scientific discourses, which predominate in medicine, psychology and demography and, in a different way, in economics, are enclosed within their own cultures of scientific enquiry. The knowledge they produce is correspondingly biased because it imposes a certain set of values (Western, economic and/or biologically based) on beliefs, processes and practices which are different, and so produces data which can be standardized but which are very partial in what they reveal. The apparently automatic association between the medico-scientific approach to ageing and chronological age is not entirely logical but seems inescapable. The implementation of policies is similarly dependent on bureaucratic boundaries related to chronological age. This is a global process that is gathering strength. It may soon be impossible to live a normal life without evidence of calendar age.

It is possible to argue that old age is very rarely problem free. (The same is true of life so this conclusion is hardly surprising.) The most reliable indicator of old age as a problem is that each generation constructs a better past when old people were well looked after. Also, each such past includes a standard selection of horror stories of the abandonment or ill treatment of elders – or of the foolishness of elders who gave all their property to their children and so had no resources left to coerce them into caring. European literature abounds with moral and cautionary tales (Lorenz-Meyer, 1996). However, there is no homogeneity within ageist cultures and respect for elders survives in some contexts. People may greatly value and admire their grandparents or their ageing parents and even in a public context elders may be deferred to. In one recent example a postgraduate course on gender was joined for one term by man of 77. He persisted in trying to impose his (extremely sexist) views on the group. When he left a student commented: 'It just shows there is still respect for age, because if he had been younger we would have torn him limb from limb.'

Older people, as individuals and groups, live out their lives against a background of multiple beliefs and draw on the different sets of discourses and cultural values which are available to them. In any culture some will favour resistance to age and death and others will favour acceptance. This emphasizes that there is no single system of beliefs about old age, but many. Some relate to the past and some are emerging and will relate to the future.

Further reading

Keith, J. (1994) *The Aging Experience: Diversity and Commonality across Cultures.* Thousand Oaks, CA: Sage.

Cohen, L., (1998), *No Aging in India : Alzheimer's, the Bad Family, and other Modern Things.* Berkeley: University of California Press.

http://www.ifa-fiv.org/mfa4.htm – The World's Living Treasures.

CHAPTER 3

RISING TIDES: DEMOGRAPHY AND OLD AGE

In terms of numbers, the great contribution of demography is to show that the world's populations are ageing. This means not just that there are more older people, but that people are living longer at all ages as well as in later life. A Eurocentric perspective encourages us to concentrate on old age, but in world terms the big drop in mortality has been among the under 15s, not the over 60s. It has been followed by a fall in the birth-rate in nearly all countries. A doom and gloom scenario linking demography and old age can be found in most gerontology text books but, before we consider the actual numbers, it is worth asking a few questions about the data.

The first problem is that demography is a Western science. It takes dominant Western concepts of old age and ageing, and imposes them across the world, as if they were genuinely universal but, as we saw in Chapter 2, they are not. It may be argued that this does not matter since it is a Western view that is needed in order to get an understanding of how the world's population is evolving. But any such understanding will be more or less limited to a Western perspective and will impose false uniformities on the data (Wilson, 1997). Figure 3.1 shows how data that are produced under different cultural assumptions have to be modified to fit demographic conventions. In cultures where views of ageing are not linked to chronological time in the same way as they are in the West, raw demographic data can look very peculiar and have to be changed to fit the dominant model. Figure 3.1 shows population pyramids for Bangladesh in 1974.

Figure 3.1a shows the ages of the population as recorded by census enumerators (who have instructions to record chronological ages and have already worked very hard to get their informants to report age accurately). The pyramid divides the total population into one-year age groups, men on the left and women on the right. There was clearly a marked preference for odd numbered ages up to the age of five and, after that, for ages ending in five and most of all for measuring age by decade. In cultures where date of birth and the number of years of life are much less important than birth order in relation to other relatives or neighbours, chronological age can be an irrelevance. Enumerators do their best to relate date of birth to harvests or festivals but the raw data have to be processed to fit Western ways of defining age chronologically,

Figure 3.1 Age pyramids for Bangladesh in 1974: actual and adjusted data
Source: Adapted from Newell (1988: 29).

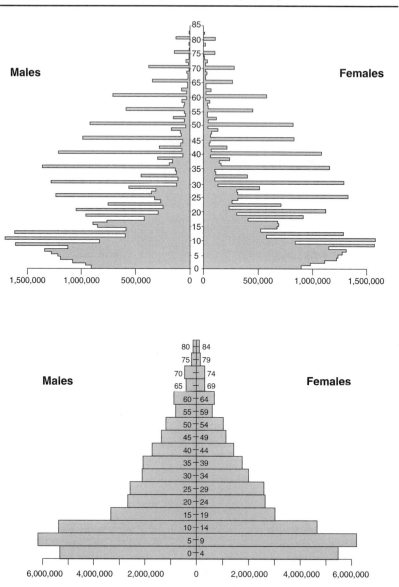

as in Figure 3.1b. These two diagrams offer a visual representation of the cultural gap that can exist in ways of thinking about age. The ideas that one group takes for granted are not universal, and they affect the way that people of different cultures present data. It is also true that, as seen in Chapter 2, definitions of old age vary greatly and it is misleading to impose a single chronological definition, whether the cut off point is 55 years, 60 or 65, to take those most commonly used in international statistical comparisons.

The other main danger of demographic data is that the false uniformity that arises from the presentation of standardized numerical data leads to even more false assumptions of cultural uniformity and policy transferability. Older people, however defined, are not uniform even within countries, let alone across the world:

> If there are so many culturally-based gender differences between men and women in late life (in social stressors relating to longevity, emotionality, experience of illness, modes of relating to other people, income, past experiences as culturally structured in the life course, to name a few), how can these be ignored? Yet we frequently talk of the elderly as a uniform or discrete group. (Rubinstein, 1990: 116)

In other words, cultural views of age, and particularly old age, vary across the world and change over time. Old age differs between men and women in meaning and impact, and across classes and ethnic minorities within countries. It also differs greatly between individuals. None of these differences is fixed. They are consciously or unconsciously contested by individuals and groups. As the following chapters show, some men and women can maintain health, income, influence, love and power in old age. Others can become disempowered, poor, sick and unloved in any culture.

If we accept common chronological definitions of old age it is easy to fall into the trap of assuming that common policies should follow. For example, starting from a Western perspective, we may take it for granted that older women and men should stop paid work at pensionable age, and so divide the population for policy purposes into those above and those below 60 or 65. Such an assumption makes some sense in developed welfare states, but it still overlooks the fact that a pension for a young elder with a full complement of consumer durables and a well-maintained home is worth much more than the same pension for someone 20 years older. If durables have broken down and are too expensive to replace, home maintenance is no longer a matter of DIY or assistance from relatives, and the cost of care needs is rising, the pension will not produce the same standard of living even in a Western country. In the rest of the world, the assumption that all elders get pensions leads to misplaced concern about the cost of pensions, (for example the World Bank publication *Averting the Old Age Crisis*, 1994). On the other hand, when work is not necessarily paid and does not cease at any defined age, and pensions are small or non-existent, age-related categories become less useful for policy-making. Further, pensions crises can be seen to be a very minor problem at present compared with debt repayments, urbanization or sustainable economic development for most countries (see Chapter 5).

Demography, then, is useful in terms of measuring numbers (quantity). Censuses (counts of the whole population) have been taken in most countries for many years. They show changes in the size of different age groups in a country reasonably accurately, even if the raw data are not strictly comparable across countries (as in Figure 3.1). They may include systematic errors that grow or reduce over time (for example the poor or migrants are usually under-enumerated), but general world trends are not in dispute. Populations have grown and are still growing in many countries. However, the rate of growth is slowing and populations are ageing.

Demographic transitions

Population ageing results from the change from high fertility and high death-rates to low or declining fertility and low death-rates. This world-wide trend is identified as the 'demographic transition'. It has taken place at different times and takes different forms in different countries. By the late 20th century it is possible to see five versions of demographic transition which result in different rates and types of population ageing.

1 Slowly falling or static birth-rates combined with slowly falling death-rates = relatively slow ageing of an already aged population – e.g. Western Europe.
2 As above, with a reduction in traditionally high rates of immigration = intermediate rate of ageing – e.g. USA, Australia, Canada.
3 Fast or very fast drop in birth-rates with an accelerating fall in death-rates = very rapid ageing – Japan, parts of Latin America and possibly China if low birth-rates are maintained.
4 Drop in birth-rates + accelerating fall in death-rates = relatively slow ageing of a previously young population – most developing countries and newly industrializing countries. Presence of a demographic bonus in the form of a growing youthful workforce. The effect of AIDS, especially in Africa, has still to be determined.
5 Low birth-rates and static or even rising death-rates = slow population ageing from an intermediate position – e.g. the former Soviet Union and Eastern Europe.

These different patterns of demographic transition show clearly that population ageing is dependent on the birth-rate. Death-rates are falling in virtually all countries but the stage and speed of demographic transition varies with the rate of collapse in the birth-rate. The transition took place much earlier in Western Europe than elsewhere but it also took longer. Japan, for example, has gone from relatively high to very low birth-rates in less than a generation, while in France the process took

Figure 3.2a Population Pyramids for Germany in 1910
Source: Adapted from Bevölkerung und Erwerbstätigkeit (1995).

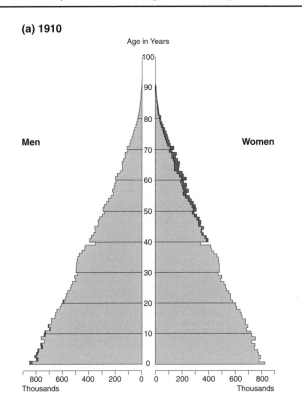

more than a century. In visual terms a country or population moves from pyramid to pillar (see Figures 3.2a and b). The diagrams are for Germany in 1910 and 1993 but could apply in most western European countries with minor modifications.

Figure 3.2a shows the population pyramid for a European population as it was when the birth-rate was still fairly high and steady, but mortality was falling. There is a very slight surplus of young boys (visible in a thicker line terminating the bars for 0–10 years and a surplus of women beginning round the age of 40. This is normal for most populations outside a belt stretching from Morocco to China (Sen, 1989). We might note in passing the small cohort of 39-year-olds (the drop in births during Bismark's 1870 war) and the rise in the years after it. Those over 60 are a very small part of the population but the small surplus of women is most marked in the older age groups.

In contrast, Figure 3.2b shows a completely different picture for the population of the same area in 1993. The dramatic fall in births that began in 1960 and stabilized at a new low level by 1970, might even be falling further. Earlier drops in birth cohorts can be seen to match the First and

Figure 3.2b Population Pyramids for Germany in 1993
Source: Adapted from Bevölkerung und Erwerbstätigkeit (1995).

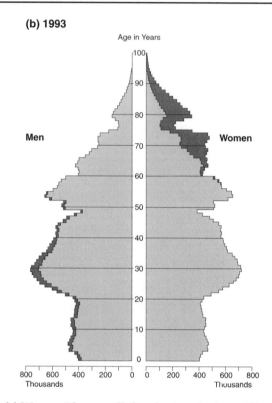

(b) 1993

Second World Wars with a small dip during the inter-War depression. The post-war baby boom, with boomers aged between 25 and 35 in 1993, started later than in the UK or USA as German reconstruction took longer to get off the ground. The dramatic increase in length of life is clearly marked and the transformation in the number of older women is one of the success stories of modern times.

Figure 3.3 shows the big changes in marital status that have accompanied changes in population structure. Lower death-rates have meant more older widows (and fewer young ones) along with the constancy of marriage for men in later life. The rise in divorce is concentrated among women once the age of 65 has been passed. A mini boom of elders was due at the turn of the century, earlier than in the UK where the increase is not expected before 2008.

Figure 3.4 shows that there are already more people over 60 in the less developed countries than in the developed. By 2035, if projections are correct – and there is every reason to think they may be – there will be nearly three times as many elders living in today's less developed countries, though hopefully some at least will have joined the developed

Figure 3.3 Age and marital status: Germany 1993
Source: Adapted from Bevölkerung und Erwerbstätigkeit (1995).

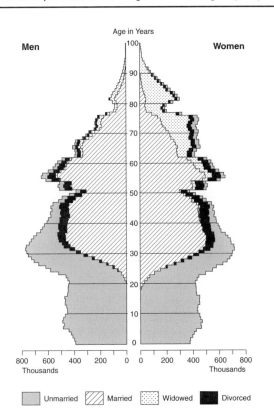

Age in Years

Men

Women

Unmarried   Married   Widowed   Divorced

world by then. In other words, developing countries are ageing much faster than more prosperous countries. The difference is that the main cause of ageing in developing countries is a drop in the birth rate rather than longer life (see below) and in most of them there will be a demographic bonus in terms of a young, healthy and better educated workforce (see http://www.unfpa.org/ on world population ageing).

It seems unlikely that this growth in numbers will cause any serious problems. In developed Western countries the numbers of older men and women doubled from around 7 per cent of the population to 14 per cent without causing any major political or economic upsets. There is no reason to think that other countries cannot repeat the same pattern. On the other hand, in OECD countries where the birth-rate has collapsed, it may be that a growth in the older population from 15 per cent to 25 per cent of the total will indeed strain political and economic systems, but this is by no means certain. Much depends on the rate at which women enter the paid labour force (and so make pension contributions), total productivity (however measured), the effects of economic restructuring,

Figure 3.4 Total numbers of people over 60 in more developed and less developed countries 2000–2035 (projections)
Source: Calculated from Bos (1994).

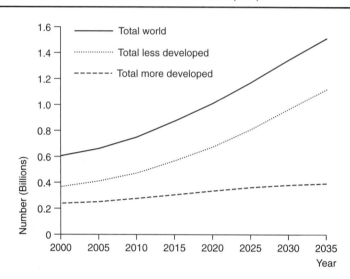

our success in developing effective polices for intergenerational integration, and political decisions on whether to tolerate large numbers of poverty-stricken elders.

Women

As the figures above have shown, women are normally in the majority in later life. This makes ageing potentially a feminist issue, and feminists are slowly beginning campaigns to improve the lot of older women. Since in most cultures women marry men older than themselves and men die earlier, a rise in older women means an increase in the number of widows (Figure 3.3). Numbers can be very high, for example in India 70 per cent of women over 65 were widows in 1980 (United Nations, 1991: 78, Table 9). High rates of widowhood in countries where the status of women is low, represent high levels of poverty and disadvantage. As birth-rates fall, the number of older women without children is also set to increase. The number of older men with no children, or who have lost contact with their children, seems likely to rise even faster as a consequence of divorce, and this will cause problems if they need care.

Life expectancy

It follows from the increase in the numbers of older men and women that life expectancy has risen. It is sometimes thought that when life expectancy at birth (the average number of years that a newborn boy or girl could expect to live if conditions remained stable) was low, there were no old people. For example, if life expectancy was 40, it might erroneously be assumed that nearly everyone would be dead by 40, grandparenthood would be a short-term activity and the problems and contributions of the old would be minimal. However, life expectancy is heavily influenced by infant mortality. When half of all those born are dead by the age of 15 (a population pattern that was formerly common but is thankfully now almost eradicated), the average life expectancy was necessarily low. Even so, those who survived past 20 still had a good chance of living to be over 60. Older people have therefore always existed and, as seen in Chapter 2, their contribution in terms of experience, spirituality or other social attributes has been recognized in all societies.

Even though life expectancies have increased and infant mortality has fallen, it is worth noting, in the midst of doom and gloom about population ageing, that the total world population remains young. For example, if current predictions are right, by 2025 the numbers of people over 60 are expected to amount to 14 per cent of the total world population. This projection depends on a falling birth-rate. At present this looks unproblematic because, with minor blips such as the baby boom after the Second World War, birth-rates have fallen consistently as women became more educated and prosperity increased. The median age (the age at which half the world's population are older and half younger) will move from 23.4 in 1950 to 31.1 in 2025 (United Nations, 1991: 11). This change of less than ten years in median age over three quarters of a century gives some idea of the time it takes for ageing to work through populations and the very high numbers of young people as compared with old.

Dependency rates

Demography's other great, but even more culture bound, contribution to the study of ageing is the concept of dependency ratios or rates of dependency. The assumption behind these measures is that the popula-tion of 'working age' has to support a growing number of 'dependants' (see Pampel, 1998 for a survey of ageing based on this assumption). The number of dependants (children under working age and adults over retirement age) is expressed as a ratio or as a percentage of the 'working age' population.

It is well known, but not well publicized, that in most countries outside the industrialized West and Japan, the ratio of the 'working age' population (usually 15–59) to the 'non-working age' (0–14 and 60 to death) is almost wholly determined by the number of children (neontic or youth dependency), rather than the number of people over 55, 60 or 65 (gerontic or old-age dependency). For example, in 1990 the dependency rate, defined as the percentage of people who were not of working age, was as high as 111 per cent in Ethiopia (more 'dependants' than 'workers'), where the demographic transition had barely begun and there were still very large numbers of children under 15. This can be contrasted with Japan where the dependency rate was almost three times lower, at 43 per cent. The difference is that in Japan the concern about population ageing had already generated new policies (Jacobs, 1998; Takahashi and Someya, 1985), but Ethiopia's old-age dependency rate can increase for many years before it begins to equal the youth dependency rate.

Problems again arise with the imposition of Eurocentric concepts across cultures. Male-dominated views of the workforce that assumed that only men were 'workers' have been shown greatly to overestimate the cost of future pension support in countries where women's labour force participation has gone up (Johnson and Falkingham, 1992). Again, the population of 'working age' may not be 'working', that is gainfully employed in the formal economic sector. Also, the terms 'working' and 'non-working' indicate the Western origins of the terminology. As Caldwell and Caldwell (1992) point out, all over the world children in poor families begin work around four years old, and elders work till they can no longer do so. In worldwide terms, people may be defined as 'old' and 'dependent' by demographers, but the vast majority of them are working. They could even be defined as productive, if productivity was measured in terms of freeing others to do paid work, or if informal unpaid work and/or self-care (see Chapters 7, 9 and 10) were counted as productive. It is only in countries in a very advanced stage of demographic transition (such as Europe and North America) that the number of *older* people is the most important aspect of demographic dependency. In the rest of the world it will be many decades before increased length of life becomes as important in population terms as decreasing numbers of births. It follows that worldwide, the greying of the population means a *drop* in the number of people of non-working age who are 'being supported' by those of working age. Furthermore, this drop is accompanied by an increase in the size and quality of the labour force as healthier and better educated young people reach working age – the demographic bonus (see http://www.unfpa.org/, on world population ageing, 1998). It is therefore hard to argue that population ageing threatens the world economy, though it may result in greater hardship for many older men and women (see Chapter 5).

A counter argument is that the old cost more than children, so the old-age dependency ratios should be weighted to take account of this. The different social (mainly education, health care and pensions) and private (household) costs of bringing up children and supporting elders vary greatly from country to country, but in welfare states the cost of pensions makes older people more expensive than children (Hills, 1993). In developing countries it appears that elders cost less than children. There are fewer of them, most get no pensions or public assistance and, when health care costs are high, few appear in hospitals (Cohen, 1998), so it is very hard to argue realistically that they are a serious burden. In all countries the entitlements of older men and women are politically far easier to ration or cut than the entitlements of children (see Chapters 7 and 8).

Burden and the intergenerational contract

The burden assumed to exist and quantified by national dependency ratios is frequently individualized in discussions of the women's intergenerational contract to care (Lorenz-Meyer, 1996). The growth of the aged population is presented as an unsustainable burden of care on mid-life women. Once again, this is a simple matter of drawing conclusions from numbers without considering culture. In the UK a very high proportion of care in old age is provided by spouses, mainly wives, but also husbands (Arber and Gilbert, 1989; Green, 1988). Daughters and daughters-in-law come next and it is frequently pointed out that there are fewer of them than in the past (Wicks and Henwood, 1984). There are two problems with this use of data. One is a matter of numbers – numbers of available children are high (Timaeus, 1986) until the baby boom generation reaches the ages when their care needs are likely to increase. In the UK or USA, this will be around the year 2025 if they become frail in large numbers at 75, and 2030 if at 80, as seems more likely on current projections of healthier ageing. Myers has stated that in America elders in

> . . . the decades ahead should have more living relations of different generations and, therefore, greater potential sources of social and material support, even though the long term trend is towards a stable population where kin availability is restricted. (Myers, 1990: 39)

In other words, there is no immediate demographic crisis of care for frail elders. Even so, numbers of *potential* carers are not the main issue. Numerous studies have shown that in advanced societies it is not the number of children that determines the level of care in later life. The concentration of caring on one 'principal carer' is a reality, not a fiction of social service departments. In most families one carer does most of the work and so as long as there is one (preferably female) child, the size of the family is not so important. The other cultural reality of caregiving in Western societies is that variety among possible caregivers in terms of sex and generation is also beneficial (see Myers, 1990 above). Men are more likely to provide transport and home maintenance (Qureshi and Walker, 1989), younger generation relatives provide emotional support (see Forster, 1989 for a fictional account of family care in the UK). The older generation may be available when mid-life main carers are at work and so on. It follows that the 'long thin family' of four or five generations may be just as efficient at caring as the traditional large three-generation family (always provided it existed as a widespread, operational, caring entity, which is doubtful).

And, finally, while on the burden of care, we may note that as people, particularly women, live longer, the age when care is needed has shifted upwards in Western countries (OECD, 1998). Men and women are less and less likely to need care in their 60s but more likely to be giving care – to children, grandchildren or older parents. Carers are similarly ageing so that the burden of care no longer falls on 'women in the middle' caring for children and parents. This is not to say that teenagers or even young adults who have not left home do not add to the work of mid-life women, but to point out that the chances of having children in nappies at the same time as caring for an incontinent parent are quite low. It is now more likely to be the 'pivot' generation who are caring for grandchildren and parents. However, if the age of childbirth continues to rise across classes and minority groups, this effect will fade.

All these considerations add up to a call for greater care in the presentation of demographic data on what is becoming known as the 'female care potential'. Leaving aside the highly contested issue of whether care is a prerogative of women, it seems very likely that the ages of caregiving and the age of frailty are changing. Demographic statistics need at least to reflect this, so that men and women over 65 are not assumed to be all in need of care, and care is not assumed to be provided by those aged 40 to 60. The OECD, for example, now presents the numbers of women aged 46–69 as a proportion of the population over 70 (OECD, 1996: 19, Table 1.1). If we ignore the apparent assumption that one shifts from caregiver to care receiver at age 70 (over 80 might be more realistic), the approach is closer to reality in OECD countries than most measures of population care potential.

Cohort variations

While demography has often ignored differences in culture, it has been interested in changes between cohorts within cultures. Cohorts are made up of all those who are born in one year (each bar in Figure 3.1a) or, more commonly, within a space of five or more years (each bar on Figure 3.1b). The members of a cohort may differ individually or in terms of class, gender and so on, but they normally share certain life experiences such as belonging to a boom generation or being young in times of war or economic depression. As different cohorts with their different life experiences reach old age, the nature of the older population, defined as those over a certain age, changes. Women who have experienced many pregnancies can expect on average to be less healthy in old age than women who have never been pregnant or who have had few children. So those who were part of the collapse in the birth-rate in the 1930s live longer than earlier cohorts who still had large families. Men who gave up smoking early in life can equally expect to live longer than those who smoke all their lives and, hence, later cohorts of non-smokers may expect to live longer than today's very old men. These differences may affect individuals but they show up more clearly when measuring large numbers of people across a given age group. One aspect of ageism is that we do not collect enough data on differences in the older population, either within or across cohorts (see below) and so important cohort differences are obscured.

Ethnic variations

National demographic data have yet another weakness that could easily be remedied, and sometimes is. Countrywide totals can obscure the cultural differences that exist within nation states. Migrants and minorities, young or old, may be made invisible in demographic tables. Often migrants reach old age earlier than the dominant majority. Culture (greater respect for old age makes it less fearsome), poverty, poor housing and working conditions may all be implicated. Or there may be something special about the migrant experience (the stresses of racism for example) which contributes to earlier ageing. An unresolved demographic controversy that is of interest to gerontologists is the question of longer life for minority groups, or, the 'demographic crossover'. In the USA, life expectancies for Afro-Americans are consistently lower than for whites up to the age of around 75. At this point Afro-Americans take the lead. Explanations for this phenomenon are still in dispute (Olshansky, 1995). One is that disadvantage over the life course weeds out all but the strongest survivors in Afro-American communities, and so at late ages they live longer. Another is the belief that older Afro-Americans consistently exaggerate their ages. A similar controversy rages over the populations (mostly in mountain districts), which have recorded very long lives (100–120 years being normal).

Questions for the future

Demographic changes have had very big effects over the past 50 years. It is almost certain that they will continue to be important, but the effects are far from clear. In developed countries the major issues must be the birth-rate, the state of the economy and the political effects of an ageing electorate. The first question is whether the birth-rate can continue to fall in countries like Germany or Italy, whether it has reached an all-time low, or whether it will stabilize or even rise. The reduction in the birth-rate has been accompanied in most countries by a rise in the age of motherhood, which is most pronounced among women with relatively good jobs. The question is whether this trend will be maintained long enough to lengthen the time between generations and possibly to cause a transition from the four- and five-generation family which has accompanied longer life expectancy back to a much extended three-generation family. Just as it is unclear how far the trends will go, or how long they will continue, it is also unclear whether they will spread to more countries or be confined to a few.

Then, as later chapters show, it is unclear how the changing composition of the population and, in particular, the growth in the numbers of older men and women, will affect economies, social structures, political life and the distribution of power. In countries where economic prosperity is not assured for all, or where the state does not take collective responsibility for income maintenance in old age, it seems very unlikely that birth-rates can fall to the low levels common in the West (see Cain, 1986a; Robinson, 1986). In Cain's (1986b) research population, older widows with no adult sons were simply absent (dead). Older couples and men with no adult sons were less common than might have been expected, given the age distribution of younger couples. Similar but less extreme processes appear to be at work in rural India and China. Birth-rates may therefore be expected to fall in all countries as more women are educated, but there will still be a need for surviving children unless adequate pension systems become universal – something very unlikely in the short or medium term.

Other public health risks arise from AIDS and any similar diseases that may appear. The effects of pollution, war and famine following natural and manmade disasters will either leave older men and women to care for the children of a decimated midlife age group and/or will cause higher mortality among the old. It is usually the very young and the old, particularly older women, who die in such disasters (Tout, 1989). Future demographic projections and the social relations that go with them are therefore unclear in many respects.

Conclusion

One problem for demographers, and gerontologists who use their data, is that the collection of data based on chronological age has ageist implications. We know that 'the old' are not a discrete group with clear boundaries and characteristics and that it is not possible to define a fixed 'threshold' which can be crossed into old age, but data are still presented in this way. Such data have their uses, for example predicting future numbers of pensioners (but not the cost, which depends on the performance of the economy) in countries with good pension coverage. At the same time these data can give a false sense of accuracy and cultural uniformity. World numbers of people over 65 group together countries where a pension is normal, and countries where older men and women continue in paid work if they can, and those where the majority work unpaid in order to survive – in agriculture or the grey economy. Variations in the health status of populations over 65 across countries may be so great as to make population aggregates meaningless. Even in the most advanced countries there is under-enumeration of some groups. In developing countries data are likely to be even less accurate. However, the trend towards older populations is clear.

As a subject demography has concentrated on measuring populations in terms of fertility and birth-rates and has shown less interest in those past reproductive age (even for men, few become fathers after the age of 65). One result has been that demographic data are popularly used by the media to fuel ageist discourses. For example, the most important determinant of demographic transition is falling mortality among the young followed by a falling birth-rate, but older people are commonly blamed. They are indeed living longer all over the world, but their impact on population growth is relatively small. In other words, the causes of demographic transitions are to be found at the beginning of the life course, not at the end. Similarly, crises in the cost of pensions and the availability of care continue to be popularly presented as consequences of rising numbers of older people. In fact, changes in the number of pensioners are far less important than the number of men and women in paid work, their productivity and their willingness to support their parents and grandparents. Pensions crises depend more on economic, political and cultural factors, than on demography.

It is also easy to forget that in the great majority of countries in the world overall dependency ratios are falling as the birth-rate falls. In countries with fully functioning pension schemes elders can be assumed to cost more than children, but in most of the world entitlement to a pension is the exception not the rule. Children cost more than elders and as their numbers fall the 'burden' of dependency on the working-age population falls too. Population ageing produces a demographic bonus as an increasingly highly skilled and healthier workforce has fewer dependants to support. The number of older people grows but there is no sign of a pensions crisis for many decades to come. There is undoubtedly an unsolved problem of supporting older people in the rapidly growing megalopolises of the developing world but this is an issue of poverty not demography.

Different demographic data will be needed in the future. As the OECD (1996: 56) said:

> ... policy indicators about the level of receipt of long term care services, must, to be most useful, be capable of disaggregation by five year age bands, up to at least 85 years of age. This must be a priority for national statistical agencies.

And there is also a need for better data on cohort variations within countries in terms of cultural and ethnic differences, rural and urban variations, class and income differences and changes within and between cohorts in later life.

Further reading

Sen, K. (1994) *Ageing: Debates on Demographic Transition and Social Policy*. London, Atlantic Highlands, NJ: Zed Books.
http://www.ifa-fiv.org/mfa3.htm – on global ageing.
http://www.oecd.org/subject/ageing/awp5_6e.pdf – on population in OECD countries.
http://www.popin.org/pop1998 – on world population and projections.
http://www.unfpa.org/ – on world population ageing.

CHAPTER 4

OLDER PEOPLE AS POLITICAL ACTORS

The big changes in the postmodern world are that there are many more older people (older voters in democracies) than ever before, and that modern communications may enable them to become more and more politically conscious. We therefore concentrate on two aspects of political power in later life. The first is the power of individual elders and the second is the rising power of elders en masse.

Power and older individuals

Most societies have had social structures that enabled some older men and women to become powerful. As Chapter 2 showed, there are practical aspects of long life such as the accumulation of wealth, descendants, experience and favours given and received which, when properly managed, add up to power and influence. This influence can be converted into political power. There are also spiritual advantages to being older in those societies where elders are believed to be closer to God or where the wisdom and religious knowledge that accompany long life are respected. These, too, can be deployed as sources of power. The hierarchies of the family when extended to the wider society also favour older people. Older leaders may be the patriarchs or matriarchs of their people, ruling over symbolic families, revered for their age as well as their symbolic status. We may think of Golda Meir (1898–1978) in Israel, Konrad Adenauer (1876–1967) in Germany or Mao Zedong (1893–1976) in China.

The symbolic power of older leaders appears to be a 'deep structure in human affairs' (Gutmann, 1988: 89) and remains strong in a very wide range of societies. Meir and Adenauer were active leaders, wielding considerable personal and institutional power,in the case of Adenauer, at a very advanced age. Other elders retain symbolic rather than actual power. In traditional societies a case was quoted by Fortes of the Tallensi:

> An old man could be blind, deaf and mentally incompetent and have relinquished the management of household affairs to his sons but he is still the head of the family and lineage, the hub of their unity, and the intermediary between them and their ancestors. However infirm an old man

may be of body or understanding he is regularly told of everything that happens in the house and his consent is always obtained before anything is done in his name, as everything that pertains to the family and lineage must be. (Fortes, 1949: 181)

This approach to power in old age, while apparently more common in societies where elders are valued simply for being old, is not confined to such societies. We have only to think of Winston Churchill or Ronald Reagan, who continued in the highest posts even when they were suffering from dementia. Murphy (1986) opens her discussion of dementia in old age using the example of Churchill in his last term of office:

This man who had previously been able to work all hours with intense concentration could at times not follow the drift of conversations or grasp the meaning of official documents. His private secretary condensed down long documents to a single paragraph. . . . Yet he steadfastly denied that anything was wrong and resisted all suggestions that he rest or step down from the job. (Murphy, 1986: 2)

Men and women who are older may indeed be wiser, but in the modern world wisdom and accumulated experience may be seen as signs of obsolescence and so disqualify rather than qualify them to lead. Traditional objections to the old appear to have been strengthened by transitions associated with globalization – the old are negatively viewed as rigid, bigoted, backward looking, and unwilling to give up power despite obvious signs of incompetence, as with Churchill. The ambivalence that surrounds those in power is reinforced by ageism and its influence is stronger or weaker depending on the strength of individual leaders and the cultures they operate within.

Changing political power

Power for some elders does not automatically mean power for all elders, even in cultures that respect older men and women. There is a difference between being respected and looked up to within a family group and achieving political power in a wider society. Power for the majority of the older population with no special status is likely to depend on the ballot box and so be confined to democracies with high numbers of older voters. Since, as Chapter 3 showed, the *proportion* of older people is going to continue relatively low in developing countries (despite very rapid growth in *numbers*, see for example Turkey in Figures 4.1. and 4.2), the main political effects of an ageing population are likely to be confined to advanced industrialized countries – the West and Japan.

There are two aspects of demographic change and political power. One is the size of the older electorate, which is predictable, and the other is voting behaviour, which may change. The age of voting is 18 in most countries and as smaller cohorts reach voting age the proportion of potential voters who are over a cut off point such as age 50 or 65 goes up faster than their share of the total population. Simple percentage changes such as those shown in Figures 4.1 and 4.2 do not automatically result in changes in power structures. Even when older voters begin to make up half the potential electorate, there can be no certainty about the outcomes. We have to ask whether older people will bother to vote, whether they will vote as a block and how will they balance the wider interests of their community or country as against their own sectional interests. And since votes are not the only source of political power, there are questions to be asked about the strength and capacity of pressure groups and lobbies and the baby boomers' backlash, or the efforts by younger people to retain power. These issues are discussed below.

Changes in numbers of voting age

The number of men and women of voting age can be calculated with reasonable accuracy in the ageing democracies of the Western world. (Even those who do not vote are potential voters and so have some political influence.) In countries where the birth-rate has collapsed, the size of the young electorate is falling but numbers in the older electorate are rising steadily. This trend is very unlikely to be reversed in the next quarter of a century.

Figure 4.1 shows that potential changes in the proportion of older voters are massive – early in the next century well over 40 per cent of all potential voters will be over 50 in many Western European countries. However, the calculations include migrants from outside the EU who are younger than the average and cannot vote in countries such as Germany and Switzerland. The actual proportions of older voters in the electorate will therefore be even higher in some countries than is shown in Figure 4.1 and well above the average in some areas within countries. Add to this the fact that older people are more likely to go to the polls than the young and it is clear that older voters will become more important in most countries.

It takes 18 years for a change in the birth-rate to result in rising numbers of young voters, but the number of older voters will continue to increase unless there is some new and major scourge which radically affects the death-rate among older voters. The effect of migrants depends on whether they can vote and where they live. Often they are concentrated in certain areas, where their effect on local election results will be greater than if they were scattered across the country.

The world has never experienced democracies with such high proportions of older people and it is unclear how they will develop.

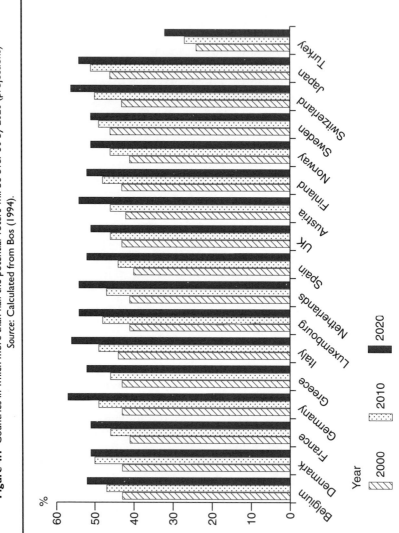

Figure 4.1 Countries in which more than half the potential voters will be over 50 by 2020 (projections) Source: Calculated from Bos (1994).

Older women, defined as those over 50, move from being approximately one fifth of the potential electorate to over a quarter in most of the countries shown in Figure 4.2. Since older women have been more or less invisible in the policy-making process up till now except as burdens or carers, it seems highly likely that policy-makers will take more notice of their wishes than they have in the past.

Older people as voters

Numbers alone do not determine voter influence. The first question to ask is whether older voters will indeed vote in local or national elections, or for the European Parliament or in referendums. (In Australia voting is compulsory in national elections but, as long as migration continues, elders will not make up the high proportions of the electorate shown in Figures 4.1 and 4.2.) In recent years voter apathy has been increasing in many countries. First-time voters and those in their 20s have high rates of abstention. Older people, on the other hand, have been consistently more interested in politics than the younger in the USA and Europe and more likely to vote (Leichsenring et al., 1999; Naegele, 1999). In America, where voting turnout is low, especially among the young, older voters have more weight than their numbers alone would suggest. Normally seniors cast 20 per cent of all votes (Binstock, 1997; Wallace et al., 1991). In the future elders will be better educated and so even more likely to vote, unless they become disillusioned with political systems. Poor health and disability have also been recorded as reducing voter turn-out, but the health of older people is expected to improve in advanced democracies. New technology may also be used to enable people with disabilities to vote. There is the strong possibility, therefore, that political involvement by older men and women will grow even faster than their crude numbers.

We can expect political parties to take a growing interest in the 'older vote', especially in areas where there are very large proportions of older voters or when they look like uniting on single issues such as pensions. Elders themselves may well respond to greater attention from politicians and media by seeing their vote as more important and so go to the polls in greater numbers. As the elders who prepared the DaneAge report on later life in Denmark said:

> . . . elderly people . . . were characterized chiefly by poverty, ill health and loneliness. . . . We do not feel as powerless or alienated as many people did in the past. . . . A change in the pattern of sex roles has especially made women more self-confident and active. (DaneAge, 1990: 40)

Japan is the other country where elders are predicted to be a very high proportion of the electorate in the near future. It differs from the West

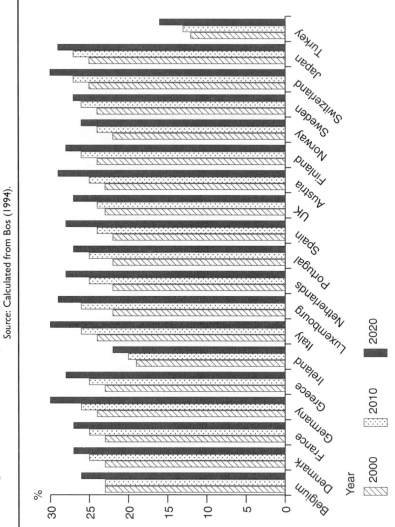

Figure 4.2 Women over the age of 50 as a percentage of total voting-age population: selected countries
Source: Calculated from Bos (1994).

in the degree of respect for older people and the strength of traditions of family responsibility for the welfare of elders. It is possible that elders will feel they have interests in common and no inhibitions about identifying with others of their age group, but so far there is no reason to suppose that elder consciousness will convert into political action at national level (Sodei, 1995).

Life cycle and generation

As with most key issues in ageing, there is a lack of research on older voters. A major problem is that most research has taken the 'older voter' as any and everyone over the age of 60 or 65. This apparently arbitrary division may once have related to pension ages but it could well be obsolete now that a large fraction of the labour force has either been forced out of the labour market or taken early retirement by the age of 55. Even if 65 does mark some kind of turning point in voter behaviour, when we ask whether it is reasonable to treat men and women aged over 65 as a single homogeneous cohort, the answer will be no. The growing importance of older voters means that new research will undoubtedly be more enlightened.

Meanwhile, two main perspectives on voting behaviour in later life can be identified: life-cycle theory and cohort or generation theory. There is evidence to support both, but no firm answers. According to life-cycle theory, the young are in favour of the new but become more conservative as they age. In the UK Dunleavy and Husbands (1985) showed that, although older people voted in much the same way as younger people, there was a minority of pensioners with higher incomes who were very much more likely than the average to vote for conservative parties. The same is true of better off retirement migrants in Australia (retirees in coastal Queensland and New South Wales voting for white Australia policies) and in the USA (Republican bias in retirement cities, Kastenbaum, 1993). Exit polls for the UK 1997 election indicated that the proportion of women voting Labour fell from 56 per cent of the 18–29-year-old age group to 34 per cent among the over 65s. None of these findings necessarily supports life-cycle theory since older right-wing voters may always have been right-wingers. According to cohort theory, on the other hand, 'We must not ask how old the elector is, but when he [sic] was young' (Butler and Stokes, 1974: 54). It follows that voting patterns are formed by generations in response to specific historical conditions (Binstock and Day, 1995) and continue into later life. This is vividly illustrated by the stories of 15 left-wing activists in *Lifetimes of Commitment* (Andrews, 1991).

The next question is how far individual voters or cohorts can change their allegiance in later life. Norris (1998), for example, notes that in the

USA, party loyalties strengthen over the lifetime. Alwin (1997) tentatively disagrees. His analysis of American data collected over time by the National Election Studies and General Social Surveys suggests that people become slightly less fixed in their political attitudes in later life. Since his oldest 'cohort' was aged 66–83(!) and his samples were small, it is not clear how much weight should be attached to his findings. Rose and McAllister (1990) see cohorts as capable of changing the way they vote and suggest that age and conservatism (with a small c) go together, so fewer old people will vote for a radical party whether it is on the right or the left. This might be the explanation for the widespread shift of older Tory voters from Conservative to Liberal Democrat in the Tory heartlands of southern England in 1997 (Geddes and Tonge, 1997).

Elders as a lobby

In the USA there is a much longer and stronger tradition of old age solidarity than in Europe, and the American experience has shown that elders can unite, especially as a lobby group and in local elections. Authors such as Pratt (1976; 1993) and Putnam (1970) or Achenbaum (1983) and Elman (1995) writing on the Townsend movement, have identified an early tradition of national movements for seniors which gathered strength in the Depression years. More recently, the American Association of Retired People (AARP) had 28 million members in 1990, which amounted to considerable commercial and political muscle (Torres-Gil, 1992). The AARP began as a group of retired teachers who negotiated better terms for health insurance. Since older people need cheap health insurance in a private health care system, the ability to negotiate discounts was a major catalyst in the growth of the AARP and hence of the American elders lobby.

Even so, elder power in America is now thought to have limitations, most obviously since the reversal of the Medicare Catastrophic Coverage Act 1988. Torres-Gil has concluded that:

> No other major legislation had ever been enacted and repealed within a year due to political pressure. On the other hand, older people were perceived, as a result, as a selfish interest group wanting expanded benefits without the burden of paying for them. (Torres-Gil, 1992: 81)

In other words, when the shift in resources from young to old was seen as extreme, the old-age lobby provoked a backlash (Quadagno, 1993) and the legitimacy of the elder lobby was successfully challenged. Torres-Gil therefore sees the repeal, in 1989, as the turning point for American elders. Henceforth, they might have more political *resources* in terms of votes, education and possibly money, but not necessarily more political *power*. In his view, their future as a block depends on how effectively the legitimacy of their demands can be maintained, and whether they move to voting as a block rather than relying on lobby coalitions to represent their interests. There is also the problem of class division, with the relatively well off members, who are the backbone of the AARP, failing to look after the interests of the less well off.

No discussion of lobby politics in America would be complete without mention of the Gray Panthers. While the AARP has been essentially mainstream and age based in its approach to politics, the Gray Panthers, founded in 1970 by Maggie Kuhn, was much more militant and from the start aimed to recruit members of all ages who cared about justice (Jacobs, 1980). Although its numbers were never large, it caught the imagination of the public and the media. In consciousness-raising terms its activities were out of all proportion to the size of its membership. The name was striking and there is an offshoot in Germany (Walker, 1999).

In UK the main lobby groups for elders, Age Concern and Help the Aged, are basically pressure groups run by younger people, even though they have many older participants. Organizations for older people such as Pensioners' Link and the National Federation of Pensioners are much smaller. As mainly working-class organizations, they have never had the same visibility or recognition by the government of the day as the big charitable pressure groups, but were undoubtedly more representative of the grassroots (Bornat, 1998). In the rest of Europe there are pensioners groups in all the EC countries (Gifford, 1990; Walker and Naegele, 1999) and some of these may yet move into high-profile activist roles. Germany and France are distinguished by wide-ranging representation of older people in civil society, for example retired members' sections in trade unions, and pensions systems which assume that elders will be represented on governing bodies. Britain has been slow to set up ways for pensioners to contribute to political decision-making but the 1998 initiative on *Better Government for Older People* (www.bettergovernmentforolder people.gov.uk) is a recognition of the growing power of older voters. The influence of pensioners' lobbies at European Community level appears set to increase.

Single-issue politics

In the future it seems likely that single-issue campaigns will become more important as ways of influencing policy. Environmental groups have already exploited this new development in both the USA and in Europe. Campaigns against oil companies, for animal rights, or over local environmental issues, can unite a range of people across classes and age groups. Older men and women may or may not bring a distinctive perspective, but their numbers will increasingly count. In these cases they are likely to be integrated into the main movements they are supporting. (In postmodern terms, older men and women now have a choice of new political identities, mixed age or age based, and their commitment can vary according to the issues of the time.) Such movements are in tune with other developments in single-issue politics. They offer older men and women the chance to join a functioning organization, and this opens up more political possibilities to older people who do not always have the time (in terms of years needed to build up a movement) to develop long-term political groups of their own.

The limitations of single-issue parties for older people were shown in 1994 in the Netherlands, when two pensioners' parties together gained 7 out of 150 seats in Parliament. They had campaigned against a proposal to freeze pensions for four years. However, their spokesman was quoted as saying that they would join a major party if it could be persuaded to take their concerns seriously, because they favoured intergenerational solidarity rather than separatism. Once the main issue of pensions was removed the parties collapsed. Experience in other countries has similarly shown both the power of pensioners and the ephemeral nature of their mobilization. In Australia (Sax, 1990), Canada (Gifford, 1990) and in New Zealand in 1998, pensioners organized to vote down means testing or cuts in their entitlements. These were not shifts in their favour, since they only maintained or restored the previous position, but they were hailed as triumphs for older voters. In the 1993 Christchurch by-election in the UK, a 34 per cent swing, the largest ever recorded against a party in government, was led by pensioners voting against a rise in fuel tax. This may be the first instance of pensioners voting in their own interests as a block in the UK.

Zero sum models of power

The above discussion presupposes a certain model of political action. Most political writing has used an adversarial or zero-sum model of age-group politics – power for one group is gained at the expense of another, and power is expressed as the self-interest of a defined group. Older voters are seen as another self-interested group, like ethnic minorities or women. Such a model appears relevant though contested (Street, 1998) in America, where there is a long history of appeals to clearly defined blocks of voters and lobbying is very well developed. It is not entirely satisfactory in a European or Japanese context, where social solidarity and links between age groups have been more in evidence, and lobbying has not been such an important aspect of political decision-making. In cultures where social solidarity is highly valued, policies for inter-generational solidarity and integration of older men and women into mainstream society are more in evidence. For example, 1993 was the

European Year of Older People and *Intergenerational Solidarity* (my emphasis) and supported by EU funds and money from the governments involved.

Structural aspects of political power

While all the above are general aspects of political power for older men and women, the actual outcomes will depend greatly on political, economic and social structures in different countries and regions. For example, Figures 4.1 and 4.2 show national totals. The variation within countries will be very much greater. In areas of high retirement migration, the proportion of older potential voters may reach two out of three in some local electorates. Similar high proportions will exist in run-down areas where the young have moved away and only the old remain. In the new era of postmodern fragmentation and targeted political campaigns, it is quite possible that constituencies with high proportions of older voters will have to be treated as key marginals and their importance will grow. Even if this does not happen, individual candidates will have to avoid alienating 'the older vote', especially in local elections.

We can therefore expect a wider growth of various government and quasi government structures that enable older people's views to be heard. (Some would say the aim was to head off trouble by defusing the complaints of older voters.) Pensioners' forums, the representation of clubs/organizations for elders at local, regional and central level in France (Guillemard, 1980) and the British initiative on *Better Government for Older People*, all come under the heading of encouraging older men and women to participate in political and civil society.

The policy of the media, especially television, may also turn out to be very important. As cases where the older vote has swung an election are reported more often, it seems likely that a popular consciousness of pensioner power will evolve. In countries where pensions are relatively high, the size of the 'silver' market will grow and members may be presented as a political block. Media reports of grey power seem likely to strengthen the passive political power of elders. By this I mean that if policy-makers *believe* that there is a block of older voters, customers or service users out there, who could be upset by insensitive action, there will be changes in policy. For example, even in Australia, where older people make up a small proportion of the electorate by European standards, the 1998 budget was hailed as a package directed at older voters to win them back to the Liberal (conservative) party that they had apparently deserted. Changes in nursing home fees and health-care contributions and more generous tax relief for better off retirees were clearly targeted benefits. Gerontologists who lament the fact that the media take a stereotypic view of old age (this book among them) might remember that fragmented power is much weaker than unified power and if policy-makers believe, for ageist reasons, that the old are all the same, this may be beneficial in the short term. However, Wallace et al. (1991) advance a contrary view, saying that even in a high retirement state such as Florida, policy-makers do not see themselves as automatically responding to elder preferences.

Electoral systems could become key determinants of the ways in which elder power is manifested. It might be argued that in first-past-the-post voting systems older voters will do best if they join mainstream parties or operate through powerful lobby groups. In America the strength of the AARP has come partly because it was able to mobilize other lobby groups in common campaigns for better pensions and health services (Torres-Gil, 1992). On the other hand, in a system based on proportional representation, the best tactic may be to form a party either specifically or mainly for older people/pensioners. Party representatives will then get seats in proportion to the size of their vote and mainstream parties will be forced to set up pensioners' sections or to take more notice of their existing pensioners' organizations as in Austria (Leichsenring et al., 1999).

Proportional representation could therefore be one catalyst for the development of separatist elders' movements. Cuts in pensions might have the same effect, even though they appear to have only resulted in single-issue campaigns so far. As pointed out in Chapter 1, retirement age produces a body of pensioners and if cuts in existing pensions go too far, being a pensioner might become a long-run political identity. The achievement of the AARP in linking mass membership to health insurance seems unlikely to be repeated in Europe, where it is taken for granted that health care will be provided by the state or under state auspices. Cuts in health entitlements are likely to unite large numbers of people, not just elders (though the virtual abolition of long-term geriatric beds was accomplished in the UK with minimal opposition).

Conclusion

Political leaders have usually been older men or women. This seems unlikely to change, even though there may be more scope for young and dynamic politicians in the future. Older leaders have not been particularly concerned with the welfare of elders in the past, and there is no reason to believe that this will change in most of the world where older people make up less than 10 per cent of any possible electorate. However, there is the possibility of big changes in political life in democracies where the proportion of older voters is growing very rapidly. In many regions or constituencies in Europe or Japan, older voters could be over half the electorate. Not only will older people have more votes but they are likely to continue to go to the polls more conscientiously than the young. We can reasonably expect that they will have higher expectations in terms of their quality of life. They will be on average better educated, more healthy, better housed and, in many parts of Europe, they will be better off financially than they are today. For all these reasons they are likely to take more interest in politics and to be more likely to vote. Older women are in the majority in later life and their influence as voters and on policy may grow.

Mainstream (American) thinking assumes that elders will act like any other block and further their own short-term interests. There is, however, no certainty that this will be so. Bengtson and Achenbaum (1993) have pointed out that societies need to balance change with continuity, and elders are usually associated with continuity. Continuity need not mean knee-jerk conservatism, however. The long-run interests of community or nation (not to say humanity) may demand a more altruistic and less selfish approach than is assumed by market individualism. While not wishing to set up older men and women as peculiarly altruistic, there is no reason to believe that older voters with adequate pensions will want to divert ever more resources to themselves. They frequently want to see their grandchildren and great grandchildren 'settled'. They are aware of problems such as youth unemployment, family breakdown, high crime rates and problems of cultural transmission. Better policies in areas such as these are likely to get strong support from older voters.

The fact that elders may not unite in a political block (something that seems unlikely in Europe) does not mean that they will not have growing political power. There are already instances where elders have united or where governments have attempted to buy votes with age-friendly policies. Elder power need not be overt or active but can be defined as passive. There are four reasons for thinking that the political power of elders will grow in advanced Western democracies. The first is that their numbers are increasing, both in absolute terms and as a proportion of electorates. The second is that there will be regions or districts with very much higher proportions of elders than the average (Scharf, 1998: 176 n.10). They are likely to act as demonstration cases where the influence of elders can be clearly seen in local policies. Third, the media are becoming more sensitive to elders as a political force. There is no reason to think that this trend will be reversed as elders become more visible in terms of market segment. Finally, as with the media, there is evidence to indicate that politicians and other policy-makers see 'the old' as a group, whatever gerontologists may say about inter and intra cohort differences, and the ageism involved in ignoring them. The vision of an ever-growing block of older voters, customers and service users will affect the behaviour of younger policy-makers. In democracies the changes should be for the better.

We can conclude that the political power of older people appears bound to increase in Western-style democracies, but not through confrontation or the types of emancipatory politics associated with black power, disability groups or feminist movements. Over the past century the weight of numbers in democracies has caused a shift in favour, first of the working class, then of women and it may be that the third shift will be in favour of older men and women. Each shift is seen as wildly inadequate by the old left and too far too fast by the new right. A very wide range of policies which favour social solidarity and community awareness are good for older men and women as well as good for the rest of the population (Day, 1992), but particularly women with young children. More grey power could therefore mean better outcomes for all in Western democracies. As things stand, the impact of an ageing electorate on political life in modern democracies is unclear, but it would be unwise to think there will be no change.

Further reading

Vincent, J.A. (1999) *Politics, Power and Old Age.* Buckingham: Open University Press.

http://www.aarp.org/intl/orgs.htm – on world list of seniors' organizations and political parties who have contacted the web site by country (some with own websites).

http://www.bettergovernmentforolderpeople.gov.uk/

http://www.helpage.org/info/index_health.html – general links index.

http://www.ifa-fiv.org/menu1.htm – 'Strategies for a Society for all Ages, a global discussion document for the International Year of Older Persons, May 1998.

http://www.ifa-fiv.org/mfa4.htm – 'Toward a society for all ages'.

CHAPTER 5

GLOBALIZATION, STRUCTURAL ADJUSTMENT AND AGEING

> Development cannot be equated solely with economic growth – it must combine the triple objectives of income expansion, social development and environmental protection and regeneration. In short, the goal ought to be sustainable human development
>
> (Kaul, 1997: v).

One aspect of human development is support for elders so in a globalizing world it is important to ask how the relations between states and markets, between paid and unpaid work and between young and old and men and women affect the position of elders. At its most basic, globalization implies that the world is shrinking and becoming more uniform in some ways, but at the same time old unifying structures are fragmenting and diversity is increasing. The speeding up of communications and transport and the growing power of multinational corporations are obvious manifestations of globalization. Then there are changes in world stock markets and currency trading which mean that any country whose economic policies fall out of favour with world (or American) economic opinion is now vulnerable to a run on its currency and threatened bankruptcy. As global movements of people, money and goods increase, large parts of the world and many aspects of daily life become more and more standardized. Computers allow ever more information to be processed and transported at ever increasing speeds, and satellites beam information and television programmes round the world. The changes have meant that in nearly all countries standards of living have risen, population increase has slowed (see Chapter 3) and there are aspirations towards greater individual freedom and democracy. Within this big picture there are contradictory forces such as the rise of separatist movements, massive refugee problems, fundamentalist religious movements and, in more prosperous areas, the rise of consumerism and individualism. In different ways they all threaten the integrity and policy-making capacity of traditional nation states.

Economic growth and rising prosperity for many is reflected in an increase in world trade (Gillion, 1993). However, although the total has risen, developing countries have lost out. On the other hand, the Newly Industrializing Countries (NICs) of the Pacific Rim and Malaysia benefited greatly, and even after the check in growth in the late 1990s, their level of development is very different from Africa or the poorer regions of Latin America. Increases in trade, and the diffusion of Western life styles via television, film and advertising, have produced massive changes in living patterns and aspirations in virtually all parts of the world. Men in suits or jeans now appear in TV news pictures from all but the most famine stricken areas, and they are almost certainly drinking Coke or Pepsi off-screen. To quote Kalache:

> No matter if the household is miserable, in a slum area surrounded by open sewers, the adults unemployed, the children not receiving any kind of formal education, a television set is still affordable. If not they can watch the round the clock programming on their neighbour's set. (Kalache, 1993: 341)

Even in the developed world, life styles have changed dramatically over the last generation. For example, in rural France in the 1970s, an older person would normally expect to have to look after rabbits and/or hens and to grow a minimum of vegetables if at all possible, as well as the flowers needed for various cultural activities. Convenience aids to living, like washing powder, plastic bags, and prepared foods, were prohibitively expensive. Bathrooms and indoor toilets were not common, and women might still do their washing at communal washplaces in the street or beside the road. By the late 1990s this had wholly changed. Livestock was more or less confined to farms, vegetable growing was in decline and a range of frozen and partly prepared food was available in the smallest village shops and at discount prices in the neighbouring supermarkets. The nation was fully equipped with washing machines and refrigerators. A similar revolution has taken place at greater or lesser speed in most other countries. These changes make life easier and are, on balance, beneficial to elders in countries where pensions are adequate, but they lead to increased poverty and marginalization when pensions are low or very different for men and women, and older people cannot all share in the general improvements.

In developing countries and where pension coverage is inadequate, older people must still do paid work or grow food whenever they can (see Chapter 7). The United Nations report *The World Ageing Situation* (1991), for example, drew attention to the very high number of elders (men and women) worldwide who worked at child care, market gardening or looking after livestock. This type of work usually goes unrecorded in economic statistics and so is either invisible or undervalued. A survey reported by Tout (1989) of men and women over 70 in Vilcabamba, Ecuador, showed that only 13 per cent were not working outside the home. ILO projections for *economically* active members of the population over 55 for 1990 (see Table 7.1) produced figures of 73 per cent for men in Africa and 63 per cent in Asia. Rates for women were lower, 51 and

39 per cent respectively. In Europe in contrast the estimates were 37 per cent for men and 13 per cent for women (ILO, 1986, presented in United Nations, 1991: 26). The term 'economic activity' excludes a wide range of activities that are essential to free other family members to take paid work – water collection, cooking, cleaning, child care and subsistence cultivation or gardening. All these activities need to be added to get the real activity rates of older men and women in developing countries. Even in developed countries, child care remains an important activity which frees younger women to take paid work (Deven et al., 1998) and before 1991 older men and women spent large amounts of time queuing for their families in Eastern Europe (Calasanti and Zajicek, 1997). It is normal, therefore, for elders to be active if we take a world perspective.

The presence or absence of opportunities for self-provisioning in later life may become increasingly important if economic and family dislocation continue to increase. Lloyd-Sherlock, for example, found that low income elders in Argentinian and Brazilian cities usually had no steady source of income but fell back on a variety of income strategies. They claimed a variety of small public benefits if they could prove they were eligible, took charity when they could, worked at informal or formal casual jobs and were helped by relatives and neighbours (Lloyd-Sherlock, 1997, 1999).

Older men and women and the services they need are liable to be marginalized in a world where new technologies allow virtually everything to move (Quah, 1996) and, in theory, to move to the cheapest and most efficient location. The world producer in a world marketplace can shift factory or service, such as computerized banking or health maintenance organization patient records (which have been exported from Europe and America to India), to wherever the relevant labour or other inputs is cheapest and most efficient. There are some services, particularly social welfare services, which may prove more difficult to move, but there have been plans to export the care of frail elders to low-wage countries such as the Gambia and to export social care expertise to Asia (Health Solutions Pty. Ltd, 1994; McCallum and Geiselhart, 1996). Older people from the UK, Germany and the Low Countries have already exported themselves to lower-wage parts of southern Europe as retirement migrants (see Chapter 6).

The most harmful aspect of globalization as far as older men and women are concerned, is the growing ideological power of the belief in free markets and structural adjustment policies. Until the crises of the late 1990s in Asia and Russia it was possible to see restructuring as an inevitable and even beneficial result of the globalization of economic activity. According to this set of beliefs, structural adjustment was simply a side effect of growing prosperity, brought about by the rapid expansion in world trade, the free movement of capital and goods and the unification of world financial markets. It was believed that the abolition of subsidies and trade barriers was essential so that goods, especially food, could be distributed more efficiently. Greater efficiency was believed to lead to less waste and so to a better life for all. The recognition of the importance of safety nets for those made destitute by restructuring (see below) has begun to undermine the purity of market ideology. The failure of the IMF in Russia after the 1998 economic collapse has strengthened countries and policy-makers who oppose its policies. Increasingly there are calls for more regulation of world markets, not less. However, it is fair to argue that the main thrust of proposed reforms is to protect Western countries and not the disadvantaged peoples or states of the developing world. An exception might be made for the movement to reduce Third World indebtedness, see below.

The globalization of competition in the world marketplace presents companies with the excuse (or some would say the necessity) to drive down wages and disband or disempower trade unions which interfere with a free market for labour. Job security, employee rights and health-giving fringe benefits such as paid holidays are eroded, if not abolished, in the name of greater efficiency. In most countries this also means that it is increasingly difficult for older men and women to find and keep jobs. Periods of unemployment and low pay have knock-on effects on pension entitlements and savings, and so affect the long-term well-being of workers who are restructured. Unless safety nets, in the form of some type of state- or employer-financed benefit, are put into place, poverty increases in the short and long term. At the same time market individualism and a belief in the need to cut public expenditure can result in the erosion of collective state benefits. Charges may be imposed for health care and even primary education, for example, in Tanzania since 1993, (*Guardian*, 19 February 1999), and scarce cash has to go to support children and young people – not elders (Tracy, 1991).

In the absence of world agreement to curb these trends, debatable short-term gains in efficiency or profits are being made at the expense of long-term social cohesion and prosperity. The USA has been most successful in reducing the earnings and social entitlements of the low-paid and unemployed and widening the gap between rich and poor – in its own population. The long-term effects on support for existing elders and on future pensions are presented as problems for individuals rather than for society in general. Seniors may live in high-rise blocks and eat dog food, or be warehoused in nursing homes but, according to market ideology, that is a matter for them and not society.

Even in Western Europe the impact of economic restructuring is likely to intensify. In the worst case scenario, world trade competition leads to increasing concentration of businesses across Europe and large scale closures of small- and medium-sized firms. Peripheral regions decline rapidly and economic union strengthens the core (the golden banana of London, Paris, the Low Countries, Frankfurt and Milan). The process of impoverishment may be slowed by national and supranational policies designed to protect peripheral regions from the worst effects of industrial consolidation and economic unification, but the general trend is inevitable. The addition of the former Soviet bloc countries of Eastern Europe can only increase the number of regions needing support without increasing the resources to support them. The main questions are how far struggling regions will be assisted by the centre, and what controls countries will be able to maintain in order to protect socially necessary employment – in other words, how far current economic orthodoxy will be fought off. In the best case, economic unification will lead to steady growth, stable prices and inflation levels, and countries (possibly influenced by an ageing electorate, see Chapter 4) will continue to implement policies for national solidarity and a better quality of life for all, including elders. Declining regions will be supported, economically and socially, and farsighted leaders will put social solidarity high on the political agenda at the same time as creating economic policies which allow European business to compete and thrive in world markets.

Until 1997 an even more positive picture could have been painted for the Newly Industrializing Countries (NICs) of the Pacific Rim or East and South East Asia. Growing labour forces, (even if reliant on immigration) (see Krugman, 1996; 1999), and falling birth-rates, the demographic bonus (see Chapter 3), made it possible for labour productivity to far outstrip the rate of growth of the older population. The extension of funded pension schemes to more sections of the population was bringing in funds for investment and offered a breathing space, while pension outgoings were low. The losers in this strict approach to pension funding are men and women who have already passed pension age and those who will reach retirement in the near future. They have not built up pension rights and must rely on their families or on payments for the destitute if they have no savings or cannot find paid work (Kwon, 1999a).

Improvements in pension coverage have been combined in a few countries with more support for families, who are ideologically assumed to provide for the old. This belief is strongly underpinned by religion or philosophy in Japan and in countries where Islam or Confucianism is strong. In contrast to world economic fashion, East and South East Asian governments have continued to support state intervention against pure market freedom (Ghai, 1992), though the 1998 crisis restricted their autonomy. However, even in the more advanced Asian welfare states (Japan, Hong Kong, Korea, Singapore and Taiwan) state intervention has been aimed to speed up economic development, encourage investment and prioritize exports, not to provide welfare (Goodman et al., 1998). However, business has increasingly recognized the importance of state-assisted education and a national health service which offers universal coverage. Taiwan achieved almost complete health coverage as late as 1995, South Korea in 1989 and Japan since 1961 (Jacobs, 1998).

The needs of elders have increasingly been recognized, especially in Japan where rapid ageing (see Chapter 3) has concentrated the minds of policy-makers. A ten-year 'Gold Plan' to promote health and welfare services for older people was launched in 1989. As costs and projections of the ageing population increased, the plan was modified to reduce entitlements and raise the contributions of older people or their families, but extra funds were still needed (Jacobs, 1998). The New Gold Plan, launched in 1998, predicts a doubling in national welfare expenditure for the ageing population (Health and Welfare Bureau for the Elderly, Ministry of Health and Welfare Japan, 1998).

In Singapore the state has presided over an attempt to share the costs of elder support between the family and business (not the state). Legislation has encouraged the retraining of older workers who were deemed to be out of date in a rapidly changing economy, outlawed enforced early retirement, and allowed employers to waive annual increments for older workers if the cost of retaining them became too high. While Singapore may be alone in being able to legislate so widely, until recently a similarly authoritarian approach to state welfare for elders might have been predicted in other parts of South East Asia. The economic setback of the later 1990s makes this less likely for the moment.

Even the less dynamic countries in Asia were to some extent protected from the worst effects of structural adjustment policies (Ghai, 1992). Larger populations mean that even the poorest countries, such as Bangladesh, depend less on foreign markets than they do in Africa. Asian countries have long histories of urbanization and the shift to city life can cause less dislocation than it does in Africa. Larger manufacturing sectors compared with African or Latin American countries mean less vulnerability to falls in the price of agricultural raw materials. Debt burdens were lower and remittances from migrants over the 1990s offered support to low-income economies. Up till 1997, large numbers of men and women from the Indian subcontinent, the Philippines (Pertierra, 1992) and other centres of emigration could find work in the Gulf States, Malaysia, Taiwan, Hong Kong, Japan or even the USA and Canada. Ghai (1992) reported that workers' remittances amounted to 80 per cent of exports in Pakistan by 1982. In India remittances officially increased from 5 per cent of exports in 1972 to 25 per cent in 1982. Remittances are hard to measure and an unknown proportion are undeclared, but there is no doubt that they contribute to economic development at a national level (Libercier and Schneider, 1996) and to the welfare of the older generation at an individual level (Nana Apt, 1996).

World trade agreements (via the World Trade Organization) and the policies of the International Monetary Fund (IMF) and the World Bank continue to prioritize the well-being of the rich of the world at the expense of the poor. Gavin Davies (1998), for example, explains how money from ordinary taxpayers in developed countries is passed to the

UN regulatory organizations in the form of national subscriptions. It is then used to enable defaulting banks in developing countries to pay back the loans they have had from developed countries. The money thus returns to the shareholders of big banks who are protected from the consequences of unwise lending. As Davies says, 'this transfer from the general taxpayer to the bank shareholder almost certainly implies gains by the rich at the expense of the poor' (Davies, 1998). The decision to call on the IMF to support a national currency is also typically followed by a package of free market measures, which are either imposed from outside or used as an excuse by a local elite to overcome popular opposition. The package is likely to include enforced cuts in public expenditure, especially on social security, a shift from progressive to regressive taxation, that is taxing the poor relatively more heavily than the rich, cuts in subsidies on goods that benefit the poor (especially food), charges for social services, including health and sometimes even basic education, a rise in interest rates and policies to cut and casualize employment over large parts of the formal economy, and possibly also dismantling of import and export controls.

The effects of these structural adjustment policies differ in detail from country to country but certain broad outcomes are well established. As Plant has said, the market is not a planning device but some of its effects are very predictable (Plant and Barry, 1990). In the first place poverty and income inequalities increase. Gylfason (1994: iii) presents the orthodox positive view: 'At first the restructuring of the economy is accompanied by a collapse of output, increased unemployment and high inflation'. He believes that the next stage is greater productivity. The World Bank is more realistic:

> Transition produces winners – the young, the dynamic, the mobile, the connected – but it also imposes costs on visible and vulnerable groups, and in many countries it has been accompanied by a surge in measured poverty. (World Bank, 1996: 5)

One problem is that many elders and others in poverty will have died long before the economy picks up in the poorest countries – a poor country does not become rich just because of a few changes in economic policy. Another is that the new prosperity, if and when it occurs, is very likely to be concentrated on those who are part of the formal labour market and so it excludes most older women and a very high proportion of older men. It is very difficult to think of an increase in poverty in any country in the world that will not have an adverse effect on older men and women. When the increase in poverty is combined with cuts in health and social services the negative impact on elders is unavoidable. IMF-led cuts in public expenditure have routinely included cuts in subsidies for staple foods such as rice (Paul and Paul, 1995) which led to the outbreak of riots in Indonesia in 1998 and massive destruction of

Chinese-owned property. Health and education become subject to charges and poorer households lose out. All these cuts have differential impacts on different groups – men and women, rural and urban, old and young (Ghai, 1997), but the impact on the life of most elders is inevitably harmful. Even in Western Europe, where resistance to extreme free market ideology is relatively strong (excluding the UK), there is unremitting pressure to cut public spending, privatize services, reduce welfare and deregulate economies. The entitlements of older people have been reduced in most countries, even if only by raising the pension age. In Eastern Europe, where inflation has decimated pensions and the dismantling of social services has greatly reduced formal support for older men and women, death-rates appear to have risen in some countries and older beggars have become commonplace.

Meanwhile, the indirect effects of the rise in oil prices, combined with the knock-on effects of the Asian crisis, have continued to destabilize and impoverish countries in Africa and Latin America. Their development and their ability to finance social policies, such as pensions and health care, are inhibited by the international debts they owe to bankers and governments of the developed world. These debts are a knock-on effect of high oil prices and the associated huge rise in income for the oil-producing countries. The massive increase in petrodollars which could not be spent locally ended up in international banks. The banks appear to have taken a short-term view that the main aim was to get the money out on loan, with interest coming in, rather than to consider how the loans would be repaid in the long run. They lent to developing countries without much thought of the consequences. The result is a completely unsustainable level of debt in many countries. Debt repayments and interest (debt servicing) rose to an average of 45 per cent of total export earnings in sub-Saharan Africa (excluding Nigeria) and 22 per cent in Latin America in the 1990s (Ghai, 1992). In Chad, for example, debt repayments before restructuring were meant to be 50 per cent of the nation's budget (*Le Monde*, 3 September 1998). Development is virtually impossible under such circumstances when hard-earned export revenue is swallowed up by international creditors. The threatened bankruptcy and debt restructuring of Mexico in 1989 was the most highly publicized result of these free market policies, but the worst effects continued to be felt in Africa (excluding Nigeria and some former French oil-producing states) (Ghai, 1992). Calls in 1998 for better risk analysis after the extent of bad loans involved in the Asian crisis became clear, indicate that banks did not become more interested in the long-term future of the world economy and have continued to lend without much attention to the risks involved.

A world market that is ideologically presented as ever freer and hence ever better is, like any other social institution, subject to political pressures, even though these may be obscured for ideological purposes.

It follows that markets are not free but are heavily influenced by the powerful, and market prices reflect their interests. Western developed countries have the greatest political power and have increasingly been able to structure markets to their benefit. Since the 1974 oil shock, advanced countries have taken care to develop a wider range of oil suppliers. They have forced down the prices of most other (non petroleum) raw materials and so recouped some of their losses at the expense of the poorest countries in the world – mostly in Africa.

A so-called free market that is rigged in favour of the developed world is one very big disadvantage facing elders in the countries of Africa, Eastern Europe and Latin America (Neysmith and Edwardh, 1984). The other, and possibly even more serious, result of economic globalization for older people is the ideological stance of the economists who work for the World Bank, the WTO and the IMF. These international bodies, heavily influenced by the USA, have often appeared to have a messianic vision of a world in which individual freedom from government interference was the greatest possible good, and certainly the guarantee of enterprise and prosperity. There have been signs of change, most notably in the World Bank, where there has been a recognition that the state should do more in terms of social policy:

> ... market development without a functioning state is not an option ... in many countries the state is still not securing the economic and social fundamentals: a foundation of lawfulness, a benign (and stable) policy environment, basic social services, and some protection of the vulnerable. (World Bank, 1997: 39)

The need to safety net the vulnerable has been recognized (Barr, 1994; Umali-Deininger and Maguire, 1995) but not specifically for older men and women. Also, as Barr (1995) points out, effective safety netting depends on the poor being manageably few, the cost being affordable and the state having the administrative capacity to deliver social benefits. Any existing shortfall on these essentials is made much worse by structural adjustment, so the chances of disadvantaged elders getting what they need are very low in most of the countries involved. In countries that have the capacity to deliver safety netting for the old, as in South East Asia and South Korea, it does not appear to have been part of the rescue packages imposed in the 1990s economic crisis. In towns, the casualization of labour and cuts in public sector wages and employment mean that many families can no longer support the weakest or dependent members and elders come nearer to destitution. Health care will clearly be impossible to pay for, as any available cash has to go towards the health and education of younger family members. Increased competition and withdrawal of tariff protection can lead to the collapse of local industries and the growth of unemployment, and with it the inability of families to provide for 'unproductive' older people as Ekpenyong (1995) showed for Nigeria.

Urbanization

Less direct effects follow from the global trend to urbanization (United Nations Department of International Economic and Social Affairs, 1991). Social systems, which traditionally supported their older family or community members in all but the most extreme circumstances, have been undermined. A collapse in the price of agricultural raw materials following the shift in the terms of trade in the 1970s and 1980s, exacerbated by economic restructuring (Gillion, 1993), can leave older men and women alone in the countryside with nothing but poverty to look forward to. As communities are weakened, traditional, trust-based activities decline. Elders who cannot cope with farming in rural areas may be forced to migrate to the cities and to try to make a living in the grey economy. Tout (1993) lists a range of schemes in Latin America which allow elders to avoid starvation (see Chapter 10).

Older men and women and development

In these difficult conditions older people are often making valuable contributions to household and family income strategies, but their input is systematically lost. Ssenkoloto, (1984), for example, describes older men and women in Cameroon who are active in local development or who have set up clubs or pressure groups to work for local elders. In Europe, elders can keep communities alive until government aid and new technologies can revitalize dying regions and villages – as may happen in rural areas in France and Germany. They may support the younger generations directly (Case and Deaton, 1996; du Toit, 1994) or indirectly. All over the world older women, and some older men, look after children while the younger generation tries to find paid work. When remittances fail or AIDS wipes out the middle generation, they support the future of their societies. If they become frail they look after themselves, saving time and money, and often when they co-habit with the younger generation, continuing to be useful round the house and garden even when extremely disabled (Nana Apt, 1996).

Despite their continued activity, the dependence of older people on collective or co-operative endeavour is more obvious and overt than it is for younger generations. This does not mean that families fail to provide. Even in advanced Western countries it is estimated that 80 to 90 per cent of all care needs are met by families or elders themselves. As Chapter 10 indicates, few countries have more than 6 per cent of people of pension age in institutional care. The impact of the breakdown in traditional structures for collective support can be measured in terms of changes in the proportion of destitute or very low-income elders, but so far this has not been done on an international scale.

Social cohesion

To the non-believer, free market policies seem designed to increase social problems rather than solve them. This reality may even be evident to proponents of the market. Thus Longman, writing on the problems of the baby boomers in America, says:

> Today's poor, undereducated youth will become tomorrow's unemployed or marginally employed workers. Rather than pay taxes to support the baby boomers in old age, they will be more likely to collect public assistance themselves. Even if the more affluent members of the next generation decide not to subsidize the working poor, we have every reason to believe that they will nonetheless be forced to commit more resources to pay for police, jails, private security guards, and other measures to protect themselves against the expanding underclass. (Longman, 1987: 22–3)

Longman could also have added, but did not, that in the USA a lot of these poor are going to be blacks and Latinos. Thus the outlook for social cohesion, business confidence and economic growth may be even grimmer than for ageing baby boomers.

'Social problems need to be addressed not only in the interest of national cohesion and solidarity but as a necessary investment for future growth' (Ghai, 1992: 1). This will seem obvious to some, and heresy to others, who see social spending as a waste of money and a perversion of freedom. The real problem is that commentators from all sides agree that it is becoming increasingly difficult to deal with social problems at both the national and the international level. Most of the social problems worrying commentators are not directly related to ageing but, rather, to health and education, the productivity of the younger generation, the maintenance of social order and social solidarity, crime and governmental instability. These may seem much bigger issues than the problems of older people, but they all have an impact on older men and women, and reducing them would improve the quality of life of elders. Day (1992) has also powerfully argued that improving the life of older people would benefit other members of their communities. This too is true, but the mechanisms for improving the quality of life of any but the better off appear to be weakening rather than strengthening.

Conclusion

The rising impact of market forces in all areas of life and in all parts of the world is perhaps the most important aspect of globalization as far as older people are concerned. Older people as a group will always be badly affected by the extension of market forces because they lack market power. The actual impact on any one group or on individual men and women will vary in time and place. Although this book argues that there are choices to be made in policies for ageing populations, globalization (like population ageing) appears to be an element of change in the world that is inevitable. Many of its effects are modifiable but there is little chance of stemming the main phenomenon. More to the point, many of its results are beneficial, popular and greatly desired by those who have not yet benefited. Economic policies are usually presented by the champions of the free market as the outcome of semi-scientific laws which must result in changes for which 'there is no alternative', or at least no alternative that is as rational. This approach hides the political and ideological components of economic orthodoxy, and the aspects of global power and national self-interest that they embody. The outcome of globalization for the majority of the world's population and for older people everywhere therefore depends on how effectively countries and regional policy-makers can fight off economic policies that fail to benefit the poor. Policies that do not implicitly and explicitly strengthen social solidarity (and enable the transfer of resources to those who cannot work) will inevitably be harmful to older men and women. The hard line market economist would answer 'Who cares?', and he would have a point. Ageism is very widespread and as a result many people do not much care about the well being of elders who are not their parents. However, most readers will join the older population. If we are to look forward to old age with any confidence, we will need a re-evaluation of the political, economic and social contributions that older men and women make to development, new methods of measuring unpaid work and the reform of pension systems (see Chapter 7).

Further reading

Ghai, D. (1997) *Economic Globalisation, Institutional Change and Human Security*. United Nations Development Research Institute for Social Development, Discussion Paper No 91, Geneva, UNRISD.

http://www.aarp.org – ageing and pensions in America.

http://www.oecd.org/subject/ageing – technical site on work and pensions with some papers on caring and demography.

http://www.hclpage.org/info/ – for older people in development.

http://www.undp.org/ United Nations Development Programme – more on ageing is to be expected as consciousness of elders' participation in development grows.

http://www.worldbank.org – for World Bank policy on population ageing and pensions.

CHAPTER 6

GLOBALIZATION, MIGRATION AND AGEING

A shrinking world, better communications and cheaper travel open up much greater opportunities to move in old age. Migration in later life challenges traditional beliefs that older people are unadaptable and unwilling to move. At its best it offers new ways of living, greater choice and better health to those who choose to move, but it is much more difficult to be positive about enforced migration. Older men and women who move because they are frail or are the victims of natural and man-made disasters are much less likely to find their quality of life improved. This is true whether they are international migrants or simply moving within their state or country.

The presence of older men and women from different cultures is a challenge to mainstream gerontology. First, migration is a process that emphasizes the importance of a life course perspective. Second, the idea of old age as ethnically homogeneous and culture free is challenged by the presence of minority ethnic groups among the aged population. Service providers become aware that culture is important (see Ahmad and Atkin, 1996). In other words, diversity in later life cannot be ignored and culture or ethnicity needs to be understood as one of the factors that shape the lives of older men and women. The concept of culture or ethnicity can then be seen to apply to the dominant majority as well as to minorities. Since most migrant groups are subject to racial or other discrimination, it becomes important to recognize that groups are not just different in culture (diverse) but also different in terms of power and influence (difference).

This chapter focuses on four overlapping types of migration and the effects that migration has on those who are left behind. First, the rising numbers of conventional life-style migrants are considered. They are mainly confined to prosperous Western societies. Second, there are increasing numbers of economic migrants who grow old after a life time working in a foreign country. Many of these become life-style migrants but have not been recognized as such. Third are those who move because they have to, rather than through choice – they may become frail and feel forced to move to be near distant children. Fourth, there are the older men and women displaced by wars, famines and the abuse of human rights. All migration has an effect on those who are left behind. Those who remain in devastated countries, as in former Yugoslavia, are the extreme examples of the tendency for the young to move on, while the old are left to form ageing communities in poverty-stricken rural areas or in the decaying centres of cities.

Life-style migration in later life

Life-style migration is not enforced, but is a matter of choice. The aim is to improve the quality of life. This aim is not always achieved but then, most people in most countries find it difficult to improve quality of life in advanced old age. The growth of large-scale amenity or life-style migration is a function of rising prosperity. Adequate pensions and affordable health care are essential before any large number of older people can begin to make choices about where to live. US experience shows that the more affluent the elders, the more likely they are to move and the further they go (Myers, 1990). Thus we have had to wait for the rise in pension levels, the expansion of pension coverage to whole populations, and the growth of owner occupation to find out that older people are not automatically conservative, but can respond in all sorts of ways to life after retirement.

Researchers have taken a rather restricted view of gender in relation to life-style migration. The supposition is that older couples move to improve their life styles while older widows and widowers make enforced moves to be near their children or go into supported accommodation because they need care, that is, only couples can normally be life-style migrants. This may be changing. Newbold (1996) found that single and divorced men and women in America were more likely to move than couples. Much will depend on the ability of older women to form their own social networks after moving. For example, Cribier (1990) and Van den Hoonaard (1994), among others, found that the social life of retirement communities revolved round couples and noted that, when the husband died, older widows became isolated or had to make new friends. However, research on older widows (Hochschild, 1973; Jerrome, 1992) has shown that they can build full social lives, especially if they move early in old age.

Large-scale movements of elders in search of better weather and a better life were first recorded in the USA (Longino and Marshall, 1990). The process has also been much more commercialized in the USA than in Europe (Hunt et al., 1988). See, for example, Stallman and Jones (1995), who offer a five point typology to enable communities to attract more retirees. Large sunset cities restricted to elders have been developed in Arizona, Florida and other states. Some are closely regulated and have fixed age limits (Kastenbaum, 1993). Others are a market response to demand by existing small townships that see a chance of trade. All these developments depend on an adequate income and the freedom to move without being tied to the labour force.

In Europe, retiring to the country or the seaside has a long tradition and, for the few, it was possible to move as far as the Mediterranean (see, for example, Warnes and Patterson, 1998, on the connections between Britain and Malta which date back to the days when it became a naval base, or Bytheway, 1995, for the British in Florence). But retirement migration only became possible on a large scale after the Second World War. The aim was for city dwellers to move to the places where they had spent their holidays (England), the seaside (France), or to places where rural members of their families had property. In London, the Greater London Council built country developments for older Londoners so that they could move to smaller homes and free their council flats for families who needed to live in the city. By the 1960s retirees were beginning to move further south and even abroad. In the UK the most popular destinations for home owners were the West Country and the resort towns of the south coast and Lancashire. There was vacant accommodation in these towns because their economies had collapsed when the native holiday trade shifted to package tours abroad. In France the seaside was again the most favoured, with a fairly well-developed scale from the fashionable Mediterranean northwards.

In England the high property values of the 1970s and 1980s brought capital gains into many lives. Where a bungalow by the sea or in a country village had been an unattainable dream, it suddenly became possible to sell a modest home and move to Spain, southern France or Italy where property prices were far lower. Most of those who moved were middle class and, as King et al. (1998) found, there was a surplus of graduates in Tuscany compared with other destinations. By 1995 there were 28,000 British state pensions paid to recipients in Spain, but the biggest increase in pensions paid abroad from 1990 to 1995 was in France, up 43.3 per cent to 11,730 and in Italy, up 43.0 per cent to 19,404 (Williams et al., 1997: 121, Table 4).

The late life search for the sun is not simply a matter of housing. For many the move opens up immense possibilities for social life in new surroundings with new people – often people very like themselves – who have moved for the same reasons. Satellite TV will keep them in touch with home and they may not even feel the need to learn a new language (Stokes, 1990) if there are enough of them to maintain social contacts (see below on older migrant workers). King et al. (1998) found that over 20 per cent of retirement migrants to southern Europe spoke only 'a few words' of the local language.

As well as 'permanent' life-style migrants (who may be forced to return to their countries of origin if they become seriously ill) there are also seasonal migrants – the snowbirds of the American south. They may be moving interstate or from Canada and may own or rent. The ability to maintain two homes implies high income or careful planning. For example, Canadians may have medical checkups before leaving for the south and stock up with any necessary medicines. In Europe, those with good occupational pensions but no property to sell could still become seasonal users of discounted hotel space on the Mediterranean (the Costa Geriatrica). The better off might aim for a home in the sun and a *pied-à-terre* in the UK.

Fagan and Longino (1993) have shown that the economic effects on the receiving communities in the USA are largely positive. The same is true when life-style migrants cross national boundaries. For example, Stokes (1990) described the interactions between American retirees and different strata of the local Mexican society. The political and cultural impact of older migrants depends on whether they can vote (as those who move within Europe increasingly can), and how they choose to conduct relations with long-term residents. Migrants may set up exclusive clubs and lament that the natives do not participate, or they may move into local politics and become highly respected members of their new communities.

As readers of this book will have come to expect, none of this is problem free, either for older migrants themselves or for the receiving areas. As long as the migrants are relatively young, well off and active they can blend into the community and few complaints are made. It is when they become less active and more socially visible that trouble may begin. In *City of Green Benches*, Vesperi (1985) details the problems of a community that became famous (a laughing stock) because of the high visibility of its older inhabitants. Rows of green benches on the main street provided meeting and sitting places where older residents and incomers could sit and pass their time. In this small town in the southern USA the climate allowed outdoor activity all the year round and the benches always seemed to be full. The city managers finally decided that the only way to revitalize the town and change its image was to remove the benches. No south-coast retirement town in the UK has gone so far, either in meeting the needs of older migrants or in instituting a backlash, but municipal ageism is always a risk.

Ageism and the local image are one problem but life-style migration has a number of other down sides. In the first place, migrants have left the areas where they passed most of their lives – areas with which they are familiar and where they have long-standing relationships with friends and relatives. The vibrant new social life in destination areas can make up the deficit and frequently results in a new lease of life for migrants who make new friends, take up new interests and contribute to their new communities in all sorts of structured and informal ways. However, friends are not the same as family if there is a need for long-term care (Bulmer, 1986). For one thing friends are usually of the same generation and often suffering from disabilities themselves. Their support may be invaluable in psychological terms (Jerrome, 1992) but they may not be able to stop a frail older woman moving to long-term residential care, whereas if she had stayed close to home, family support might have been adequate. Researchers (Cribier and Kych, 1992) have identified the need for more services in retirement areas and areas of out migration, but there is little evidence that the need will be met.

One answer lies in specialized continuing care communities which have been relatively well developed in America. The 'sunset complex' can include care as needed and a nursing home for those who become very frail, so entry is for life. Such arrangements should be possible in other countries but they are rare. It may be that cost and culture both act as deterrents. In the more age-graded society of America, well off elders are willing to move to what are in effect ghettos for elders, while in Europe they have shown greater resistance to age segregation and the market of rich elders is very much smaller.

Ageing labour migrants

While life-style migrants at the upper end of the income scale have been the subject of research, those at the lower end have been largely ignored. As mentioned above, there is no reason to believe that economic migrants will return 'home' when they reach retirement age (Castles and Miller, 1998). In Europe the numbers of older men and women from different cultures are set to increase greatly in the early years of the next century. In many groups such as Greeks in the UK (Cylwik and Wilson, 1996) or Turks in Germany (Wilson et al., 1999), older men still predominate, but this is likely to change in the near future. Some older migrants have no choice but to stay where they are, in subsidized rented accommodation with minimal pensions. Others, particularly women, choose to stay where they have put down roots near their children and grandchildren. As one Cypriot woman said:

> There you have got the weather and everything. But if you are missing your children that doesn't make it better, does it? If the old people are there and the children and grandchildren are here. (Cylwik, unpublished interview, 1997)

The alternative for those who have accumulated enough savings or pension entitlement is to return to their countries of origin where they may have already built a house. Increasing numbers are following better off life-style migrants and splitting the year between two homes (Wilson et al., 1999). Noiriel (1992), who conducted a study in 1989 on older migrants in the Parisian region, also found a widespread pattern of return to the country of origin for longer or shorter periods, depending on where the family was situated.

As seen above, there are gender differences in the way that these choices are made. In most migrant societies older men are more likely to wish to return definitively than older women (Noiriel,1992; Potts and Grotheer, 1997). The second generation who need baby-sitters or child care may also put more pressure on their mothers to stay. Women are also likely to value the greater freedom allowed them in the country of migration and to be less willing to give it up for the restrictions on their social life that may still exist in their native places. As one older woman said:

> I'll tell you the truth, it was my intention to come, and return to Cyprus. But later I liked it. I found the environment pleasing, the restrictions in Cyprus and you know I found that women were more modern (had more freedom) (translator's amendment). She didn't have the stranglehold of her parents and relations not allowing her to go out. . . . I found that women had many more rights in England than in Cyprus. As a moral woman I did not want to abuse my freedom. I got a job in Lyons the cake shop selling cakes and enrolled at the Pitman college. (Cylwik, translation of unpublished interview, 1997)

Older women migrants who become eligible for any form of welfare benefit may also wish to keep a personal source of income. The compromise position is itinerant retirement or seasonal marital separation. Both are very hard to document within existing statistical definitions, but are increasingly recorded (Arasse, 1992). For example, Buton (1992) found that older hostel dwellers (known in France as *célibataires*), were happy to make extended visits to their wives and families but chose to stay in France long term.

Health can be even more important for older migrants in retirement than for others. A life time of poverty and poor working conditions can result in early onset of the medical problems often associated with old age (Maria, 1993; McNeely and Cohen, 1983; Markides and Miranda, 1997). Many migrants in France appear to retire early on health grounds. Others are forced out of work but must remain in France until pension age so that their pensions can be paid in their countries of origin (Besnard, 1993). However, countries of origin usually lack good health services or may charge for them at rates that cannot be financed on a pension (see McHugh and Mings, 1994). Migrants who have built up entitlements to health care may have to keep their resident status up to date. In Canada and France, those who stay away for more than six months lose entitlement to health care. However, on the plus side, many countries of origin have a much better climate in winter and so, just as the snowbirds move south to Florida in America, retired migrants may visit their birth places during the European winter.

In the words of one mid-life migrant: 'Migration is like a chronic disease. There is no cure' (author's interview, 1996). This negative view highlights the problems that many older migrants face if they try to escape racism in the country of destination and return to their place of origin. They are foreigners in the country of destination but equally when they return to their place of origin they can find themselves referred to as 'the English' (Greek Cypriots), 'Hawaiianaos' (Philippinos who left for Hawaii) or some other term implying alienation. Likewise, the personal narratives of older Ghanaians who had moved to grow cocoa but decided to return to their family villages when they became old, show that returning 'home' is not always a solution for migrants. The returned elder might have ceremonial status but if they were not able to contribute generously to their new family's needs, their status did not stop them being seen as a burden (Nana Apt, 1996). This is not to say that a happy return home is impossible. Many returnees live out their later lives as highly respected members of their communities. Pertierra (1992), for example, mentions the town where street lighting was provided by a respected returnee.

Migration and frailty

Moves associated with frailty are inevitably constrained, or simply moves where there was no choice at all. The move to residential accommodation is the most obvious example of an enforced move. In terms of migration, American elders are likely to move three times – once at retirement, again with minor disability and finally with major chronic disability or widowhood (Longino, 1990). The last two moves will ideally be local but can involve long distances if older people choose to move near distant children, or if the children take the decision to move their relatives to a place which is more convenient for them. Migration which is led by the younger generation depends more on their prosperity than on the income levels of elders.

The ultimate benefits of late life migration depend on how active the migrants remain, and how well they are looked after if they become disabled. Matthews (1979) has pointed out that it is much better to age in a community where you have been known as a young, or at least an active, person for many years and by many people. The quality of love, care, respect and other aspects of relationships are likely to last better if they were built on foundations of long familiarity. In contrast, to enter a community as an old or disabled person risks being identified first and foremost as old or disabled rather than as a person. A close and supportive family may compensate to some degree, but not fully, for the loss of friends and familiar places. For many older men and women there is no ideal option but an awareness of the problems involved in relocation and the need to work through the many losses involved can help towards a more positive outcome.

Enforced ageing in a foreign land

Itinerant retirement may be the most satisfactory option for many older migrants but it is not an option open to all. Those who are trapped in areas of high unemployment, crime, drug dependency, poor housing and poor schools are unlikely to accumulate enough resources. Their children, caught in economic restructuring, recession and the fall in demand for unskilled labour, may be unemployed and drift into crime. Even if outcomes are better, older men and women may find themselves isolated in a different culture that they are unable to pass on to their descendants. Chantreaux and Marcoux-Moumen quote the following cry of pain:

> We have lived in poverty for them, we have suffered, we have lost our health and they [the French] are going to take them from us. Our children are going to marry their daughters. They will increase their population. Our daughters and our sons have gone, and we, we have been left behind like waves in the sea. We no longer know whether it is our duty to fight or to fly. Our children are like the fruit of a tree. They will be harvested by French men and French women. (Chantreaux and Marcoux-Moumen, 1991: 187–8; my translation)

Increasing numbers of men and women of all ages are being forced to move because of war, famines and loss of human rights. We can add to these the illegal migrants who grow old in very impoverished circumstances and who are forced to age in place, often a hostile place. Another special case are the older Germans and Greeks from the former Soviet Union or Japanese from Latin America who have returned 'home' to countries they have never known and languages they barely speak.

Finally, there may be large-scale movements of older migrants from the newly industrializing countries of the Pacific Rim and Malaysia. It is unlikely that they will be welcomed in their home countries unless economic conditions greatly improve. Tout (1989) reports on the problems of elderly refugees and of older women left behind when younger generations migrate. He shows that many older refugees remain unidentified and under-enumerated. They do not come to relief centres, either because they are too weak to walk so far, or because of the general agreement that children and younger adults should have priority. They will be very unlikely to get any form of counselling or psychological help with the traumatic events they have passed through.

Those who remain behind

Migration has traditionally removed young men from their communities for a shorter or longer time. This could often be beneficial (remittances, education and training and adventure could all bring personal and social benefits), but only if it did not seriously unbalance the community. In Europe in poor rural areas and the old areas of mining or heavy industry, local economies have collapsed and with them job opportunities for the young and middle aged. The young leave and the old remain in disproportionate numbers. Like retirement zones, service needs are high, but unlike retirement zones they are usually among the poorest areas in their countries and local governments are not able to provide the quality and quantity of services needed to support an ageing population.

Inner-city zones can also contain large numbers of older migrants, left behind when their more prosperous children moved to better housing and living conditions on the edge of towns and cities. If drug dealers and new waves of impoverished people move in, as in most European capital cities, the quality of life for elders can become very poor. In other parts of the world, in the mega cities of Latin America or West African cities, or in rural South Africa, older women may be heading three generations of women-only households, with no services but those they can produce themselves (Chaney, 1989; Chant, 1997; Moser, 1996). Tout (1993) offers some cheering examples of what can be done by self-help, but not even the most optimistic observer would suggest that it is enough.

Policy issues

Ageing migrants find themselves positioned at the junctions of two sets of policies or lack of policy. In the first place there are policies for later life – often more noticeable as policies of inaction rather than positive frameworks for action. In the second place, older migrants are affected by policies (or again the lack of them) on race and ethnic diversity (Ahmad and Atkin, 1996; Pensabene, 1987). Ageing in migrant communities has been largely ignored. Either older migrants are expected to fit into any mainstream services that exist, or the migrant family is believed to 'look after its own'. Policies for older migrants are not solely a matter for the dominant majority. Migrant groups and individuals, young and old, resist racism and disadvantage in different ways, and both passively and actively. For example, the outcome of policies for assimilation and integration depends as much on migrant individuals and groups as on the dominant majority. Policies which strengthen migrant groups and cultures are essential for the well being of elders but may threaten the status quo of local politics.

Assimilation

The policies of dominant ethnic groups can be divided into assimilation and integration as they apply to minorities. The terms may have slightly different meanings in different policy contexts, but always imply a deficit model of minorities. Any problems are seen as largely their own fault. With better understanding of the country, its language and customs, all will be well. Assimilation implies that migrants will simply disappear by being absorbed into the dominant community (and its class system). Clearly this has happened in the past since most nation states have a history of inward migration but have been able to see themselves as relatively homogeneous. Historical records may show that migrants such as French Huguenots in England were discriminated against or that the Italians and Portuguese were looked down on by the French in the 19th and early 20th centuries but now Huguenot survivals seem limited to unusually spelt surnames, and many Portuguese and Italians are wholly absorbed into French life and are to be found in most parts of the class system, not just at the bottom. The model has been well described by Markides et al. (1990) for America. They define minority status as the experience of disadvantage – according to this definition most European immigrant groups to America have had a *sociological* minority status at some stage but are now part of the dominant culture. The important conclusion which they draw from this observation is that minority status is a dynamic not a static characteristic. Smaller, more visible communities, such as black slaves have also been absorbed into British, French and Arabian life over time. In countries where immigration is more recent the process is not so far advanced, see for example Burnley et al. (1985) for Australia.

Integration

Some migrant groups have maintained their distinctive identity over many years or even centuries. Chinese and Hindu Indian migrants in most parts of the world have remained largely separate from the communities they have migrated into. A certain amount of economic success and strong sanctions against marrying outside the community seem to be important attributes for long term community survival. These groups may be able to force de facto integration policies on the native community. Integration in such situations implies that members of a migrant group are not confined to one segment of the labour market, that they can benefit from the education and health systems and any other universal aspects of civil society. In other words, nations become pluralist and diverse rather than homogeneous. Racism and discrimination do not go away, but they no longer wholly define the life chances of migrants. Members of Jewish communities in most countries have been able to choose whether to integrate or assimilate. As identities become more diverse it is possible to be both assimilated and to maintain a distinctive ethnic identity, at least in developed countries with pluralistic policies of citizenship. For example, there are Americans who see themselves as 'hyphenated', as Korean-Americans, Italian-Americans and so on, but only in certain situations. At other times they may simply feel they belong to the dominant culture and will be allowed to do so.

Simple deficit models of assimilation or integration appear to be held in more or less similar form by dominant majorities in all countries of destination. The main difference lies in whether migrants have been expected to stay (for example in North America, Australasia and UK) or to return 'home' (most continental European countries). The comfortable assumption seems to have been that since no policy measures were deemed necessary for integration or assimilation in the past, it is the failure of present-day migrants to assimilate that is at fault.

Problems arise when assimilation, not integration, is the national policy but large sections of the native population (as well as many migrant groups) are opposed to it. In France, for example, migrants have traditionally been expected to become French in culture as well as legal status. (Those from overseas French Departments and Territories are already French citizens.) In colonial times many did indeed become citizens of the secular state and were widely respected by the elite as French men and women. More recent north African and Senegalese migrants who maintain their Islamic religion and compete for jobs with lower-paid natives have been prevented from integrating by racist local government policies, for example in housing, and by the racism of French society (Besnard, 1993). The religious chasm may grow in importance if anti-Islamic feeling is not reduced. Mainly secular states are intolerant of organized religion and Christian states are still intolerant of other faiths. Migrants who build mosques have been accused of differentiating themselves in a way that is hostile to French society and tradition. They fail to assimilate to the norm of a secular republic. On the other hand, Ferjani (1993) has pointed out that when north Africans decide to build a mosque they are integrating and beginning to regard foreign soil as something on which it will not be blasphemous to build a place of worship. They are caught between outdated policies which assume assimilation and popular realities which reject it. Integration has also proved very difficult in increasingly racist societies with far-right parties. In Germany, where the concept of blood is deemed more important than citizenship in determining nationality, even the grandchildren of migrants were denied German nationality until 1999.

One rationalization of the disadvantages suffered by older migrants is that migrants assimilated perfectly well until there was a welfare state to identify their needs and to spend contested amounts of money on meeting them. This, as Fishman (1988) has shown, involves a fairly distorted view of the past when migrants were often as unpopular or more so than they are today. Sayad, the arch proponent of *miserabilisme* (the devaluation of migrants by writing only of their disadvantages and shortcomings), says:

> ... immigrants exist only in the discourses that are produced about them. They exist only in so far as they 'present problems' and ultimately they exist only through the problems which they present and which cause them to exist. Immigrants only exist from the moment when the society of migration identifies the problem of 'migrants'. (Sayad, 1993: 43 (author's translation))

In America a similar discourse links ageism to the need for social security and Medicare to be paid for by the state (Bengtson and Achenbaum, 1993).

Jeopardies

Certain writers have pointed out that older migrants and older migrant women suffer from double, triple or multiple jeopardies. Ageism, racism, sexism and structural disadvantages related to class combine to make their life chances especially poor. Norman (1985), for example, identified older migrant women as triply disadvantaged. Markides and Mindel (1987) cast doubt on jeopardy theories by showing that older black Americans are not necessarily sicker and that they report higher rates of life satisfaction than older whites. While not denying that migrants may be disadvantaged as groups and as individuals, any theory that sees migrants as defined by their disadvantages is suspect. The extract below from an interview with an older migrant in France shows how migration can be seen as a benefit:

> *Robert* (interviewer): Your life is complicated isn't it? Two wives, children here, children over there (in Senegal), a little mixed race daughter.
> *Respondent*: No not at all, it's a gift from God.
> *Robert*: Yes but there are people who stay in their village, its simpler.
> *Respondent*: That's not good. It's not good at all. If you stay in the village you are a hick, you don't know anything at all. Because I, if I had stayed in Senegal, if I had been born over there, grown up there, what would I know? Nothing, Nothing but Senegal. (Robert, 1992) (author's translation)

He goes on to explain that experience of life in different countries is worth more than book education and that he wins the arguments when he returns to Senegal on visits because he knows more.

Jeopardy theories and other views of migrants which concentrate on racism and disadvantage have the strength of making oppression visible but the enormous weakness that they leave no place for the views of migrants themselves. Older migrant men and women are unlikely to see themselves as wholly oppressed, even if, like elders everywhere, they lament the lack of respect among the younger generation. In most migrant groups, women traditionally gain more power and influence as they age (Chaney, 1989). This improvement can be weakened by migration, but at the same time migration can open up new possibilities for women. The other gap in miserabilisme is that it does not allow for the ways in which migrants take charge of their own lives and resist or alter conditions in the country of destination. It also assumes single identities and multiple disadvantage among older migrants rather than understanding identity as diverse and varying according to circumstances, surroundings and purposes.

The importance of diversity

Polices which aim to assist older migrants are unlikely to be successful if they do not take account of diversity within and between migrant groups. Migration results in changing family structures, for example women-headed families, common in Latin American cities and parts of Africa, or ageing single men who live alone without relatives. Even without these extremes family networks are reduced or altered by migration. Support which might have been forthcoming can be lost. However, the negative consequences of changes in the family can be overemphasized. There is evidence, for example from France, that single men living in hostels who are usually seen as intensely deprived, actually choose to live as they do, visiting their transnational families from time to time, conceiving children and enjoying prestige in their communities on visits back 'home' while continuing to spend years in the male company of a hostel. It is important therefore to start from the perceptions of each migrant group, rather than the stereotypes imposed by the dominant majority.

The same is true when considering the position of older migrant women. Migration may reduce family and community networks which are essential mechanisms of women's power in some cultures, but it may also open up new sources of power which can be integrated with the traditional. Older women (and older men) may take up the 'ethnic career' noted by Simics (1987). They become keepers of culture and tradition and acquire respected community roles. There are other differences in power within migrant communities. Some are structured in ways which oppress community members – possibly older women or those who deviate from strict norms. Others build up strong organizations which can provide clubs and services for older people. Members may fear the gossip and control involved, but still enjoy the enhancement of identity.

Conclusion

Older migrants make up a rapidly growing proportion of the population in countries of destination even though they may still be a small group in numerical terms. They are different from elders in the host population and differ among themselves and these differences need to be recognized when formulating policy. Life-style migration illustrates the importance of considering diversity in later life. While the idea of an age-restricted sunset city in Arizona is a nightmare for many, the fact that these settlements are commercial ventures indicates that they meet the needs of large numbers of better off elders. Others prefer to move where they can fit into an existing mixed-age community, with or without a high number of retirement migrants. The more adventurous move countries and either learn a new language or join existing expatriate communities, for example in Mexico, Spain or Greece. Still others will not migrate but will simply sell their homes and move to a smaller house or flat in the same area, possibly in order to be nearer their grandchildren. Such a range of possibilities was unthinkable in earlier times when incomes were lower and the benefits of globalization still unthought of. Migration is not a majority option but it shows that if choices are offered, older people will take them up. Amenity migration also highlights the contrasting lifestyles of rich and poor and the effects of poverty in later life.

While life-style migrants in prosperous Western countries have been most studied, in future the largest numbers of older migrants will be in countries of the Pacific Rim, India and the Gulf states. In many countries they will not be allowed to remain once their working lives are over and will be forced to return with no pension and possibly little familiarity with the changed conditions in their countries of origin. Illegal or clandestine migrants will face even worse conditions. In some cases such as the Philippines, the majority of migrants are women (Campani, 1995).

Economic migrants who grow old in Europe and North America are increasingly likely to spend different periods of the year near different parts of their transnational families. They will be joined by elders from developing countries, whose children have made good in the developed world and can afford to invite their parents for extended visits. The outlook for elders who grow old in a foreign land depends on the strength of their family and community networks as well as on their own abilities. A working life marked by racism and discrimination (which is the norm for most) does not equip them well in terms of pensions. If their children (or close relatives) have not bettered themselves through the sacrifices of their parents, the outlook for elders may be poor. Refugees and asylum seekers are likely to find ageing particularly hard. Policies which enable communities to provide ethnically appropriate services when families cannot are essential, but need to be based on an understanding of the power divisions within different ethnic groups.

Further reading

Migration studies usually concentrate on migrants of working age. More literature should become available as economic migrants age in greater numbers.

http://www.un.org/instraw/studies.htm – some information on older women and on migrant women.

CHAPTER 7

MATERIAL RESOURCES IN LATER LIFE

In most of the world pensions are not an issue because very few older men or women have any pension at all. To the young in countries where pension systems are well developed, the subject may be dull or confusing but, as more and more money is tied up in pension funds, we can expect them to get a higher profile. We might ask what links the following tabloid headlines: 'Millionaire Found Floating Beside Luxury Yacht'; 'National Heritage Lost as Art Prices Spiral'; 'US Birth Rate Collapses'. The answer of course is pensions. We do not know if Mr Maxwell (the millionaire) drowned himself because he had siphoned millions of pounds out of his workers' pension funds, but certainly the money disappeared. The huge amounts of money which accumulate in pension funds are an enormous temptation to rival firms, or debt ridden entrepreneurs, or (when they are public funds) to governments. The money has to be invested somewhere. When the British Rail Pension Fund managers decided to buy art treasures as a hedge against inflation, large amounts of new money flooded into the art market. Prices rose faster than government and taxpayers financing state-subsidized museums and art galleries could keep up, but private collectors from abroad were able to buy what the public sector could not. Finally, if old age can be financed by a pension, there is no need to have children. Longman (1987), for example, accuses pensions of causing population ageing and hence national moral and economic decline. He says:

> As support in old age has come to depend less and less on the affection and prosperity of one's own children, or even on one's having children at all, individuals have correspondingly less incentive to reproduce themselves and to sacrifice on behalf of their children. One result is the falling birth rate. (Longman, 1987: 28)

Support in later life

Pensions are the key to income and material security in later life, but even more so they are the essential support of a new life stage. Demographic change in the shape of rising life expectancies may result in more people experiencing old age, but a good pension is what changes the nature of that experience. The freedom to live without having to earn money or to produce goods for sale is something unknown in human history except for the very privileged few. Even today there are not many countries outside Western Europe and North America where pensions provide a majority with a reasonably high quality of life. In the countries where there are universal or near universal pension schemes which offer a decent standard of living after retirement, pensions are by far the most important aspect of policy for old age. They typically make up a very large item of government spending.

Early retirement is a popular policy wherever pensions are adequate. Johnson (1988) has tracked the drop in labour force participation as pension coverage improved in the UK and has shown that workers were increasingly willing to retire even though pensions were well below earnings. Most European countries when faced with high youth un-employment have considered retiring older workers as a way forward. There is no evidence that the young unemployed are suited to the jobs vacated by older workers and the policies do not appear to have worked: workers who are forced out of the workforce without a pension can lose 10 to 15 years of pension contributions and will suffer from low pensions for the rest of their lives. They will also fail to pay contributions to pension schemes and so make it more difficult to finance present or future pensions. They will need some form of social assistance and so act as a drain on public expenditure. On the other hand, those who retire early on an adequate pension will be better off personally but they will still be a drain on pensions funds at a time when they might have been paying in. As the OECD (1998) says, early retirement (or enforced exit) from the labour market is an expensive policy option.

The first point to note is that universal pensions are a fairly recent invention. Germany was the first country to start a 'universal' scheme (for men only) in the 1890s. Most other developed countries have moved slowly to universal coverage (pensions for all workers and support for those who cannot work) during the past 50 years. Pensions have from the beginning been accompanied by prophecies of doom. There have always been those who saw pensions as a burden on workers and employers, not as earnings forgone or as a collectivized version of the normal duty of children to support their parents. These different views of the money trans-ferred in pensions have important ethical dimensions. All are logically sustainable but it is the first, pensions as a burden (an unsustainable burden in most discourse) on the young, that has become universalized.

Small pensions

While a pension that is a living wage might be an impossible ideal in most countries of the world, this is no reason for having no pension scheme at all. Led by Kerala and its Communist government, the southern states of India have had near universal pension systems or safety nets for the aged poor for some time (Tracy, 1991; United Nations, 1992). Since 1996 the safety net has been extended to all states of the Indian Union. Very small allowances are paid monthly via post offices to low-income elders. In a country where family and community are enjoined to care, a personal income, however small, can make a huge difference to the negotiating power of elders. Such systems have become much easier to deliver with computerization. The experience in South Africa is the same. An efficient system is more or less impossible without computerization. In the past this was less important since pensions for black South Africans were rationed by the inefficiency of their delivery (Burman, 1989), but with the end of Apartheid the government was committed to increasing the take up. As Case and Deaton (1996) note, old age pensioners in South Africa were supporting large families and the money was effectively assisting children as well as old people. Such schemes which are essentially delivering low levels of non-contributory social assistance for older people can be expected to grow in the future.

Work

Before we move to a full discussion of pensions it must be recognized that in most countries of the world the vast majority of older people work in some capacity for as long as they are able. Their work may be paid or unpaid. This is a problem for policy-makers because only paid work is counted as productive activity and measured in national accounts and visible in Table 7.1.

The table shows that over half of all men over 55 were defined as being economically active in the poorer continents, but a much lower proportion in Europe and North America. In developing countries almost all other older men and women will be working but their work is unrecorded and so invisible (Hendricks, 1995). This is true even when

Table 7.1 Economically active population aged 55+ in 1990 (per cent)

	Men %	Women %
Africa	73	31
Asia	63	16
Latin America	56	12
North America	41	19
Europe	37	13
USSR	35	8

Source: Based on 1990 projections in ILO (1986).

the work of elders leads directly to productive activity, for example child care that allows a daughter or daughter-in-law to enter the labour market. In most societies there is more work (unpaid) for older women than for older men, though if men can work on a small holding or market garden they can continue being productive for many years.

Once pensions are instituted fewer and fewer people take paid work (Johnson, 1988) after retirement age. They may not have enjoyed their work and they have been willing to take a lower income to be free of it. Alternatively, they may be forced to retire (the structured dependency thesis), or they may be too ill to continue, or they may wish to work but an ageist labour market offers no jobs. It is, however, cheaper to encourage older people to stay in work than to pay pensions and many countries have policies for helping older people earn (UN, 1991). Throughout the Western world there are moves to raise pension age, but when labour markets are ageist a delay in pension eligibility only means that older men and women have to fall back on public assistance until they can claim their (reduced) pensions.

Family

Families give support to older people in material and emotional terms just as older people support the younger generation. When work is short and pensions small or non-existent, that is over most of the world, the family is the main source of material support for older people. This is usually a two-way transaction with elders, both men and women, but more frequently women, since they live longer and have more domestic skills and lower expectations of leisure, helping out. They may trade or garden or farm, but are mostly likely to look after children and do housework. There are cultural differences in attitudes to family support. In many countries, as far apart as Ghana or Japan, large numbers of elders still expect the young to provide for them and are aggrieved if they fail. In others older men and women expect to be largely independent of their children and would think it shameful to accept more than token contributions from their families. Obviously this last cultural position can only develop after the establishment of a universal pension system.

Commerce and industry

Large employers have contributed to the welfare of their workers in most countries. Employer contributions to pension schemes were institutionalized with the development of welfare states. However, there are other ways in which the commercial sector can support income in later life. Welfare policies in East Asian states have aimed at incorporating employers by raising the retirement age and legislating incentives for businesses to employ older workers. This approach is best developed in Singapore. Japanese schemes for paying older workers low wages to do mainly unskilled work also come under the same heading (Bass and Oka, 1995; Campbell, 1992). Such initiatives could well be extended in countries where the family is meant to provide welfare but state activity in support of commerce is widely accepted.

Pensions

Pensions are basically a way of equalizing individual or collective incomes over the life course. They enforce saving during the years of work. In this they are like other social insurance schemes, which workers pay into so that they have a source of income when they cannot take paid work for any reason. Pensions are different from unemployment benefit, invalidity benefit, and so on because a pension has become a predictable need in developed countries, now that virtually everyone lives until retirement age. As life expectancy increases pensions are not only predictable but also need to last longer, and so cost more.

Pensions are essentially about individual as opposed to family responsibility. In countries where social insurance does not exist or has not eliminated the risk of having to provide for adult relatives, the pensions debate looks very different. As Scherer says:

> Many analyses of social insurance in terms of market failure assume that each generation is somehow separate and alienated from the next, and that intergenerational transfers are zero sum processes in which one generation's loss is another's gain. But since these systems to a large extent replace intra-family transfers which would take place in their absence this is a narrow and misleading view of their function. Whether or not they are legally responsible for their welfare, children remain concerned about the welfare of their parents. This is one of the reasons why those who seek to reduce the coverage of old age income security often have to proceed stealthily in all countries. (Scherer, 1996: 20)

However, taking the orthodox view, there are two main ways of looking at pensions. Either they are *deferred earnings* or *savings*, money that a worker has earned but which was not paid to him or her at the time of earning it. The other way of looking at pensions is to see them as *transfers* from members of the generations in work to the non-working generations. These two models are important: are pensions earned, or are they simply a burden on the productive young? In most countries trade unions have been involved in setting up pension funds and have made sure that both employers and employees contribute to the fund. (Pension schemes for the self-employed took much longer to establish.) The unions agree to accept lower current wages on the understanding of future support for retired workers. This approach has been much more clearly part of union policy in countries such as Germany than in the UK.

To some extent the view of pensions is a matter of generation. Elders often say they have earned their pensions. If they also fought for their country, as most male European pensioners did, they are very likely indeed to see their pensions as earned. In the UK they may also draw attention to the excessively low level of the current pension (see Bosanquet et al., 1990). On the other hand, men and women of working age who have been conditioned by the media to see the older generations as a burden on their earnings may see them as little different from the other claimants their taxes support, such as the unemployed or single parents.

Pensions: why the problem?

There does not appear to be any perfect pension scheme. Combine this technical uncertainty with the huge sums of money involved, and it is not surprising that pensions are a highly contested area. Most possible schemes have advantages and disadvantages. However, the first problem which appears to be common to all schemes and across all countries is that young people are generally uninterested in pensions and unwilling to start saving at an early age. They suffer from economic myopia – they do not think about pensions. It is only the exceptions who take their pensions seriously and the majority seem to find it hard to think of themselves as being old and so put off saving. The result is that voluntary pension schemes lead to poor coverage (not everyone joins) and low pensions (few people make big enough contributions for long enough). Voluntary (private insurance based) schemes therefore have to advertise heavily and are mainly directed at the well off, who have surplus earnings and can afford to set side enough money for a better future (and to provide a profit for the private insurers who need the funds to invest).

Even when contributions are compulsory many people will try to get out of paying. This is not just 'myopia'. Those who avoid paying may be very hard up and so unwilling to put away money for an uncertain future. Women workers, in particular, appear to put the short-term needs of their children way before their own long-term needs. Readers might ask themselves what they would do, or have done in the past. Not many will have behaved as pension specialists would wish them to. It follows that any pension scheme that aims to give all citizens, or all workers and their partners, a decent income in old age has to be compulsory. Workers must be forced to contribute each week, month or year, or many will not do so, particularly when they are young.

The way that contributions are organized and the type of fund are much more variable. All pensions are funded by money that is removed from the economy in some way. The main choice is between fully funded (FF) schemes and pay as you go (PAYG) schemes, and between defined contribution (DC) and defined benefit (DB) schemes. In funded schemes contributions are saved, either in a personal account or in a pooled fund, and invested. The scheme, in theory, only pays out what has been saved, but there can be many changes in the value of money and investments over the life time of a pension. The funds have to be invested in some way and can all be lost in a stock market crash, or if they are fraudulently removed (the Maxwell case). Even if the funds are preserved there are problems with inflation. In a defined contribution scheme (much the most common for FF), a pensioner will get the value of his or her contributions, as it is at retirement age, and should then buy an annuity to last the rest of his/her life. Government should guarantee some minimum protection from inflation and so reduce the risk if the scheme is a private compulsory one. Chances are high that many pensioners with below-average incomes will never contribute enough. They will need a safety net, usually a government scheme with a defined benefit (minimum payment which can be raised in line with inflation or not, as political needs dictate). Women who live longer will need to pay more to get the same level of income as a man from their annuity and few will be able to afford it.

The other difficulty with funded schemes is that the funds can, and should, become extremely large. Longman (1987), for example, pointed out that, according to US Department of Health and Human Services calculations in 1985, the Old Age Survivors Insurance and Disability Insurance funds would have a surplus of $9.3 trillion or 26 per cent of the total US GNP by 2020. There are obvious problems arising from such large funds. As mentioned above, when the British Rail Pension Fund decided to invest in old master paintings, the result was a massive rise in prices of old paintings, big profits for auction houses and major problems for national museums trying to keep their art heritage in the country. In countries such as the UK with a big stock exchange, there is always the fear that pension fund holders (mainly insurance companies) will unbalance the stock market (Schuller, 1986). Or, as with petrodollars (see Chapter 5), the funds will unbalance the economies of poorer countries and cause further disaster.

Another problem is that the huge build up of funds when stock markets are rising gives a false sense of security and leads to pension holidays (no contributions are made for the year). Sometimes these holidays are extended to employees but usually it is employers who take the decision to cut or eliminate their contribution to the fund. Obviously the temptation to raid a large fund is very great indeed. In the private sector, old-established, good employers who have built up large pension funds can find themselves taken over simply for the fund. Regulating these activities has proved extremely difficult in the UK. Very large vested interests are involved and it has taken a string of scandals to get even minimum safeguards into place.

Inflation greatly magnifies any problems relating to the size of funds and also endangers the pay out for future pensioners. They do not share the profits from inflation once they have retired (unless their pensions are inflation proofed which is rare outside the public sector) and so the value of their pensions falls steadily. The final difficulty with funded schemes is that it takes time for the fund to build up. At the national level it can be politically difficult to enforce contributions to a fund at the same time as workers are supporting existing pensioners via pay as you go schemes. It follows that funded schemes have their best chance of expansion in countries where the pension system is poorly developed or where demand from retired workers can be ignored. The funded schemes established in Taiwan and South Korea, for example, leave current pensioners dependent on their families (Kwon, 1999a and b).

The alternative to funding is pay as you go (PAYG). This type of scheme has been much more attractive to governments in the past because it can begin paying out as soon as it is set up. Workers pay contributions but these are not banked as in a funded scheme. Instead they are paid out to existing retirees. Since there have always been many more people in work than retired, contributions could be set at a politically sustainable level. The problem in most countries is that PAYG schemes have now been in operation for over 50 years and they are caught between a rapidly growing pensioner population and a falling labour force as smaller cohorts begin to come through the system and unemployment rises. This probably would not matter if economic growth were still assured but since it is not, doom and gloom abounds. The casualization of employment makes the contribution problem even worse. Men and women in part-time or short-contract work or self-employed may not be paying into pension schemes or are paying for themselves without an employer's contribution. Revenue therefore falls even lower than it would if all were in standard employment. Women are likely to lose out most severely since they typically have interrupted employment careers and, still more seriously, may work in poorly unionized areas where pensions are not offered. Changes in women's participation rates in the labour market kept PAYG schemes viable in Northern Europe but fears for pension schemes have now returned. Extreme forms of the crisis that can hit PAYG schemes can be seen in declining industries in France. Early French pension schemes were industry based, for example in coal mining or steel production.

Now that these industries have collapsed, a tiny number of employees is contributing to funds which have very high numbers of pensioners and early retired, sick or redundant workers on the books. A state subsidy and transfers from other more viable funds have been the only way to keep paying pensions.

The private sector has not been particularly interested in providing national pensions. As with private health insurance, the costs of providing for low earners are too great and the profits too small when compared with what can be achieved by restricting business to the upper ends of the market. As a result the state usually has to guarantee certain aspects of a private or voluntary pension scheme, such as a degree of inflation proofing and extra payments when systems cannot find enough money, as, for example, in the French coal miners pension scheme (above). The state also has to provide poverty-level pensions for those who cannot afford to pay into the scheme. Such schemes need not be funded. They were often PAYG in the early days but the present supposition is that private schemes will be funded in the future.

Collective schemes make it easier to set defined benefits (e.g. a minimum pension level for all). The risks are pooled and so contributions for the most vulnerable can be lower. Private firms cannot offer defined benefits except as a minority top-up package because the cost of premiums for low-paid men and women would have to be covered by very high premiums from the highly paid – something that is likely to be politically and commercially unacceptable. It is difficult to see any advantages in individualized schemes except that, as individualism increases and willingness to care for others declines, it may be that individualized schemes will be more popular. However, such policies are also self-fulfilling and encourage a breakdown in collective social responsibility. Problems then arise because it is not only older people who benefit from social cohesion, though they are arguably the greatest losers if it weakens.

Some redistribution of pension income is inevitable in any collective scheme. Those who die early effectively transfer their contributions to those who die late. The element of redistribution can be greater or smaller. A subsidy to an insolvent scheme paid out of general taxation is one method already discussed. More often those with the lowest earnings receive pensions which are partly financed by the contributions of those with higher earnings. There is usually a redistribution from men to women, but even so women end up with poor pensions in most countries.

Flat-rate schemes where all contributors receive the same pension can function with a relatively low level of contributions. This was the original British model. Lloyd George, when thinking of introducing the first pensions in 1908, visited Germany to see how Bismarck's system worked and came back shocked at the level of contributions demanded (9d or 4.5p a week). He decided that the British working man would not put up with anything like that and set his contribution at 3d a week. Beveridge continued the tradition, saying: 'It is dangerous to be in any way lavish to old age until adequate provision has been assured for all other vital needs, such as the prevention of disease and the adequate nutrition of the young' (quoted in Hill, 1961: 12).

Flat-rate pensions favour equality but it is usually equality at a low safety-net level. A flat-rate pension that actually lifts pensioners out of poverty (that is gives them around 50 per cent of average earnings, as in Sweden or the Netherlands) is very expensive and usually judged to be politically impossible in countries which have not implemented it long ago. When flat-rate benefits are low, the rich top up their pensions and so equality suffers. A state flat-rate scheme therefore favours the private insurance industry which will cater for the better off. Low pay-out flat-rate schemes are the archetypal way of losing middle-class support for welfare.

In earnings related schemes, workers and employers pay more as earnings rise. Pensions are set to reflect earnings differentials and so differentials in working life are carried over into old age. The strength of this type of scheme is that all income groups have a stake in it and the weakness is that it perpetuates and validates life long earnings inequalities. It is the type of scheme most strongly associated with European states, often described as corporatist, often Roman Catholic, and places more emphasis on social solidarity than equality. Private funded schemes are necessarily earnings related in their entitlements.

The objection to state pensions is not that they are inefficient. State PAYG schemes are probably the most efficient that exist in terms of low administration costs and good coverage, but state schemes are part of government expenditure. It is obvious that a shift to the private sector would reduce the money accounted for as government expenditure and do wonders for the type of government financial performance indicators that are so important with globalization. As long as global fashions in economics persist in seeing government expenditure as harmful there will be very strong pressures to privatize as much pension expenditure as possible. The main advantage of PAYG schemes is that they are easier to control politically. There is no build up of funds and so less temptation to corruption, either by government or the private sector. However, they do not have the advantage of generating savings that can be used for capital development (as long as they are not exported). State schemes of whatever type are easier to regulate because the systems for accounting for public money are already in place. Private sector schemes have proved very difficult to regulate. State schemes are also more efficient because administrative costs are usually lower than in the private sector and there is no need to produce a surplus (profit).

Generation contract?

Pensions as burden are usually presented as part of the generation contract. The two sides of the contract are the men's contract, which is about cash contributions and benefits, and the women's contract, which is about caregiving (Lorenz-Meyer, 1999). For example, should this shrinking work-age generation in the USA or UK have to pay the full cost of today's larger pensioner cohort, when they are very unlikely to get the same amount of money back from the young when they are old? There is no evidence that workers are actually very concerned with this, as opposed to their general concern with the level of taxes. Minkler (1991) presents evidence that not only are they not concerned but that even in America, the public appears to believe in intergenerational solidarity. However, the cohort inequalities pose a number of interesting academic problems, so there is a literature.

As things stand, pension levels now and in the future are most strongly influenced by the performance of the economy (world or nation) and political decisions. If employment falls, or if men's full time jobs are replaced by low-paid, flexible or part-time women's jobs and productivity does not rise substantially, contributions fall. They either fall because the labour force has reduced, or because the low-paid or flexibly-employed make few or no contributions. In a PAYG scheme the solution has to be immediate. Pensions will have to be cut at the risk of pensioner votes, or the government will have to subsidize pensions from taxation, maybe alienating a wider constituency. In a funded scheme the problem is postponed until today's contributors begin to retire with inadequate funds. The political attractions of funded schemes to governments that are encouraging the casualization of the labour market are clear.

When a pensions crisis is perceived or manufactured, the remedies are to raise contributions, to change eligibility (for example raise retirement age or reduce or fail to implement pension protection for women who care for children or elders) or to cut benefits. All of these are very unpopular. Increased contributions are liable to be seen as a tax and as such, ideologically as well as politically unpopular. Raising retirement age is a long-run policy that benefits from myopia. As long as voters do not see themselves as retired it appears that they will not campaign strongly against raising the age of retirement. The problem is that the benefits are long term also and so do little for the current crisis. Finally, cutting benefits has been shown to be politically impossible in a range of countries. The solution is to raise pension levels more slowly than inflation. One way is to link pension increases to changes in prices rather than earnings (which normally move ahead faster). This has been achieved in the UK and will result in widespread poverty in the next century if it is not reversed. An attempt in the Netherlands to hold pension levels steady for a given number of years failed (see Chapter 4).

The World Bank (1994) has contributed to the pension problem in a strange document entitled *Averting the Old Age Crisis* which, despite the fact that there is no crisis, proposes a blue print for the world. It advocates a pension system with three pillars: mandatory publicly managed pillar – safety net, PAYG; mandatory privately managed pillar – mainstream, FF; and voluntary private – extra top ups for the rich, FF. This structure shows an attempt to deal with the problems raised above. Fully funded mandatory private pensions have been shown to fail large proportions of the population, therefore put in a safety net. Wide coverage is expensive and unattractive for the private sector, therefore add a high-profit, possibly less closely regulated sector for the rich. There is no evidence that this type of pension structure is either effective or efficient in most countries. (See the very full discussion given in Schulz, 1993; Lloyd-Sherlock and Johnson, 1996 or Williamson, 1997 for the USA.) In Chile (the World Bank's successful model to be copied by all) the private pension funds have made a loss in several years and 40 per cent of the working population remains uninsured. One ethically doubtful aspect of the World Bank scheme is that, if it were successful, the savings of workers in the developing South would have to be invested. Since stock markets are poorly developed in the South they would need to be transferred, for example to New York or Hong Kong, and no doubt invested in rich countries rather than improving economic development back home.

Hazards for pensions

The chances that economies will remain stable over a working life and until death thereafter are almost non-existent. Change in the value of money, in stock markets, in employment and the employment market, in productivity and pensions policies can be taken as absolutely certain. Fraud, government and private raids on funds, and major revolutions are less likely but cannot be ruled out over a time period of 60–80 years. It is therefore not unexpected that young workers are frequently said to lack trust in any pension system. Add their well-known myopia and their insecure employment and it is not surprising that saving is uniformly agreed to be too low.

For those who do contribute to pension funds, inflation was the main worry in the past. The value of a pension can be protected by linking it to changes in the level of earnings or prices. These are political decisions. In some countries indexation is a constitutional right, but only for national pension schemes. In others it is a matter of government discretion each year. Earnings indexation allows pensioners to share in national prosperity (as in most of Europe). Price indexation means that pensioners get relatively poorer but, in theory, maintain their living standards (their pension will still buy the same basket of goods), as in the UK since 1982. Given the rate at which consumption needs change, price linkage may be little use to pensioners. The shift in need from black and white to colour TV is one simple example for the UK. In 1960 colour was a luxury, now it is eccentric to be without it.

Growth of pension coverage

The history of pensions in most countries is that highly unionized male workers, such as railway men or miners, are the first manual pensioners. Civil servants, including the armed forces, are the first white-collar pensioners. Schemes slowly extend to include all workers. In France farmers came in late and among the last groups to be covered by the 'régime générale' were clergy and prostitutes. Migrant workers may be covered if unions decide that insisting on proper benefits is one way to stop migrants undercutting home labour or, they may be excluded from many benefits.

Conclusion

Most older people everywhere are workers. Some are low paid but most are not formally paid at all. They work to support themselves and because they feel a need to contribute to the income strategies of their families, rather than being a burden. At present we have no standard ways of measuring their work and their contribution to economic and social development. Nor do we know how much families do to support the very old and frail who can no longer work in countries with underdeveloped pension systems. The development of statistics on unpaid work will go some way to answering these questions. In the future we can expect many more older men and women to be pensioners. The funded pension schemes in South East and East Asia will begin to pay out and will extend their coverage, and the very low social assistance pensions of India and higher ones in South Africa are likely to be copied as more countries can afford the cost and develop the information technology needed to deal with very large numbers of very poor elders.

In the developed countries pensions have transformed the lives of millions of older men and women for the better and produced a new life stage. In other words, pensions are a success:

> The reality, in contrast to widespread perception, is that public pension systems in the advanced countries are doing reasonably well. Like all major

institutions with a long history, they need to be changed to take account of new circumstances and those projected in the future. However they have shown themselves capable of change. (Ross, 1996: 50)

Despite their success it is fair to ask how far countries use their pension schemes to concentrate poverty in later life, and how far they simply continue the existing distribution of poverty into old age. In the first case, most elders will have low pensions (equality through levelling down), but some may have been able to save during their working lives. In the second case, pensions are linked to earnings replacement rates. For example, if all pensioners get 50 per cent of their final earnings as a pension, the differences in earnings will be translated into later life. Women, who may have been out of the labour market and so depend on their husbands, or who have been low paid, will have lower pensions than men. Any inequalities will be further reinforced as the rich will have taken advantage of savings schemes and tax breaks, and the poor may be in debt. Most countries, therefore, have some form of redistribution or collectivization of pension risks. The UK, where the full pension is currently (1999) below the social assistance rate, appears to have policies that both concentrate poverty in old age and carry forward inequitable distributions.

Unemployment (either ideologically reinforced, as for women in many countries, or due to low economic performance or economic restructuring) has disastrous effects on PAYG pension schemes because the size and productivity of the current workforce determine the viability of the schemes. Stock market collapse and the economic decline that is likely to follow economic restructuring have a greater impact on fully funded pensions, but all pensions are vulnerable to economic collapse. Argentina, for example, still has much of the administrative framework that was set up in the 1930s when it was an advanced welfare state and good pension schemes were put in place. Economic conditions have brought about the failure of the welfare state and pensions are now inadequate for many (Lloyd-Sherlock, 1997).

In the future when older people are fitter and live longer, phased retirement may become a more widespread choice and be better supported by anti-discriminatory legislation, pension scheme structures and recruitment practices. Policies to encourage later retirement, or at the very least a slowing in the trend to early exit from the labour market, seem to be essential (OECD, 1998). However, the simple expedient of raising the retirement age, which is widely being adopted in the face of the 'pensions crisis' is liable to shift the cost of older workers from the pension fund to social assistance unless jobs are available and age discrimination is effectively outlawed.

Futher reading

OECD (1997) *Family Market and Community Equity and Efficiency in Social Policy*. Paris: OECD.
OECD (1998) *Maintaining Prosperity in an Ageing Society*. Paris: OECD.
http://www.europa.eu.int/comm – for Europe.
http://www.helpage.org – for developing countries.
http://www.oecd.org/subject/ageing – technical site on work and pensions.
http://www.imf.org – for International Monetary Fund recognition of population ageing and the need for social policy.

CHAPTER 8

HEALTH AND ILLNESS IN LATER LIFE

Older men and women can be perfectly healthy even though their metabolic rates slow down and their strength declines. Some mental activities also slow or change. However, they decline from different levels and at different rates. In favourable environments the changes will hardly be apparent, and the benefits of old age may often mean that life improves and that the older person is happier, and so more energetic, than when young. Normal ageing may therefore be a time of reduced energy, but most people have a great deal of surplus capacity in all areas of daily living and they can continue to function very well. It will help if they can shift from heavy to lighter work or physical activity. However, this is an individualized approach to health, and in population terms health will vary as the structure of the older population changes (see Chapter 3). In theory a population reaches a point of epidemiological transition when the main sources of ill health shift from acute infectious and parasitic diseases (for example tuberculosis and malaria) to degenerative and chronic diseases (heart disease and cancer). As with the various demographic transitions discussed in Chapter 3, the idea of a simple epidemiological transition is contested, most notably because in very unequal societies the poor will still be suffering high infant mortality and communicable diseases, such as tuberculosis, even though the rich may indeed be dying of cancer and hypertension.

The World Health Organization defines health as a positive condition and not simply as the absence of disease, but any discussion of health comes up against the problem that 'health' in a social policy context almost always means 'illness'. Since old age is also stereotypically a time of ill health, it is not surprising that we know little about healthy ageing. What we do know is that the relationship between health, illness, frailty, old age and the life course is complex at individual and at population level. Basic assumptions or even 'facts' that seem entirely obvious in one culture will not necessarily be the same in another. Chapter 2 showed that in many cultures a healthy older person is not seen as 'old' unless they become disabled in some obvious way. In Japan, on the other hand, very large numbers of older people are classified as bedridden and hence in poor health by Western standards. Since 1986 the rate of bedridden elders appears to have remained steady at around 4.7 per cent of the population over 65 even though the numbers over 65 increased from 13 to 18 million over the decade (Ministry of Health and Welfare of Japan, 1998). In the UK, by comparison, only 2 per cent of over 65s were unable to get in and out of bed (Victor, 1991). We cannot assume that Japanese people are physiologically twice as likely to become immobile in later life than others, but it is quite possible that there are cultural reasons for late life immobility.

At present (1999) we know that people are living longer on average, but there is no consensus on whether longer life means a longer period of disability. Is being old simply a matter of survival with more and more incapacity, or is the quality of life as good or better than in the past? To those who believe that old age is synonymous with disability, the answer is obvious. They assume that the longer people are 'old', the longer they will be disabled, and the more they will cost in terms of health and social care. This is a widely held popular view. Like most stereotypes it is not completely without foundation. Since more older women than older men report limiting health conditions and disability and since there are more older women, there are plenty of examples of chronic illness and disability among older people. Research has so far produced contradictory results – some samples show more disability and some less as life expectancy increases (see Ebrahim and Kalache, 1996). Given the levels of diversity among older men and women (which studies rarely take into account) and the limited studies undertaken, contradictory results are to be expected.

Health as a life course issue

Individual health status in later life does not simply happen but rather it develops over the life course. It therefore reflects changing cultural, social and economic conditions, genetic make-up, health beliefs and behaviours, chronological age and, of course, luck, among other things. Lack of reliable research means that the actual impact of all these factors on late life health status is very far from clear. As things stand we do not know what makes up good health in later life or what is to be expected as a goal to aim for. We can, however, start with a Western stereotype of a 'survivor' – someone who has lived longer than average life expectancy:

'He makes you WANT to be 91'

Let us imagine a man in his 90s, active in mind and body. Well able to look after himself but supported by a female relative, who might be his wife but equally can be a daughter or niece. He is probably of average or above average height (now a little reduced) but still upright in his bearing. He has material resources, maybe an adequate pension or savings and one or two interests or hobbies and takes some exercise every day, come rain or shine. He has retired long ago and does not cling to power. He is probably wise and certainly cheerful. He has lived a good life life. He may smoke (though this is unlikely) and drink but not to excess, and he will hopefully die of a heart attack or fatal stroke.

A healthy old age, in fact (Western version). Other cultures would expect less activity and more contemplation, and in yet others such a man would be seen as 'not yet old'.

Older women are statistically more likely to suffer from disabling conditions than men of similar age and it is less easy to identify a stereotype of healthy old age for women. The stereotypical grandmother, looking after and indulging a tribe of grandchildren, is a social image and refers to younger women aged 50–70 rather than the over 80s. Some women do look after their great grandchildren but they are then more likely to come into the category of 'marvellous for her age' than 'in good health'. Social stereotypes of exercise for older women are mainly limited to gardening. Housework is the most commonly recorded form of exercise but is not usually seen as such (Sidell, 1995). It seems likely, however, that older women are consistently more socially active than older men even though they may take less exercise – see, for example, a Canadian national sample that showed older women doing more shopping, eating out, visiting friends and going to clubs or playing cards. Men walked more and went for drives more often. Men over 80 (the ultra-fit survivors very often) were more social in terms of going out than women (Government of Canada, 1993).

Health capabilities in later life

As these examples tentatively illustrate, older men and women carry in their bodies a history of personal and social influences on health. Poor nutrition, parasites, lack of medical treatment, overwork and, for women, early and multiple pregnancies, can all shorten average life. In Europe the poverty of the Depression years, a fall in birth-rate, the great improvement in nutrition thanks to rationing in the Second World War (or conversely, starvation in some countries), the changing incidence of smoking across class and gender, the impact of migration and new environmental pollutants, all work to improve or undermine the health of cohorts. At the individual level, genetic make-up and life long health behaviours are important, but individuals operate within structures of gender relations, income distribution and public health provision or the lack of it, and these influence their personal choices in measurable ways. Rising incomes and better standards of nutrition have combined with the elimination of infectious diseases to change the health of whole societies (McKeown, 1976), but the problems of minorities remain (Markides and Miranda, 1997).

It is against this background that we consider the capability of older men and women to lead healthy lives. One powerful legacy from the past is the expectation, almost the demand, that older people are passive, accept the disabilities of old age and are grateful for what they get. In the near future older men and women may be less passive and more willing to campaign for better health and social services. At present health services in particular do not appear to be willing to see older patients as partners in care, but that is likely to be one way to design better and possibly even cheaper care in the future (DaneAge Foundation, 1990; Ortendahl, 1997). More health prevention and more appropriate health policies are likely to be needed in all countries (Kalache, 1988).

Income

Problems of income in later life have already been mentioned in Chapters 5 and 7 where the importance of economic globalization in impoverishing older men and women in many countries was considered. Globalization, in the shape of economic restructuring, works *directly* in lowering GNP (in Africa, for example) and preventing countries from implementing social policies that would provide a safety net for marginal members of society. It also works *indirectly* by undermining traditional social structures that supported older men and women who could no longer provide for themselves. Low income is associated with poor health in later life, as in childhood. For example Black et al. (1988) showed clear health gradients for England and Wales in terms of mortality and morbidity by class. (Class was used as a proxy for income because occupational data are easier to collect accurately than income data.) In the USA disadvantaged minorities have consistently worse health than the better off (Markides and Miranda, 1997). More egalitarian distribution of income/resources is associated with reduced mortality in most countries. When more detailed longitudinal research is available on income distribution by gender, age, class and ethnic group, it will be easier to see the influence of income on mortality and possibly even on morbidity (sickness) (Wilkinson, 1996).

Diet

A big problem for very large numbers of older men and women, and even more for older widows, is simply one of getting enough food. It is a known 'fact', for example, that older people (especially women) need less food than the young. As Chelala (1992) points out, *energy* requirements fall in old age but *nutrition* needs hardly alter. Malnutrition 'is a social construct as much as a biological state or process, an economic input as well as an outcome' (Harriss, 1995: 225), but it is also a very real and underresearched hazard of later life. In India, as far as is known, it is 'normal' for food consumption to decline after the age of 44 (Harriss, 1995). For many poorer women this will mean a drop from what Sen has called low-level starvation. Furthermore, in a joint household the oldest woman is likely to be the one who fasts most often. (However, as Harriss (1995) says, fasting can mean a change of food rather than a reduction of intake.) When incomes are low and life is a struggle, for example in the former Soviet Union, as well as in those countries usually described as developing, the food needs of older people are almost certain to take second or third place to those of the so-called productive age groups, and children. This tendency can be seen in extreme form in famines where it is typically the old and children who die.

Even in prosperous countries where malnutrition has supposedly been abolished, it is possible to be undernourished in later life. First, pensions or social assistance may be set too low and what was adequate in the early years of retirement can be reduced by inflation or by the rising costs of chronic illness or disability. In such circumstances disability is liable to be increased by lack of money, which then intensifies disability. The number of American jokes about elders eating dog food is one indicator of the effects of low income on diet. Good food costs more. It may also be further away, in inaccessible shops. Elders may develop vitamin deficiencies due to the absence of fresh fruit or vegetables. Those who live and eat alone are particularly vulnerable to loss of interest in cooking. Older men may never have cooked, so even if they can buy fresh food they may not bother. Disability can in any case make peeling vegetables or carrying heavy shopping an impossibility. Older migrants are another group who can easily suffer from poor diets. The food they would like to eat is usually expensive (being exotic) and their ability to eat healthily on a low income in a foreign land may be limited.

Once basic needs are met there are problems in defining a 'healthy diet'. Consensus is lacking even within cultures and certainly across them. Beliefs on diet have changed since today's elders were young. For example, red meat with fat, eggs, full cream milk and butter were once key items in a healthy English diet. In many cultures fatness is seen as a sign of health. New developments in prepared meals for freezer and microwave are a great help to elders with disabilities but they are not always prepared with health in mind, and the long-term effects of additives and pesticide residues is still to be determined. Scrutton (1992) is one of many who see them as disastrous. Finally, poor teeth, badly fitting false teeth and sore gums are problems which can affect elders in almost any country. Unchewed food is hard to digest and the effects can range from a drop in the quality of life through to being life threatening.

Shelter

In health terms, the ability to keep warm and dry is probably the next most important factor in colder countries. Poor quality housing in cold countries usually means high heating bills, so that older women and men may end up choosing between warmth and food in winter (Salvage, 1991). Owner occupation can become a burden to older people on an inadequate pension (Means, 1988). They may have no alternative but to wait while window frames rot, paintwork peels and water seeps through the roof. Women who never learnt home maintenance are the most disadvantaged. Late life health hazards include dripping taps, leaking roofs and out of date and dangerous kitchen appliances and all may afflict owner-occupiers and tenants with bad landlords. In the USA where elders are often housed in tower blocks, broken lifts can lead to serious isolation, depression and inability to leave the home.

Housing is not widely seen as an aspect of public health outside slums, but in ageing populations health in later life would be greatly improved by a policy that required all new homes to be easily convertible for use by people with disabilities (OECD, 1992). It is also in the interests of the community to repair the homes of older people and so keep property values up. In many areas there are voluntary schemes which provide handymen as needed. Governments may legislate for grants to help elders repair or modernize their homes or convert them to disability access. Such schemes are fine in theory but the prospect of builders in the home can be a deterrent to the most able bodied, and a nightmare to frail elders. Support in avoiding 'cowboy' builders and in dealing with the contracts, mess and likely problems may be essential before those who most need home improvement can even begin to take advantage of such schemes.

In the megacities of the developing world 'housing' for old people can be extremely limited. They may squat in a corner of a family shelter, or they may be the head of an all-woman household of several generations living in bad conditions (Chant, 1990; Lloyd-Sherlock, 1997; Moser, 1996). Their position is always precarious. Necessary health measures can be as basic as somewhere to store food away from flies or to keep out mosquitoes but, as with food supplies and medical care, when many of the population lack these basic necessities, special housing for the elderly is not likely to be a policy priority. It follows, therefore, that co-residence with the younger generation offers the best chance that many elders will have of improving their housing (Lloyd-Sherlock, 1997). The effects of co-residence on autonomy, and on other aspects of well being, are discussed in Chapter 9, but in most countries and in most families, they are limiting rather than enabling.

Social integration and autonomy

Social integration and a degree of individual autonomy are widely agreed to be highly desirable for good health in old age. In terms of social integration:

> We need words to keep us human. Being human is an accomplishment, like playing an instrument. It takes practice. . . . It is a skill we can forget. (Ignatieff, 1984, quoted in Stevenson, 1989: 10)

Apart from the few people who are genuinely happy on their own, social interaction is one of the things that makes life worth living. Such interaction need not be particularly harmonious, but as long as it is not abusive (in terms of psychological or physical abuse), it is a key aspect of healthy ageing. It follows that family, friends, neighbours and professionals can all contribute positively or negatively to healthy ageing. See Kendig et al. (1991) for a range of examples.

Autonomy is less universalized as a culturally desirable attribute of living than social contact. It implies that individuals can, within limits, call on whatever help they need to enable them to do what they want. For example, car drivers can continue to take part in social activities even if they are disabled, but non-drivers will need assistance (Eisenhandler, 1993). In other words, people with disabilities may make choices, but they are only autonomous if assistance is readily available. However, in cultures where elders are expected to be passive and contemplative and where such behaviour is facilitated, if not actively encouraged, autonomy may be less important for health.

Acceptance of inactivity should not be confused with tolerance of reduced capabilities. In some societies, elders, and particularly women, are not expected to make material demands. They may develop spiritual or interior lives that complement self-denial in the material sphere. However, Sen (1993) and Nussbaum (1995) have powerfully argued that just because reductions in autonomy (capabilities in their terminology) have social support, they should not be assumed to be beneficial. It is common for disadvantages to be internalized so that in countries where hardship is common for all, worse conditions for older people may be accepted as 'natural' by everyone. Widows, for example, especially childless widows (Cain, 1986b), may find it very difficult to make claims for health or even livelihood. Hence, even if older people support their own marginalization, impoverishment or lack of health care, this should not be taken as automatically good for them, either socially or in health terms.

Age-friendly environments

In most countries the possibilities for making the environment more friendly to people of all ages, but especially mothers with young children and frail elders, have hardly begun to be explored. Safety and freedom from crime are still not routinely considered as elements of public health but the disabling effects of fear can strike at any age. Chronic illnesses of old age such as degenerative heart failure, emphysema or arthritis can be more or less disabling according to the environment, as well as the stage in the disease. Men or women suffering from these conditions may be able to live as part of their communities, going out, shopping and socializing, but only if they have the right housing and a supportive environment. In most Western countries lack of public transport or the nature of the transport itself imposes very great physical demands on older users and is a seriously disabling aspect of the environment. The alternative of the private car is unaffordable on a UK state pension and, in any case, may be medically inadvisable. In developing countries only a slight impairment in health status can have highly disabling consequences. For example, women who have to collect water or fuel over long distances can find a minor infection enough to make independent living temporarily or permanently impossible.

Exercise

In the past old age was seen as ideally a time of rest, and possibly contemplation, in virtually all societies, but in today's sedentary, car-bound Western countries, exercise is recognized as essential for health. As noted above, in the stereotypes of health, exercise for elders is not always easily arranged. In many cultures or sub-cultures older bodies are a bad joke and not easy to display on poolsides or sports fields. The result may be 'seniors only' times or other segregated activities. In other societies the need to rest may conflict with the need to feel useful or even to survive. Bialik (1989) describes how older Mexican women of all ethnicities felt that they had to be useful in some way. At the extreme, the concept of exercise is alien when everyday existence is so physically exhausting that it threatens health. This applies particularly to older farmers and labourers in all parts of the world.

Unhealthy behaviours

Aside from enforced unhealthiness, older men and women do not always choose to live as healthily as experts would like. To some extent they may know best, since health fashions come and go. Alternatively, smoking, overindulgence in alcohol, betel nut or other drugs can be seen as a privilege of (mostly male) old age and so irrelevant to health promotion strategies. Both men and women may ignore symptoms of illness and join with so many doctors in putting health problems down to old age. If funds are short and medical treatment expensive, as it is for so many elders, they have no choice but to ignore their symptoms or fall back on their own medical treatments. Cohen (1998) notes that he was not able to recruit a sample of older Indian patients because so few were brought to clinics in Varanasi by their relatives.

Illness in later life

In the developing world elders are still prone to the diseases of under-development. Parasites and infectious diseases can result in chronic low-health status and can also kill in later life, especially if combined with low food intakes. Those who live long enough may suffer fractured hips, heart disease, cancer, stroke, diabetes and respiratory diseases, just as they would in richer countries (Chelala, 1992; Sen, 1994), but the incidence is lower and treatments that could be taken for granted in the West will not be available. In developed countries the frailty of old age makes older men and women slightly more likely than the rest of the population to fall ill with curable diseases, but only slightly more likely (Victor, 1991), and it is the chronic conditions and disabilities that differentiate the old from the young. Chronic diseases do not kill, but neither can they be cured, though they may be alleviated by orthodox or alternative medical treatments. Chronic heart failure, joint problems (arthritis), circulatory problems and depression are among the high risks of old age. Migrant groups typically have very high rates of diabetes and heart problems.

Chronic diseases are a source of growing profit for the pharmaceutical industry whose ideal customer should stay ill with a steady, long-term need for high-cost medication. Polypharmacy (prescription of many, often incompatible, drugs) is a common outcome and can itself cause ill health.

> The difficulties associated with drug therapy in the elderly stem from the fact that illness in the elderly is often multiple in nature – the temptation is therefore to treat every problem that a patient has with a drug. . . . Certain drugs are notorious for causing problems. (Cayley, 1987: 23)

Andrews and Brocklehurst (1987) summarized health problems as 'four geriatric giants':

Immobility – much reduced since hip and other joint replacements became common

Instability – falls and fractured hips

Incontinence and constipation – the former a major reason for breakdown in home caregiving, the latter a common cause of hospital admission, confusion and incontinence

Intellectual decline – widely feared and elevated to a new scourge (Alzheimer's disease) in the USA.

These conditions may be present alone, together or combined with other illnesses. They greatly complicate diagnosis and treatment. For example, depression in later life can mask other conditions and itself be hard to diagnose (Iliffe et al., 1994).

Health costs

As the numbers of elders and the range of possible medical interventions increases, nagging questions about the costs of an ageing population become more insistent. Much of this concern is exaggerated, as with the cost of pensions, for political reasons that have nothing to do with the welfare of older people. It is now becoming widely accepted that the main health care costs of elders occur in the last two to four years of life (OECD, 1998). This does not appear to be a new development. In 1892 Booth wrote:

> Canon Blackley found by an independent inquiry in twenty six county parishes, that no less than 42% of those who died had relief and were a cost to their parishes during the closing years of their lives. I cannot think that the average all over the country would be so high, but 20% would not be an improbable estimate. (Booth, 1892: 165)

It follows that, as life expectancy increases and the size of the older population grows, death-rates rise more slowly and may even fall, as they have in Australia. The rise in medical costs which is driven by population ageing is much slower than the rise in total numbers of old people. At the same time, cost increases driven by advances in medical technology appear to be unremitting and much larger than the costs of ageing (Robinson and Judge, 1987), though it may be politically expedient to blame the aged. Other important points are that a very small drop in the average length of institutionalization at the end of life has a dramatic effect on health care costs (OECD, 1998).

However, within this general lack of panic there are a number of health care issues that might be raised. The first is changes in the mix of very old and younger old in different countries. In developing countries, for example, the 'old old' (those over 80) are growing fast, but from a very low base. In developed countries it is clear that people over 80 are more liable to be admitted to hospital and may have to stay longer, either because they have multiple problems or because they have no one to look after them when they come out of hospital (they are often widows). At present the numbers over 80 are so much smaller than the numbers over 60 that their total costs are lower but this may change. But as far as can be seen, given modern medical technology and practice, the cost increase would not be uncontainable (OECD, 1998).

Medical technology

Changes in medical technology are usually seen as driving medical costs up but for older patients they could well have the opposite effect. Already, artificial hips have enormously reduced the costs of caring for elders who used to be wheelchair or bed bound by arthritis. Day-care cataract operations have reduced the incidence of blindness in later life and are much cheaper than inpatient cataract operations. Cuts in the drugs bill for elders *might* have similar good effects. There appears to be no doubt that older people in developed countries are over-medicated and that the effects of polypharmacy are harmful and raise the costs of caring for an ageing population, both in the short term and in the long term. At the same time it can be argued that, as newer and more expensive drugs come on the market, there will be enormous pressure from the pharmaceutical industry, relatives and even older people themselves to prescribe. For example, a long-term inhibitor of Alzheimer's disease and similar chronic conditions would net very large profits for pharmaceutical companies. The impact of technology on the cost of elderly care is therefore much less clear than it is for acute medicine in general.

Rationing health care

Whatever the rate of increase in the health needs of the older population, their access to medical and nursing care is certain to be rationed and the method chosen will influence their access to health care. As mentioned above, in many developing countries very few elders appear in medical facilities and this method of rationing is likely to continue wherever health care is not free to all and easily accessible. A South African elder told HelpAge International 'At times we are abused by the nurses who say "Why are you coming to the clinic? You are old. Are you afraid of dying?" Such things make us afraid to go to the clinic.' (HelpAge International – South Africa, 1999). In the British NHS rationing was previously hidden and was largely a matter of medical prestige and prejudice. However, age discrimination has always been present and is expressed in discriminatory policies (Henwood, 1993). In Sweden, for example, the municipalization of hospitals can lead to lack of medical expertise in elder care (Hedin, 1993; Ortendahl, 1997). In the UK GPs and consultants are able to explain to older patients that certain procedures are medically inadvisable at their age – whatever it might be. So for example, men over 55 did not get kidney transplants in the UK for many years. In state-funded systems, the other main method of rationing is the waiting list. Access is restricted and total costs held down by maintaining long waiting lists. Take for example the case of the 95-year-old who was told that his operation would come up in four years' time.

Rationing that is justified by costs and benefits of treatment rather than medically determined need will also discriminate against older men and women. The types of evaluation used by health economists, which discount future earnings against the costs of the procedure (QALYs, for example, see Williams, 1994), are bound to show that any measures to improve health in old age are ineffective in cost terms. If unpaid care-giving by elders were brought into the equation the calculation would look more positive (it might also be closer to reality), but it would never justify treatment for older people as opposed to wage earners.

Where medicine is privately funded, as it is in large parts of the world, price is the main rationing mechanism. Only the very richest elders can expect to pay for all the medical care they may need in later life. Private insurers have refused to provide cover for such bad risks as average income elders unless they are given massive government subsidies, and even in the USA the Medicare system for older people is state funded. In developing countries, distance needs to be added to these rationing systems. When communications are poor, expensive and uncomfortable and medical facilities are far apart, sick elders are not going to be able to travel to them. We can conclude that any system of rationing is liable to work against health care access by older people but that rationing by price is the most harmful.

Systems of medicine

Biological or medical models of ageing have tended to obscure positive ageing in favour of models related to disease and decline (Estes and Binney, 1991). It is possible to argue that allopathic or Western medicine has been caught off guard by ageing populations. Medicine, as popularly conceived, is still about curing the young rather than improving the quality of life for the majority of patients (who in developed countries are not, or soon will not be, the young). The current system has a strong scientific bias and a focus on individual body parts rather than the body as a whole. We do not know how suitable it will be for looking after an older population. However, other systems, for example Chinese, ayurvedic or unani, have even less experience of geriatric care. They do, though, take very different views of illness and health and may well have much to contribute.

Conclusion – societies for healthy ageing

We can conclude that old age is not a disease and nor is it a disability. There are diseases *of* old age and there are diseases *in* old age but the process of ageing is not one of disease. A healthy old age is therefore possible, but much more research is needed before health in old age can be clearly identified and age appropriate services planned in different societies, and for different groups within them. Longer life may or may not lead to more years of disability but it will not automatically result in unsustainable increases in health expenditure. Longer life on its own is likely to have only a small impact on health costs in the short and medium term because high expenditure is concentrated in the last two years of life, and longer life means slow increase in death-rates for the immediate future. Longer life with greater levels of disability will cost more, though the ability of health services to ration care for elders can never be underestimated. In personal as well as policy terms the object must be to maximize years of health and minimize years of sickness or disability, but the gruesome fact is that dead elders are cheaper than live ones so preventative healthcare can be expensive.

In health, even more than in illness, the influence of society is as important as the actions of individual men and women. As with other social benefits, a first and most important step to improved health status is for older men and women to be valued by their societies. In a healthy society there will be ways of making sure that all age groups have access to the attributes of healthy ageing mentioned above: social integration, autonomy, and adequate income, diet and housing. It follows that the more ageist a society the more likely it is that elders will lose out as a group, even before other divisions such as gender, class or ethnicity are considered. A more equal distribution of income, the universalization of education, especially for women, better town planning in the growing conurbations, better housing, water and sewerage disposal will be the key factors in the future.

Further reading

Markides, K.S. and Miranda, M.R. (eds) (1997) *Minorities, Aging, and Health*. Thousand Oaks, CA: Sage, on America.

http://www.paho.org/ – for Latin America.

http://www.who.int/ageing/ – the World Health Organization on ageing and health.

http://www.un.org/esa/socdev/ageipaa.htm – International Plan of Action on Ageing – includes health.

http://www.bmj.com – articles in vol. 319 by Alison Torks, Shah Ebratium, et al.

CHAPTER 9

FAMILY AND COMMUNITY
IN LATER LIFE

Popular wisdom has it that you have children so that there will be someone to look after you in your old age, and in most countries of the world where pensions are minimal or non-existent and care services are likewise non-existent or degrading, popular wisdom has a point. Even when pensions are good and services well developed, families are still important for most of those who have them. In fact, we can identify a worldwide dominant discourse that expects families to look after their aged members, and that further assumes that everyone has children. However, the overarching simplicity of such a discourse is misleading: the term 'family' can have many meanings (see Chapter 2). It underpins a range of assumptions that translate into different communal understandings and different types of social policy.

Families or individuals?

We have first to ask how people think and feel about their families. The answer has far-reaching consequences for the lives of older men and women. At the extremes, the choice is between whether the *family* or the *individual* is the basic unit of society. The dominant, though not the only answer in most Western societies, is that the individual is the basic unit, and that families are made up of individuals. In contrast there are large parts of the world where it is assumed that the family or lineage is the basic unit and the concept of an individual is relatively undeveloped, especially for women.

> In Black Africa you do not know where the family begins and where it ends. It is a greatly extended family, a vast structure, more solidaristic than in Europe. . . . It is not just *individuals* linked by blood but *people* who have been entrusted to the family by friends and have stayed on, and neighbours who maintain multigenerational relations with the family are also members. . . . It is a structure which is much less rigid than in Europe. (Sine, 1984; 315 my translation and emphases)

By contrasting individuals and people, Sine is indicating that 'individuals', and the assumptions of independent activity and choice that go with the term, are different from 'people' who can be seen as interdependent and defined by their relationship with others, rather than by their own activities. The African family, always allowing the existence of such an overgeneralization, is only one form of holistic family. Others appear in different dominant discourses, so that in India, for example, the boundaries of the family are more clearly drawn than in Black Africa but the individual remains less important than the family as a whole.

The dominant discourses that prioritize either individuals or families as the basic units of society inform the assumptions that underpin social policies. Discourses about old age are very different depending on whether the dominant discourse sees the individual or the family as the key unit of society. The first difference is that if the family is a collection of individuals of different ages, the concepts of intergenerational competition, contracts and inequalities beloved of Western academics (Johnson et al., 1989; Laslett and Fishkin, 1992) make perfect sense. If, on the other hand, the family is an ongoing and continuous unity that develops over time, the idea of division between the generations is basically an irrelevance (see also Scherer, 1996 quoted on p. 90). The second major distinction is between the values given to independence/ dependence versus interdependence. In the individualized family, independence is usually highly valued and dependency is something to be strenuously avoided. Independence is maintained by being able to return or reciprocate any favours, gifts or services. Family relations in this model are either based on reciprocity or contractualized. As long as older men and women can fulfil the norms of reciprocity they can see themselves as more or less independent but, if they feel they have nothing to offer in return for support, they are likely to feel disempowered and a burden. They are also more likely to be described as a burden by those who finance or care for them. The alternative model sees interdependence as an essential part of being human and takes it for granted as a 'natural' aspect of family and community relations. In such a culture, the idea of parents as a burden is unlikely to be developed in public discourse or in policy. This does not mean that the labour of looking after a frail elder or the cash involved in supporting them is not felt to be a burden, only that such a discourse is likely to remain muted. It may be spoken about by younger women, or a subject of dispute between husband and wife, but it is not likely to appear in official documents.

Readers might like to consider where they fall on the continuum of individual versus family as the key component of society, first in terms of logic and second in terms of emotions. There is no need for the two to coincide: intergenerational competition exists everywhere and older people can *feel* a burden, even in societies where custom and religion, as well as policy, support social solidarity at the expense of individuals. Equally, family solidarity can be strongly *felt* in the most individualistic cultures. Feelings are stressed here even though they may be masked by the individualized language of contract and intergenerational reciprocities. Whatever the dominant discourse, any society includes a range of different ways of thinking and feeling about family relations, and often they will be inconsistent.

Family boundaries

The next difference is not so much ideological or conceptual as practical. Where, as Sine says above, does the family begin and end? In the West the choice is often between the two-generation nuclear household and the 'extended' family of three generations. This is to confuse household (those who live under one roof) and family (those who see themselves as closely related) in some cases but, in others, it is to ignore differences in the meaning of the term 'family'. For example, in Europe means testing as applied to families usually refers to fathers of young children though, occasionally, it applies to the children of older people as in Germany and technically in France. In Japan, brothers and sisters as well as children are required by law to support indigent elders. Cousins, uncles and aunts may be as much family in Africa or India as siblings and parents are in the UK.

Where families are the main source of support in old age, the need for children is often recognized by formal and informal arrangements for childless couples to adopt, and for procedures which allow other relatives to substitute for those who are absent. Keith (1994a) describes the Herero in southern Africa:

> Herero feel that old people 'ought' to be given children to care for them. A scene characteristic of Herero villages is of an old woman seated in her floral finery under a tree, surrounded by several children who scurry to obey her requests to feed the fire, push the churn, bring water, wash clothes, make tea, and do anything else she needs. (Keith, 1994a : 22)

In other societies nieces and nephews will take on many roles expected of children, and brothers and sisters may offer the support normally expected of a spouse in old age. As Harris (1983) showed for Wales, this happens in Europe as well as in developing countries, but it is less formalized. Older men and women in most cultures appear to take more interest in family than younger age groups and so their perceptions of the family may be more comprehensive than the dominant community view.

Finally, there are many who have no functioning family or whose children have died before them. Brathwaite (1989), working in Barbados where respect and care of the elderly are assumed to be the norm, found that only half the population he surveyed could rely on relatives. Many elders with low pensions had no extra support from their families and found it hard to afford an adequate diet. One third had no children and a quarter of those with children had no contact with them. Most did not feel able to rely on neighbours. Twenty per cent worked and most others said they had been forced to retire. Rising divorce rates further threaten intergenerational links. Divorce accentuates the problems that older men often have in maintaining social links (see Riggs, 1997) as they are more likely to lose touch with their children and grandchildren.

The family as a site for work and care

As with the above example from Barbados, rhetoric or dominant discourse can diverge from reality. The family, though usually presented as a site for the care and protection of the old, is also the site of continuing labour in later life, especially for women and especially in countries where pensions are non-existent or inadequate. Older men and women continue to work (see Chapter 7) for as long as they are able unless the family has a surplus. Child care is the type of work most often associated with old women but when so much work is unmeasured and invisible – housework, laundry, gardening, stock keeping, participation in local affairs – it is easy to underestimate the contributions of elders. Actual physical work may decline and older women with married children may spend more time directing the work of the next generation – as senior wives or mothers-in-law – and older men traditionally take part in a range of religious and political activities that are seen as important. If older men and women continue to work and also share a roof with succeeding generations, it is very likely that resources will be pooled within the family (pooled does not mean shared equally) and inter-dependence is the norm. On the other hand, in rural areas where the young have left for the cities, work in the old family home is a way of maintaining independence. If an elder becomes frail and in need of care the transition can be gradual in co-resident households. Even very disabled elders can still be useful about the house in small ways but, for those who live alone, sudden illness or inability to cope may bring about a dramatic change. They may have to move to the city to be with children, or go into residential care. Tout gives the following sad example:

> Mrs S., very old. 'When I was at home I had a field and managed to do all I wanted, but here in town I am hardly able to take a walk. I cannot walk because I am old, and besides, in town there is a danger of cars. I always tell my son that I want to go home to live the life I am used to. I am, however, too old and sick and no one is prepared to come with me. I have no future but to wait for death'. (Tout, 1989: 121)

Friends and neighbours – the community

Friends, as opposed to family, come into their own in later life once income is secured and elders do not have to depend on their families for survival. Knodel and Chanpen (1998) found only one couple in their survey of elders in northern Thailand who had a real choice of where to live. In that case the husband had a good civil service pension and they had chosen to leave their children in the capital city and move back to their place of birth where they had many friends. As the authors say, they lived alone but 'they did not feel that their children had deserted them'. In all other cases elders lived with or very close to at least one child, indicating the importance of material support in later life when there is no pension system (Knodel and Chanpen, 1998). Even so, friends are important in terms of social integration in later life. They may be easier to talk to than the young. They may also be more understanding and emotionally supportive (Jerrome, 1992; Matthews, 1979) than younger generations and in some cases they may be caregivers. Abrams is among those who found that friends gave way to family when care became long term or highly personal (see Bulmer, 1986). In other cultures the distinction between family and friends or neighbours may be less clear and in all societies neighbours may substitute for family. The difference is that in most societies they have a freer choice of whether to care for a frail elder than a family member and will be less heavily condemned if they fail.

Caregivers

If self-care is impossible, the choice is between family (the most common option all over the world with the possible exception of Scandinavia), friends or formal services. Nydegger (1987), taking an anthropological perspective, places societies on a continuum between those where family caregiving for older people is seen almost wholly as a matter of duty and those where it is seen as a matter of love. As she says, there are countries, such as China, where the ideal of duty is the main driving force, and countries such as the USA where, at least in ideological terms, caregiving is a matter of affection. Duty gives the available relatives (and more rarely neighbours and friends) no choice but to care, but love can, in theory, offer a choice. Feminist writers and the carers' lobby in the UK have shown how women who become carers usually feel that they have no choice, even in a society where love is meant to be the main motivation in personal relationships, but those who refuse to care are less often studied and they may, indeed, have exercised choice. Of course neither of the extremes can predict what any individual carer will do in China or the USA or any other country, nor do they indicate where other countries will fall on such a continuum.

Concepts of love and duty are also useful when considering who will be expected to care and what social pressures are likely to be brought to bear (Twigg and Atkin, 1994). It seems possible to divide the world into cultures where daughters-in-law were expected to be the main carers for elderly parents and cultures where it was daughters. This statement is made in the past tense because there is evidence that these simple distinctions are breaking down (see, for example, Koyana, 1996 and Lee, 1997 who both give evidence of a reduction in family care in Japan and Hong Kong respectively). The growing number of young married couples who live on their own away from the husband's parents mean that care by a daughter-in-law is no longer automatic. It also seems reasonable to suggest that where daughters-in-law are assumed to be the main carers, duty will be the main motive.

Not all caregiving is unremitting burden. Much of it is life enhancing for caregivers as well as recipients (Abel and Nelson, 1990). Even if the burden is heavy there is the sense of self-respect that comes from duties well carried out and social norms respected. Caregivers who have had a reasonable relationship with the care receiver and who are not over-stressed are the most likely to gain from the experience. However, this does not mean that caregiving is unproblematic. For one thing, it is often invisible because it is done by women (see below). For another, there is the possibility, or in many societies the near certainty, of isolation, loss of health and income, and the possibility of knock-on effects: no pension, no friends and broken relationships. Such a transition to burdensome caregiving can be sudden (a stroke, perhaps) but it is more likely to be episodic or imperceptible in ways that make the idea of a choice of whether to care or not meaningless (Twigg, 1996; Twigg and Atkin, 1994).

Policy frameworks

The outcome for those who are cared for and for those who care can be summarized in four sets of ideologies (see also Millar and Warman, 1996). The first is that care is a matter for individuals in old age as at younger ages. Older men and women should have saved or insured themselves for long-term care. As a universal solution, this is financially impossible and the policy aim is then to get as many people as possible to provide for themselves and to set up some form of safety net for the rest. The safety net provision is likely to be of poor quality: it must act as a deterrent and encourage the improvident to save; and, since users of the safety net will be poor or without family, they are devalued and so is their service.

A second alternative is that the family, rather than the individual, should provide for old age. Religious sanctions, such as exclusion from Paradise for those who do not look after their parents, can be expressed in policy terms through laws that oblige family members to support each other. Such laws exist in Germany and France but are rarely invoked (Scharf, 1998). In Japan or Singapore they have more force. Family care is likely to be supported by very strong social and religious sanctions. Islam, Confucianism and Christianity all expect children to honour their parents and look after them. At the same time most societies have let-out clauses which may or may not be usable by potential carers. For example, Qureshi and Simons (1987) noted that having children and having a full time job could be a socially acceptable excuse for not taking on a heavy caregiving role. This may become increasingly important. Wirakartakusumah et al. writing on Indonesia remark tartly:

> ... more and more women are entering the labour market. It is therefore necessary to instil among men that they are also responsible for the main-tenance of the elderly. Men must learn how to care for the elderly in the same way as they learned how to care for their children.
> (Wirakartakusumah et al., 1997: 112)

In Japan children may take jobs far from home (Kobayashi, 1997) and so be unavailable for hands on care. It is also possible for better off women to employ others as carers, especially in countries where (migrant) female labour is relatively cheap.

The problematic aspect of cultural support for family solidarity and support of the aged, is that governments may take an ideological approach to care of the elderly which makes supportive policies difficult; though even in Asia where the ideology of family care is strong, support services exist (Dixon and Kim, 1985). If the society is characterized by strong religious or moral imperatives to honour parents, the government may assume that parents are being cared for and all evidence to the contrary is liable to be ignored, or seen as subversive or even anti-national. Instead, governments and public emphasize the caring nature of their societies in opposition to the widely believed myth that elders are all institutionalized by heartless, materialistic families in the West. Certainty on these points will be familiar to anyone who has taught students from different cultures. Asian, African and Latin American students are frequently sure that huge numbers of old people are in homes in the West, but virtually none in their own morally superior cultures. They have a point: the rate of institutionalization in Western countries appears to be around four to six times as high as in developing countries or NICs, but still only 6 to 8 per cent as against 1 to 2 per cent of the relevant populations (see Chapter 11). However, if governments deny the need for residential care or for support to family caregivers, the impact on elders and on women carers can be disastrous. Tout offers a long list of tragic cases who have come to the attention of HelpAge International. For example:

Mr B., aged 77 years. Marital status: widower. Family: a son aged 36 and two stepsons. Mr B. was living with his son in a rural village. The son's family was existing on a hand to mouth basis, and when the family could not provide food for the father he was taken to live with a stepson. He is suffering from chronic cancer and needs a lot of attention. The hospital cannot keep him as a chronic case due to shortage of beds. The common law wife of the stepson is now objecting to having to care for Mr B., and wants him moved. Mr B. has no income and no possessions except the clothing he is wearing. (Tout, 1989: 116)

As noted above, the existence of a family can never be assumed and even when kin exist they may not be supportive (Nana Apt, 1996).

Third, even though the state has taken over financial support for older citizens to a greater or lesser degree, depending on the effectiveness of the pension system and the level of social assistance for those who have small pensions, it may still leave most caregiving to families. Pensions, when adequate (see Chapter 7), change the nature of old age. They allow retirement for leisure (McCallum, 1990) and the possibility of self-care and 'intimacy at a distance', once there is no financial imperative to share a roof with the younger generation. A pension alone, however, cannot pay for long-term care and elders with failing health either need savings to pay for care or must fall back on family care. Advanced welfare states usually tend towards this mix of pensions and the exploitation of women.

The fourth model is under threat as populations age and costs rise, but has been identified in Scandinavian welfare states where pensions are relatively good and elders and their families expect care services to be financed or provided collectively. Women still provide virtually all care but they are paid for much of it, either as welfare staff or as informal carers with care allowances. Families continue to support their older frail members, especially socially and emotionally, but with the help of home care and various types of residential care services.

Policy outcomes

A golden age of family and community caregiving appears to be one of the enduring myths of human society (Lorenz-Meyer, 1996; Stearns, 1977). We can interpret this as establishing two important facts. The first is that it has been normal for younger people (possibly always women) to look after frail elders (see for example Troyansky, 1982, who disputes the negative picture painted by Stearns). The second is that this process has always had a potential for conflict. Within these generalizations there are major cultural differences in who provides care and what they provide (see, for example, Kendig et al., 1991), and how they feel about it. As noted above, the ideal in many Western societies is for independent self-care. For example:

One hears a note of self-reliance, independence, and dignity among the elderly. These people want to maintain themselves as long as they can. (Peterson, 1989: 177)

When carried to extremes this can mean that frail elders have very restricted life styles (Qureshi and Walker, 1989). Couples may be better able to preserve their independence and refuse offers of assistance. Two people, even with multiple disabilities, may make a better job of daily living than one. For example, the man who says 'I'm the eyes and she's the arms' (Wilson, 1995), is referring to the fact that his heart condition means that he has difficulty walking, let alone carrying anything, but he can make sure his blind wife does not get run over in the street and does not get short changed in the shops. Neither, or both, are carers and the fragility of their lifestyle is evident, but as things stand they are self-caring and independent of their children.

Self-care

As with the above couple, the vast majority of older men and, particularly, of older women are able to lead worthwhile lives and to care for themselves with very little help from others, but their own care work remains invisible. Self-care in advanced old age is not just looking after oneself, which is something most people have been doing to a greater or lesser extent all their lives. For frail elders self-care means the extra work, or the different strategies that older men and women need to enable them to live their lives as near normally as possible (Wilson, 1994). As with all disability, the need for self-care will vary with the environment. Older people in unfavourable environments will have to spend more time on self-care or change their lives more radically than men and women who have more supportive living conditions. As examples we can compare an older woman who has to walk a mile to fetch water from a well or standpipe with someone who has water on tap. More time and, possibly, more journeys will be needed as strength declines. Self-care may even cease if the journey becomes too demanding. Similarly, a person who has to go down steps to reach a toilet or a kitchen may be able to continue as self-caring if there are grab rails beside the steps, a stair lift or if she is able to move up and down in a sitting position. If not, meals on wheels or a commode and someone to empty it will have to be provided.

Co-residence

For many governments co-residence with younger family is the ideal social policy for ageing (Tracy, 1991). Co-resident elders may be almost invisible. Their work within the household and contributions to economic and social development are uncounted, their share of household resources is assumed to be small and any work of caring for them is performed invisibly by women relatives. If older property owners (usually men, thanks to gendered inheritance laws) who need care are also supporting large numbers of the younger generation over long periods, so much the better.

Some governments already facilitate co-residence or variants of it such as granny flats, known in the USA as accessory or ECHO apartments (Weeden et al., 1986). For example, the Singapore government subsidizes those who build accommodation for older relatives on to the family home (Cheung and Vasoo, 1992). There is, however, no evidence that co-residence is the preferred option, either for elders if they feel they have a real choice, or for younger family members. Even if sons favour co-residence, this does not mean that their wives, who are most likely to have to do any of the work involved and to cope with any emotional problems, are equally in favour. There is also no evidence that co-residence improves the quality of care. For example, Day (1985) found, in her survey of elders in Australia, that those who lived with relatives felt they had less independence and were less happy, on average, than those who did not.

Other problems with co-residence are much rarer but should not be ignored. In the first place physical or emotional abuse is more likely, particularly when sons who have not left home, or who have drug or alcohol problems, become carers of frail elders (Biggs et al., 1995; Steinmetz, 1988; Wilson 1993). This finding may not hold across cultures but it seems possible that more research will show that it does. Older homeowners may have more power or independence but they may also find themselves subject to abuse by sons, daughters or grandchildren who want the house and are prepared to neglect or institutionalize a burdensome elder. If the house is not their own and their usefulness to the family has passed, they may find themselves confined to one room or one area. Elder abuse is not confined to co-resident households or even within families (McCreadie, 1996; Pritchard, 1992), but it does appear to be more common when elders live with others than when they live alone.

Co-residence is declining fastest in rich individualistic countries. In Northern Europe it appears to have always been less common than nuclear family units (Wall, 1995; Wall et al., 1982). In Africa co-residence can mean many different arrangements but rarely means living under the same roof. Knodel and Chanpen (1998) showed that in northern Thailand co-residence is the rule but that the administrative definition of co-residence can cover everything from completely integrated three- or four-generation households, to elders who live completely separately. In other words, the meaning of co-residence and the degree of support that is exchanged across generations can vary very widely. It *may* be universally true to say that older men and women in general prefer 'intimacy at a distance' to actually sharing a kitchen and home. Even this qualified statement would be challenged by many policy-makers, and by some older men and women in developing countries where family solidarity is deemed more important than individual wishes.

Issues

Being cared for

The feeling of being old may be constant or it may come in intimations that grow more and more persistent. For most older men and women, there are times (when they are ill or have an accident or when their environment deteriorates) when the activities of daily living get more difficult. For some this may constitute a stage – something that is difficult to reverse. For most, these periods will be to some extent self-limiting and they will settle down again to live without extra assistance. Limited autonomy can give way, slowly or suddenly, to dependency or the end of autonomy. For others who get increasingly frail, interdependence becomes more and more one-sided until it is hard to see it other than as dependence. Reciprocity becomes more and more difficult to maintain. Take this excerpt from an interview:

> *Interviewer*:   And does your family help you?
>
> *Respondent*:   Oh yes they would do anything for us. Anything.
>
> *Interviewer*:   But you do not ask them?
>
> *Respondent*:   No. I would never ask. (author's interview)

Later in the interview, she explains that her daughter refuses money for shopping and so cannot be asked, and causes embarrassment when she shops unasked. Here the daughter is violating her mother's independence and so restricting her mother's autonomy. In such circumstances being cared for can become depressing and depersonalizing.

There is little evidence, but it appears that elders who have a choice are deeply divided over whether they would prefer paid carers or family members if they become frail. However, paid carers are rationed by price, by bureaucratic procedures and by poor quality, so the choice is rarely a real one. Frail elders are also divided in their attitudes to care. They do not all want to be independent or even interdependent. Some may take service by others as their right. All professionals can recall examples of elders who have not fought for autonomy or interdependence but have willingly assumed the role of dependent elder, making constant demands for help and assistance.

The long, thin family

Changes in the shape of the family from short and wide to long and thin have yet to show their full effect on caregiving. Those who have researched carers in the UK have consistently found that although large families are presented in story and myth as sharing care, when actual carers are interviewed they very frequently express resentment that their brothers and sisters do so little. More detailed studies have suggested that caregiving tasks are gendered and related to generation, so that men may do certain tasks while women do others, though either can substitute. Men's contributions are not always recognized as 'caregiving' even though they may greatly improve quality of life for frail elders – both materially and emotionally. The presence of a son or nephew who will maintain the home or garden or help an older person with transport and luggage when going on holiday brings great happiness to many. In the same way, different generations may make different contributions – grandchildren may be available at different times from mid-life carers. Retirement-aged carers (the growth area) may not have 'all the time in the world' but they are at least more likely to be available for longer hours.

It follows, therefore, that the long thin family may be able to cope, at least practically (Myers, 1990). Emotional adjustments may be greater. Caring relationships already last longer than when so many died young and widowhood was the main cause of single parenthood. It is not yet clear whether caring will be more intensive in the future. If individualistic ideologies triumph, families or, more simply, women will be thrown back on their own resources for long periods of caring. On the other hand, if elder lobbies become stronger or more notice is taken of the wishes of older people themselves, there will be more paid carers and more support in the community for those who give and receive care.

Widows

In a wide range of societies widowhood has been recognized as a particular hazard for women (who marry older men who die sooner, see Chapter 3). Special arrangements exist, from marrying a brother-in-law, which is only one of a range of possibilities in Africa (Potash, 1986), to preferential widows' pensions in welfare states. In India, Agarwal (1998) has argued that widowhood should be seen as a life stage not an accidental happening or a static category for women and as such planned for and socially protected.

Selective abortion

New developments in selective abortion will have a marginal, but possibly non-negligible, effect on caring in countries or classes where daughters are less valued than sons. Sen (1989) has suggested that when poverty is reduced, parents become more willing to rear daughters. Surveys in Japan which show that parents prefer daughters because they feel that daughters are more likely than sons (daughters-in-law) to look after them in old age bear this out (Japan Research Institute on Child Welfare, 1993). Japan has traditionally been a culture where sons and daughters-in-law were responsible for the care of parents, but this is changing. Koo (1987) identified a similar trend in Korea. If Japan is an example of a new trend, the ravages of selective abortion may yet be limited. The fact that abortion will probably only be available to better off sections of communities also suggests some self-limitation.

Generation contracts

In individualistic welfare states, different generations are sometimes assumed to be contracted to support each other. Such contracts can take two forms: parents have supported children so children reciprocate when parents retire; or, today's workers support today's elders on condition that the next generation of workers supports them. The men's side of this generation contract has been collectivized into the pension system. This means that the link between material living standards in old age and the presence of children has been largely broken in advanced welfare states (see Chapter 7). Pension systems are everywhere seen as problematic (World Bank, 1994), but individual men are not expected personally to support older relatives. This is a major structural change in relations between generations and within families. In contrast, the women's side of the generation contract remains largely invisible and personalized. Women's care for older people has not been collectivized to the same degree (Lorenz-Meyer, 1996), though many women are now employed in state-run or state-subsidized caring services. The carers' lobbies have had great success in gaining recognition for unpaid care work and most welfare states now make some provision for supporting caregivers, but caregiving is still very much a matter for family and friends (women), with family far more important than friends. It seems likely that only Scandinavia provides enough home care to meet demand but, with less than 20 per cent of people over 65 receiving home-care services even there, more services may be needed. The exception was Finland with a rate of 24 per cent in 1990 (OECD, 1996). According to Kovalainen and Simonen (1998) and Kovalainen (1999), the privatization of municipal home care in Finland has resulted in an expansion in the number of women entrepreneurs who run home-care businesses. For the UK, Abrams (Bulmer, 1986) showed that neighbours were helpful but only very rarely provided long-term or personal care. This seems to be a normal pattern for Europe, but in other parts of the world and, particularly, in cities, it may differ. Ihromi (1989), for example, says of Indonesia, the 'lower-middle class people in cities also rely very strongly on aid from neighbours, and sometimes receive more aid from neighbours than from relatives' (Ihromi, 1989: 140). In cohesive stable communities older men and women without families may, indeed, be supported by their neighbours (Keith, 1994b; Nana Apt, 1996; Tout, 1993) and, as noted above, the definition of the family can be fluid.

Conclusion

The structural changes outlined in Chapter 5 appear to be affecting caring relationships worldwide (Kendig et al., 1991). This statement assumes that at least some of the current changes are real and not just another wave of nostalgia for a past golden age of caring, when family care was better than in the globalizing, individualizing, postmodern world. The rhetoric of family care (mostly done by women) that informs policy is often at odds with reality – a problem when good policies are needed. Present day policies reflect differing ideologies of the importance of the family versus the individual. In very large parts of the world the family is still seen as a more important building block of society than the individual. Polices still reflect assumptions of co-residence across generations, sharing of work and caregiving and, as a consequence, non-existent or rudimentary service provision. In democracies where women are increasingly joining the paid labour force and co-residence is in decline, and the numbers of very old people are rising, reality may force governments to think more constructively about policies to support frail older people and their caregivers.

Stress, resulting in forms of social breakdown, can come from the economic hardships and dislocations imposed by structural adjustment. Increases in poverty make caring that much more difficult (as with Mr B. above), and reduce the chances that it can take place. Equally stress can come from the globalization of consumption patterns and the individualization accompanying prosperity. Young couples are widely perceived as too materialistic to support their parents and as diverting scarce money to their children. Many grandparents would support them in their concern for the future generation. Both love and duty have always been precarious, though largely successful, motivators to care. It is possible to argue that love may survive poverty better than duty survives individualization. So far, the overwhelming evidence is that women do continue to care for elders whenever such care is feasible and, very often, when it is wholly infeasible by any rational calculation.

Throughout Western Europe, policies to value carers are beginning to take shape. Token payments and assessment of support needs can be seen as getting care on the cheap, as exploiting the good will that exists in the community, and as a way of further dragging down the low wages of paid care staff. On the other hand, it can also be seen as the long overdue recognition of an important role in society. First, caregiving has costs and payments can reduce those costs. Second, the payment, like child benefit, is a token contribution by society to those who help it to function. The alternative to payment is a tax credit but this is useless to the very poor, the unemployed and to women if it goes to husbands. In work oriented welfare states, protection of pension rights during time spent caring is an essential policy measure.

The alternative to these versions of individualism is the assumption that society collectively shares a responsibility for welfare, not simply for frail elders but for all groups. In a collectively oriented society, the presence of systematically disadvantaged groups is not so much a warning to others to work hard, save more or return home (for migrants), but a blot on the social landscape to be reduced, even if it cannot be wholly eliminated. The Scandinavian countries, particularly Denmark, are usually taken as models for collective action in support of family carers. Scandinavian feminists have seen the change as a shift from private to public patriarchy on the grounds that women are still responsible for caregiving and men do not do their share. However, it would be hard to argue that market-oriented welfare states, such as the UK or USA, can begin to rival the care systems provided by public patriarchy, or that family care alone can offer elders an equivalent quality of life in other countries.

Whatever may be the benefits of collectivized provision for elders, it is clear that most countries are not able (if they are clients of the IMF or World Bank) or not willing (politically speaking) to fight the growing orthodoxy that unpaid care is best. Even in Scandinavian countries families are being expected to provide more. This means that it becomes increasingly important to measure unpaid work (including the work of older women for their families and others). Until this is done it will be impossible to get a clear picture of who is caring for whom among the older population, and prejudice and exploitation will continue unchecked.

Further reading

http://research.aarp.org/ppi/publist.html – AARP. Good for American long-term care including home care.

http://www.helpage.org/info/index.html – Helpage International. Good on older women in developing countries.

CHAPTER 10

SERVICES FOR ELDERS

Three aspects of services concern us most in this chapter. The first is that services for older men and women are big business in large parts of the world (see *Observer*, 26 November 1989). The second is that older men and women provide services for each other and for other age groups. And the third is that formally organized health and social care services are essential assistance for frail older men and women if they cannot rely on their families or neighbours for all aspects of unpaid care. Formal care services, along with health care, are also essential to support and back up the women and older partners who care unpaid. As noted in the previous chapter, governments prefer to rely on family care rather than provide services for frail older people. However, there are older men and women, especially older widows, who have no family. They must rely on the state, charity or NGOs if they are unable to support themselves through work.

Services for elders as big business

One contribution of postmodern theory is an awareness of the older body. The well-preserved, young (at heart at least) and well-financed older body can be seen as a site which symbolically validates participation in the global consumer society (Featherstone and Hepworth, 1991; Featherstone and Wernick, 1995; Gilleard, 1996; Harper, 1997). The mainly middle-class and masculine ideal of a self-directed life project (Giddens, 1991 or Laslett, 1989 for a positive view of the Third Age) implies the consumption of products that stave off old age – like hair transplants, cosmetics, health care and exercise – and others that indicate that the body is still 'young' – foreign or adventurous holidays and active membership of clubs and societies (Featherstone and Hepworth, 1991). The ideal, as far as business is concerned, is that older people should maintain their bodies as middle-aged bodies and, possibly more important, they should maintain the high spending patterns of the late middle-aged. This becomes increasingly difficult in countries where pensions are low.

The above considers postmodern ageing from the point of view of consumption. Looked at in terms of marketing and production, the over 55s are a lucrative market in most affluent countries and they generate employment in a wide range of service industries. Even if they have acquired the necessary consumption goods over a lifetime, they are an expanding market for services of all kinds. They have a range of lifestyles that are characterized by more free time, less strenuous activity and a polarization of income (Kaplan and Longino, 1993). The services they buy reflect their new leisure time and new interests. Even in the UK, where pensions are low by European standards, about 60 per cent of newly retired men and 38 per cent of women were getting money from an occupational pension in 1994 and so did not have to rely wholly on the state (Disney et al., 1997). They might also have a lump sum with their pensions or, for the 73 per cent of young elders who were home owners, they could also trade down to a smaller, cheaper property (Disney et al., 1997). It is this well off section of the older population who are the focus of market research and a target for an increasing range of products, from high-cost holidays to special TV programmes. In America, the American Association of Retired People (AARP, a non-profit organization) has 28 million members and enormous commercial power. The Association can negotiate discounts and affect share prices.

However, marketing is a problem in ageist societies (Sawchuk, 1995). Travel companies, mail order firms and manufacturers of garden supplies and aids to living have been very successful in targeting pensioners. Targeting a service by age group avoids the problem of a conflict of images: a service that is seen as 'for the old' is unlikely to sell to or attract the young in an ageist society. This is fine as long as new customers can be recruited as old ones die, but not if the market will shrink. The other problem is that most services are used by other age groups as well as pensioners. The drawback of these mixed-age services is that all but the very richest elders are at a financial disadvantage when they use the same services as other age groups. They have less money and will not be the priority market. They may not even be the market of choice and cannot expect to have their needs met as top priority. With growing numbers of better off elders this may change.

One approach to the marketing and image problem is to segregate service users by time of day rather than attempting to mix old and young. Keith (1994a), for example, describes how the street cafés and services of Momence, a small town in Illinois, are occupied by different ages at different times – first the early workers, then the school bus drivers, and then the older people. At midday, age groups were mixed but older people had their regular tables in restaurants. Matinées, off-peak travel and pensioners' tea dances are part of the same process, which helps to spread the cost of staff and equipment over the day. Take, for example, public transport, where there are generous reductions to attract elders during off-peak times when they do not compete with better paying customers. Trains and buses with low-level entry, and the elimination of steps and stairs at access points, could greatly increase the number of older men and women who could use these services, as well as helping mothers of young children and younger disabled people. This is slowly being realized, but there is a fine line between exploiting vulnerable older consumers and meeting their needs. A final point is that as age increases, the number of men decreases, and this affects the nature of services. Private profit-making services need affluent consumers (mostly men) or high subsidies.

Non-profit organizations

Non-profit organizations or non-governmental organizations (NGOs) come into their own in less-developed countries and in NICs. They range from very large international bodies funnelling expertise and cash round the world, to small self-help groups of local pensioners. Some, such as OXFAM or St Vincent de Paul, are for all age groups and others, like Helpage International, are specifically for elders, though they aim for spillovers to other age groups. In poor countries charities, local and foreign, may be the only service providers working for elders. In NICs there is an ideological bias in favour of charitable or private-sector enterprises rather than state-financed services. In many other countries there is no infrastructure of social services. There may be no infra-structure of health for elders either (with exceptions such as Kerala in India and Sri Lanka). Pensions are either very small or restricted to former civil servants and members of the armed services (Tracy, 1991). Elders and their families rely on self-help. In such circumstances, any service specifically for older people should include some form of income generation if it is to have a long-run beneficial effect (Tout, 1989).

The problem is not so much how to get schemes started, but how to expand them and how to keep going once the initial phase has passed (see Tout, 1989: 19). For example, elders in Kenya, when asked what they needed, said kerosene (Ekongot, 1993) but this was a widespread need in the district. Kerosene can only be sold retail if there is considerable investment in bulk transport, bulk storage and equipment for measuring and selling small amounts. Such investment is beyond the means of a group of elders, or even the local religious community, but an outside donor can provide the necessary capital. In this case a religious organ-ization got a grant from HelpAge International and was able to set up as a retailer of kerosene. The profits, which soon paid for the capital outlay, then went to elders in the district. The money could be expected to continue for as long as kerosene was needed and no other middleman was able to undercut the religious group.

The example shows the problems that face small charitable enter-prises, especially when they are trying to provide income for older people. They need a monopoly in order to make a secure profit and can easily be driven out if another trader can undercut the price. For example, elders can sort or recycle rubbish but it is likely that children can do the same work faster or for even less money. Once a project for elders has built up the market for recycled products, an entrepreneur who employs children can move in and put the elders out of business by charging less or taking a smaller profit, because his profit does not have to be shared with his workers.

All income generating schemes in low-income countries are at risk because in very poor countries it is always hard to get a market niche that no one else will try to take over. Many schemes may have to be continuously subsidized or they may have to confine themselves to providing very small supplementary incomes that are too low to attract a rival entrepreneur. In either case, the results are not encouraging for foreign NGOs that believe in localization, self-help and handing over to grass-roots organizations. The options may be starkly confined to long-run subsidy or collapse.

The conclusion from the experience of HelpAge International is that there is a long-term role for foreign NGOs in developing countries, but that enabling local people is better than putting in an alien service. If a long-term subsidy is essential, it should still be possible to hand over most aspects of a project to local management. Equality of access and financial probity are likely to be important considerations in some handovers. A project can easily be subverted if local vested interests take it over and restrict access by the poor or some other disadvantaged group. A charity has little incentive to hand over a project if that means the initial aims will be compromised by local prejudices. Attention to local power structures is particularly important when aiming to assist vulnerable people such as destitute elders or widows. They can easily become victims of local elites who may genuinely believe that good things should not be 'wasted' on older people. In such cases a full project handover may be impossible (Tout, 1993).

In future, more NGOs that are locally generated and independent of overseas funding are likely to develop as the number of elders increases and more of them form their own co-operatives and associations. Ssenkolot (1984), for example, reports the case of a Cameroonian local government pensioner who organized the local state pensioners into a pressure group and a club.

In developed countries the new generations of active and affluent elders with time to spare have also led to a massive expansion in services and activities, with a corresponding increase in jobs and investment. Older men and women provide services for each other, for example the University of the Third Age (U3A), which now has branches in most affluent countries. Courses taught by elders themselves or by hired staff allow them to catch up on education or to take up new interests. Then there are clubs of all types, often subsidized by a grant from government or a charity or, increasingly, by sponsorship from related private-sector businesses. In Japan, 41 per cent of elders belonged to semi-compulsory clubs in 1993 and there are silver employment agencies (which provide short-term, low-paid work), which are more convivial than commercial agencies but aim at supporting the work ethic and keeping older people active (Bass and Oka, 1995; Campbell, 1992). In France, government subsidized Third Age Clubs are locally based, meet local needs and depend on local initiatives (Guillemard, 1980; Tester, 1996) and in the USA there are Senior Centers set up under a range of auspices. In Australia clubs, for ex-servicemen (with a monopoly licence to install poker machines) are among the largest businesses in the voluntary sector. Other non-profit organizations concentrate on services for frail elders (see below) but all are big employers.

As well as running or helping to run services for their own age group, many elders are important in non-profit organizations with a more general membership. Retired professional men are in particular demand as highly skilled volunteers, for example as treasurers of sporting clubs and charities. In China, retired public servants are most likely to take paid work in the private sector rather than volunteer. Their education, experience and people skills are greatly needed since so many of the younger age groups lost out on education and professional experience during the Cultural Revolution (Kwong and Guoxuan, 1992). In all countries, active older men and women can continue as leaders or com-mittee members well past official retirement age. Their role in economic development has been routinely undervalued but, in many societies, they have the time to learn new knowledge and the local prestige to educate younger community members. There are many other campaign groups and voluntary services in all countries which rely on the good will and hard work of their older members to keep going.

However, even as we record all this activity it is worth remembering that there are other approaches to old age. Poverty and poor health can mean that many elders cannot be as active as they want, and even though the idea of retirement as a time for rest and contemplation has been out of fashion for many years, it still exists among certain groups or individuals. Noiriel (1992) noted that, while older French natives were likely to see retirement as a time of activity, older migrants very often reported attitudes reminiscent of earlier times when working men saw retirement as a well-earned rest. Older women have rarely had such an option in the past and most will still not have much choice but to keep on looking after husband, home and/or grandchildren. Those who do have good pensions can look forward to active and interesting lives: here is an extract from an interview with an 80-year-old UK woman who did not marry but had a career in public service and has a good pension.

What do you enjoy about life?
 I like meeting people. I enjoy my contact with my church. I do tapestry

work, as you can probably see. Early in my retirement I did welfare work for the local clubs. I was one of the secretaries and enjoyed that very much and there were a lot of rented houses then and quite bit of poverty and you know single parent households. So on the whole I think I enjoy people, I enjoy reading, I enjoy walking and gardening. That's about it I think. Theatre, especially the National Theatre when one can go to a matinée as a subsidized pensioner which is very useful. (author's interview; See also p. 165 for Enid)

Needs-based services and the frail older body

In developed countries there are services for active and affluent elders and services provided by elders for themselves and others, and all age services that have very large numbers of older users, but these are not what usually spring to mind when services for older people are mentioned. It is more likely that the key words will be 'need' and 'frailty', and the services will deliver health and social care. At this point we can return to the body, but an older (usually) and frailer body. The overtly old body is a devalued body (Featherstone and Hepworth, 1991). In literal terms the older body is despised by many. As one husband said, describing how a specialist hospital doctor had looked at his wife, 'As if it's a bit of meat on a slab, and it's going off, you know' (author's interview, 1989). In terms of services, the body is fought over like a battlefield, with contested boundaries that are nearly all negative. In more symbolic terms, each service marks out its area so that bits of the body 'belong' to different services. Devalued bits to devalued branches of welfare: the sick brain to psychogeriatrics, feet to chiropody/podiatry, teeth (if any) and dentures to dentists, health problems that cannot be cured, redefined into social care (Latimer, 1997), and so on. On this interpretation, older bodies (men and women) exist only to validate the status relations of the services that provide for them. Here, the body belongs to the politics of devaluation, which affect elders to some degree in most societies, and strongly in advanced Western countries. The low status of the older body rubs off on to the workers and intensifies the problems of low pay, inadequate training and poor management that will be familiar to those who have much contact with the caring services.

Despite the controversy over whether longer life means a more disability free life (see Chapter 8), it seems clear that, as populations age, there is growth in services for older people who have difficulty with Activities of Daily Living (ADL). Such services have varying names – community/domiciliary/in home/ambulant care – but are characterized by staff who go out to the homes of older people and deliver some form of health or social care. Day centres and day hospitals come halfway between ambulatory or community services, and institutional care. Grouped housing enables all these forms of community care to be delivered more efficiently (see Chapters 6 and 11). Basic needs such as housework, shopping, meals delivery, personal care, getting people out of bed and taking them to the toilet, bathing, home nursing and other health care such as physiotherapy or chiropody, and sitting services to relieve informal caregivers, are provided in varying ways and amounts. The service mix differs from country to country and from district to district. There may be additions like specialist elder abuse teams, or carers' support groups and respite care aimed at the carer rather than the frail elder.

As the OECD (1996) notes, the job opportunities produced by the growing needs of frail elders are substantial. In deprived areas where elders have been left behind (depressed rural districts and inner cities), health and social care services may be biggest local employers. Such benefits are often overlooked, both in economic terms but also as aspects of solidarity which can bring young and old together in stressed communities.

Developed countries differ in detail but there are certain common themes. First, a mix of organizations provides services, with non-profit agencies or government predominating. Private profit-making agencies can only supply mainstream services if they are heavily subsidized, although they may be very important in serving rich minorities. However, the rich may choose to employ domestic helpers, legal or otherwise, rather than turn to agencies. The main roles of the state are planning, service regulation and, increasingly, monitoring for quality. As opportunities for exploitation by private profit-making companies increase and competition for contracts drives down costs, there is a growing chance that vulnerable older men and women will be ill-treated or exploited by service providers in their own homes. Governments have a basic need to avert bad publicity from scandals and their role in regulating services and checking on quality is likely to grow as elders often find it difficult to exercise what rights they have (see Richards, 1996).

The rhetoric in all countries that aspire to modern social policies is about service choice and service quality. The reality in most is that services for frail elders are strictly rationed: by tests of need, by price, by poor quality or by long waiting lists, and choice is very limited if it exists at all. In the words of a UK social worker in 1997:

> 'For example, you do an assessment and assess need, and then you have to come back and decide that there is no finance to meet the needs of people that you went out to see. You went out to say yes, we are definitely going to give you so-and-so, because in the legislation it says you have a choice. And quite obviously there is no choice.' (author's interview, 1997)

Only the Scandinavian countries, particularly Denmark, come near to providing care for frail elders as a right. However, in other countries such as Australia, elder care is the subject of overt government strategies for access and equity, for social justice and for user participation in decision-making. These strategies are presented in the language of individual rights (Orme et al., 1994). Such an approach is valuable because it takes the stand that older people have the same rights as younger citizens. Few frail older men and women will have the emotional and material resources needed to exercise such rights, but some may be assisted by advocates or service brokers (as in some Canadian provinces). As with other disadvantaged groups, conferring rights does not result in equality, but it is an important step.

Policies for care services in developed countries

There are common themes running through the policies of virtually all countries which provide services for frail older people. Services aim: to enable older people to achieve maximum self-sufficiency; to help them live in as normal a setting as possible; and to enable them to participate in society.

These are worthy, citizenship-oriented aims. The actual meaning of these aims in terms of the way services are delivered and who gets them varies according to the professional culture of the country. As Baldock and Ely (1996: 203) say, 'Home care is culturally and emotionally loaded, and accepting it requires important readjustments in self-image and identity'. In the UK and America and, possibly, in Australia, the rhetoric is that users are customers with power and choice. The reality is that most users are poor, frail and frightened of being victimized by their service providers, whether private, non-profit or state. Many will have made the shift in self-image referred to by Baldock and Ely and do not see themselves as able to complain.

A second set of aims is more service oriented: to target services on those most in need; to co-ordinate services so that there is no duplication and users do not fall between services (e.g. good hospital discharge planning); to monitor outcomes; and to cut costs of elder support/care and reduce institutional care.

These goals conflict in many different ways and highlight the difficulties of providing care services. Maximum self sufficiency or normality is virtually impossible to achieve in an institution, but highly dependent people are extremely expensive to maintain if they live in their own homes. It is cheaper to provide services to people who are grouped under one roof than to send staff out round the countryside, or to get stuck in traffic jams on the way to individual homes. It is also much easier (though still difficult) to monitor service quality and prevent abuse by staff if services are delivered centrally rather than in the privacy of individual homes.

Issues

Abuse

As with family and institutional care, abuse by services and their staff is an issue. Institutionalized abuse (practices that are not intentionally harmful but have abusive effects) are always a possibility where frail, vulnerable and devalued people are being served, often by low-paid, low-status staff, or by well-meaning but untrained volunteers. Religious groups can be very coercive and authoritarian, though they do not have a monopoly of social control. Then there is more deliberate abuse. Staff who steal or defraud or physically abuse those they are 'caring for' (see Wilson, 1993, for examples in a mental health service).

Unmeasured costs

The cost of caring – in stress and strain, in lost income and higher outgoings, and in long-term reduction in pension levels – is taken as invisible or unimportant. More and better quality services to support informal caregivers meet a growing need but they are also a way of making sure the main cost of caring stays with informal carers (mainly women and older husbands) rather than falling on the state. There are no accounting procedures to balance the costs of self-care or the work of relatives and neighbours against the cost of formal services. The result of care policies in the UK has been that frail elders and their carers struggle on, assessed as 'low priority' or 'able to cope' for months or years. All too often this goes on until a crisis, such as the collapse of the carer, causes both to go into expensive institutional care, or results in a very costly package of services which does not provide rehabilitation but only staves off entry to an institution for a few months. In many of these cases some help of a minor (and relatively cheap) nature, given earlier and for longer, would have avoided a crisis and possibly allowed the elder to reach the point of death (or even to recover) without being institutionalized. The quality of life of elder and carer would certainly have been improved.

Finance

Although virtually all countries think that they are spending too much on institutional care and would prefer to spend less on domiciliary care, the levels which are 'too much' vary widely from country to country.

As Figure 1.1 (p. 10) showed for pensions, the history of services in a country is very important, though often ignored. Cuts, or even increases, must start from the existing level and there is a long-term inertia about elder care. We can assume that it will be many decades before government expenditure on elders in Greece begins to approach that in the Netherlands, even though the differences in numbers/proportion of elders is small. Similar policies will not necessarily bring convergence if they start from different points. It appears that no country is politically willing to provide everything that all older people need to enable them to function as well as people in younger age groups.

Ways of cutting costs are about shifting boundaries from: institutional to domiciliary care (but this is only cheaper if informal care and self-care fill the cost gap); health to social care (see Latimer, 1997); state to private care; subsidized to full cost services; and formal (paid) to self- or family care.

The exact mix of these shifts and the mechanisms used will vary from country to country (see Foster and Kendig, 1987; Giarchi, 1996; Gibson, 1998) and even across local government units in some countries where there is a lot of local autonomy. (Local autonomy is the norm outside the UK.) A shift to domiciliary care is always easy to reinforce because so few frail elders want to move home, particularly when they have reached crisis point and have no psychological resources left to cope with a move. The shift from health to social care can be a matter of shutting long-stay hospital beds and replacing them with cheaper nursing home beds, or a constant redefinition of health needs as social needs and hence as the responsibility of social services (Latimer, 1997). Both methods have been used extensively in the UK since 1990.

Pensioners are not rich so, with very few exceptions, they cannot afford to pay very much. Raising charges is an indirect way of shifting the boundary between paid care and self- or informal care. Minority ethnic elders are at particular risk of cuts. Their services may be special initiatives in the first place, or already substandard, as in large parts of the USA (Markides and Miranda, 1997).

Planning for service economies

Just as some pioneers of the NHS in Britain had the comforting belief that health needs could be met and then costs would fall, so it sometimes seems that planners of care services for older people believe that there is a finite demand that can be shifted around between services, with the aim of achieving the most cost-effective and cheapest mix. And this even before the rising number of older people is considered! The reality is that there are very high levels of unmet need, embodied by older men and women who care for themselves in increasingly difficult circumstances but have no wish to access services which are insensitive or inappropriate. And, at the same time, there are constantly rising expectations: in most countries women who care for older people are less willing to be taken for granted and young elders expect more from old age than in the past.

As new needs have been identified new services have been set up – usually with the aim of shifting users from high- to low-cost services. For example, community-based terminal care has been justified in terms of reducing high-cost terminal care in hospitals (Coolen, 1993). Specialist services for men and women with dementia or their carers are also believed to cut costs. However, Coolen (1993) has shown that in the Netherlands new projects have created new demand rather than shifting the balance of care from one sector or one service to another. It seems highly likely that his findings would hold in other countries. However, as long as unpaid care and self-care are not costed, it should be possible to reduce costs in formal accounting terms by reducing services. This is not, however, a recipe for service quality.

User empowerment

The welfare states that have moved most strongly towards market principles have placed a new emphasis on user choice. This has resulted in a great increase in power for active service users who can band together, for example young disabled people. To some extent the shift in power from professional to service user that is implicit in new rights to complain, statutory user involvement in management (as in Ontario) or user involvement in care planning, have been helpful to frail elders. The postmodern emphasis on consumers and choice has offered new fields for advocacy and there is a growth of organizations among service users in most countries, but there is still a long way to go.

Who provides?

There is no common pattern of service organization. The history of each country has been different and in some cases the history of each region. Much depends on the dominant religious group and its attitude to provision for older men and women. In many countries there is little choice between care in the family and care in an institution. However, most welfare states have some community services, even if they are mainly confined to home nursing. In Belgium and the Netherlands where there is pillarization (pillars depend on religion and/or language – so there will be French and Flemish, Catholic, Protestant and Humanist Associations for most social care tasks), voluntary sector agencies are very important. In Germany in the past home-help services could only be accessed via the health service. In some US states and most of southern

Europe there is no public home-help provision at all. In other countries the state has been the main provider as well as funder. In recent years this has begun to change and in Anglo-Saxon countries the fashion has been to cut state expenditure where possible (difficult where the service users have so little money) and to confine the state to financing services rather than providing them.

While in Scandinavia it has been normal to think of the state as the fairest and least biased provider, with an emphasis on service before profit and a chain of accountability upwards to politicians, in the USA state provision is stereotyped as corrupt, inefficient and an erosion of civil liberties. Other countries fall inbetween these two extremes and in any case rely on non-profit or voluntary organizations. Non-profits may be large institutionalized bureaucracies or smaller agencies who can be close to their users (usually seen as a strength) and/or highly selective and inequitable (a weakness) in the services they provide. New demands for properly specified contracts, performance indicators, best value and monitoring of outcomes, all place big pressure on small NGOs which may not have the staff or the expertise, or even the wish, to comply. They may be forced out by bigger service providers.

Quality issues

The OECD (1996) divides countries into those which aim to achieve quality through national standards (such as Australia, Japan and Spain) and those which see competition via the market as the best way of ensuring customer responsiveness, as in the UK or New Zealand. National standards depend on enforcement to produce quality and the market for care services needs to be regulated if it is not to produce scandals. In either case, there needs to be some form of state involvement if standards are to be maintained and exploitation and scandals avoided. The profit motive is not a recipe for quality services when consumers are disempowered (see Meyer, 1993). As Day et al. (1996) showed, it is very difficult to ensure quality in such services and the number of scandals seems likely to increase. The intangible or unmeasurable aspects of service quality depend ever more strongly on good management and co-ordination between different professionals and agencies (Baldock and Ely, 1996). The quality of the service depends on the 'moment of truth' (Normann, 1991) when service provider and user meet in a personal relationship. As Normann says, this is as true of airline staff or bank clerks as of home-care staff. The difference is that while the encounter is fleeting in most private-sector services, in long-term care it can determine the quality of life of the service user.

Co-ordination of services

Co-ordination is a common aim in all countries where care services are at all complex. However, there are no foolproof mechanisms (see Opie, 1992 for US experiences). Given that most frail elders have multiple needs and generic elder care workers are not the norm, it is not surprising that there are problems. These can range from turf wars, for example the social versus the nurse-led bath (Twigg, 1997) or between residents and day centre users in multi-purpose residential facilities (Wright, 1995). As with most boundary issues in welfare services, the question is not one of staking out a territory so much as off-loading a client group or set of care procedures. So home helps may refuse to change the dressing on a leg ulcer and nurses will refuse to fill a thermos. These small daily disputes mean that frail men and women are likely to deal with a range of staff from different services and many find it extremely stressful.

Conclusion

In countries with large numbers of elders, there is enormous scope for the provision of high-quality services and products to go with the new life stage of young, relatively affluent pensioners. Private services can be directed at the upper end of the income distribution and non-profits at the rest. There is an expanding need for preventive services that improve the quality of life for older people, bring fellowship and connections with others, and help them to maintain fitness. Some potential developments depend on new services but many others are simply a matter of reorganizing provision so that older men and women have better access, or access in off-peak times. For example, the impressive case of Dundee University, which opens its sports hall to older people at 8 a.m. in the morning when few students are willing to drag themselves out of bed, and with the help of an exercise leader and minimum clerical back-up, are able to have 800 older people a week enjoying aerobics. Unsurprisingly, the measured health of the participants improved against the health of the control group (McMurdo and Burnett, 1992). Much remains to be done in centres and clubs.

Older men and women are not just consumers of services. They also provide them via the voluntary sector and NGOs. They make up the membership of many organizations and help to run services. In the future it seems likely that their membership and importance will increase in mainstream organizations. In developing countries, NGOs are likely to continue to be very important since governments are unwilling to 'undermine' the family as a caring unit by providing for elders. However, when poverty is widespread there are special problems in finding viable ways of supporting co-operatives and other organizations working with and for older men and women. It may be that a long-term subsidy from a larger organization will be needed and problems of local autonomy arise.

Whatever the service mix for frail elders in a country or region, the staff delivering services find themselves working with common themes. In nearly all countries governments, who must pay for most services to low-income groups, aim to hold expenditure steady, while need rises as the older population grows. The constant urge to economize and to shift users from high- to low-cost services can only lower the quality of life of frail elders. It is relatively easy to increase the amount of self- or family care by closing beds, rationing services, changing eligibility criteria, making access procedures more impenetrable and lowering the quality of a service. Users vote with their feet and either refuse the service or never try to get it.

All services for frail elders suffer from lack of usable theory and adequate technologies for controlling quality, managing services and co-ordinating care across agencies and professions. The future lies with more co-operatively run services and more advocacy (Dunning, 1998), with a recognition that services are co-produced by elders and agencies and that elders need to be included as partners, and with subsidized self-help (Rondinelli, 1998).

Abuse, whether deliberate or institutional, is an ongoing problem, though one that is often unrecognized. Ideally, the future will allow older men and women more power over their services. In developing countries co-operatives may be one way forward, assisted, if necessary, by NGOs. In developed countries problems of care co-ordination are still a long way from being solved.

Further reading

http://research.aarp.org/ppi/publist.html – good for elders as consumers and for long-term care including home-care in America.

http://www.eurolinkage.org/euro-Europe.

http://www.helpage.org/info/index.html – good on new projects and on older women in developing countries.

CHAPTER 11

INSTITUTIONAL LIVING IN LATER LIFE

More friendships, more social activity, more help in emergency, and higher morale are consistently observed in settings where old people are available to each other as potential friends and neighbours. (Keith, 1982: 2)

The challenge for those who enter institutional care, and for those who provide it, is to realize that potential. The problems are immense and the myth of residential care as an evil to be avoided at all costs is strong across countries and cultures. In countries where residential care is virtually the only service for frail older people that exists outside the family, the good and bad myths of family versus institution are most starkly opposed, but institutions have a poor image virtually everywhere in the world. The reality, as Keith says above, can be very different, but there is no doubt that good institutional care is expensive compared with relying on unpaid informal care (mainly by women), or allowing the destitute to die.

In developed countries, especially the USA where almost 2 million people were living in nursing homes in 1995 (Kane, 1996), institutional care is already big business. Finance is available for low-income elders from Medicaid with funding by the states and Federal government. It is heavily means tested and elders have to 'spend down' before they are eligible. At the margin nursing home bills are paid from private cash, either by the elders themselves or their families. It seems certain that demand will grow elsewhere, despite the many ideological and practical problems outlined below.

Staying put

Virtually everyone is agreed that older people want to remain in their own homes for as long as possible. This statement assumes that they have homes of their own, or that they can share comfortably with their families. Neither need be true, and homeless elders exist everywhere. Tout (1989), for example, found that institutions in Latin America, which he thought were very poor quality, still had waiting lists of destitute elders. The second assumption is that 'as long as possible' means 'forever' or 'they'll carry me out feet first'. For some it does, but for many there is a choice between relying on family or neighbours and entering an institution. In Europe they may even prefer a place in a 'home' to a constant stream of 'helpers' walking through the front door – unreliable, changing every month, often disrespectful or even abusive. Survey research appears to suggest that a steady minority, usually between 10 and 20 per cent of those questioned, would prefer to go into some form of institution if they could not manage on their own. They either know they have no other means of support, or prefer institutionalization to feeling that they are a burden on their families. For example, a nationally representative sample of those aged 20–64 in Taiwan found that 10 per cent said they would choose institutional care in old age if they had the choice (Wu and Chu, 1996). Chen and Jones (1989) reported that even in Sinapore 4 per cent of elders said that they would like to enter a residential home – many more than the places available – while in the Philippines the rate was as high as 25 per cent. The British experiment of making residential care free on demand for all those on low incomes between 1982 and 1993, resulted in an increase of 29 per cent when the actual numbers are reduced to account for the increase in the older population (Laing, 1991). Qureshi, working in Sheffield, found that 3 per cent of people over 75 positively wanted to enter residential care and 18 per cent said they would be willing to do so should the need arise (Qureshi and Walker, 1989). It is not clear how these preferences would translate into actual demand for bed spaces (even if finance were to be available), but very few countries provide institutional care for more than 5 or 6 per cent of older people. Table 11.1 lists high providers but the rest of the world approaches Portugal in providing for 1 per cent or less of the over 65s.

The figures in Table 11.1 are not exact comparisons because definitions of institutional care vary between countries and because the dates differ. In Japan, for example, residential care homes are widely seen as unacceptable but hospital care is not. Many elders are therefore institutionalized in hospitals and some change hospital every three months in order to qualify as normal patients. Such practices are expensive and nearly all governments tried to cut the rate of institutionalization during the 1990s.

When most of the world has residential places for barely 1 per cent of all older people, the statistical basis for the fear of institutionalization looks weak. Very few people will get the chance to be institutionalized for more than a few months at the most. In America about half of those admitted stay less than three months (half die in homes or hospitals and most of the rest go back into the 'community'). Only 11 per cent of all people over 65 admitted will spend a year or more in a nursing home and 5 per cent will spend five or more years (Kane, 1996). Similarly, in Australia only 10 per cent of residents (not of the population) were expected to stay more than five years but 63 per cent stayed less than a

Table 11.1 Estimated proportions of older people in some form of institutional care in different countries (c.1990)

Country	All aged 65+ %	Of which in nursing homes %	Aged 85+ %	Of which in nursing homes %
Australia	10.4	2.6	40.5	20
Austria	4.7	2.6	18.1	11.4
Canada	8.1			
Denmark	5.7		24.0	
Finland	7.2	3.0		
New Zealand	6.3		33.2	
Norway	7.1	4.8	51.4	33.5
Portugal	1.8		4.6	
Sweden	5.4	2.9	23.3	12.5
UK	5.1	2.1	22.4	7.4
USA	5.4		24.9	

Source: OECD, 1996, Table 3.2

year in 1992–3 (Liu, 1996). Table 11.1 also shows that, despite what is widely believed in Asia and Africa, it is not the normal European practice to institutionalize the old. Even for those over 80 – the age at which entry becomes more common in Europe and America – well over half of all older men and women live outside any form of institutional care. In Norway in 1992 (OECD, 1996) 50 per cent of the population over 85 were in some form of institution, but no other country reaches this level of provision.

Different institutions

The basic characteristic of institutional care is usually taken to be some form of common residence. It is perfectly possible to suffer all the most feared aspects of institutional care when living 'in the community' or even in the family – dependency, depersonalization, loss of freedom, ill-health, marginalization and social rejection (Gavilan, 1992). Despite the problems associated with institutionalization, there is a genuine demand, however limited, for different forms of collective living with care provision. The range of possibilities is very wide, from sheltered housing which merges into residential homes, to nursing homes and elderly care wards in hospitals, with many variations and mixes, depending on the country and the financial arrangements made.

Each type of institution has advantages and disadvantages from the point of view of residents. *Sheltered housing* is confined to richer countries and has the great advantage that it offers tenancy agreements or owner occupation and so allows individuals more rights and more control over their own income. Residents may want the security of someone to answer an alarm in emergencies but otherwise can look after themselves. The disadvantage is that they can still be forced to move if they become too frail. The boundary between sheltered housing as a choice of retirement home – the type of move discussed in Chapter 6 – and sheltered housing as institutional living is unclear and fluid. Residents in the very large, purpose-built communities exclusively for older people that exist in the sun belt states of America are unlikely to think of themselves as institutionalized. Smaller schemes where residents start off fit but age together are more likely to develop characteristics of residential homes. There are also sheltered schemes with extra care built in from the start – often called 'very sheltered' in the UK. Such schemes may be the most popular in the future (OECD, 1996). They allow a degree of autonomy, enable tenants to keep more of their income than is possible in full residential care, save service costs by grouping frail people together, and give the peace of mind provided by alarm systems. In old style sheltered schemes a warden lived on site and there might be a communal lounge or reception area and a variety of services or activities. Each living unit was linked to the warden via an alarm system. Residents 'looked out' for each other and there might be many communal activities and friendships. Communal activity, however, cannot be taken for granted even in sheltered housing and the social life of schemes needs to be fostered in some way. Hochschild (1973) describes a Californian tower block where residents manage a full social life in *The Unexpected Community*.

Improved technology now allows many different systems of surveillance and greater sophistication is to be expected in the future. Alarms can be diverted to a central control which sends out mobile wardens to meet emergencies. In post earthquake Kobe, Japan, for example, public housing projects for elders incorporate technology to alert emergency services if no water is used for 24 hours. This alarm system can be switched from community service to hospital depending on the time of day. More is to come in terms of computerized technology and there are proposals to monitor whether the fridge is opened or the toilet is flushed. Many people will not be happy with this level of surveillance.

The main problems with sheltered housing are the ability of elders to pay rent and the fact that residents have no right to remain if they become too frail, unless the scheme includes nursing care (Mackintosh et al., 1990). There are also wide variations in quality and cost, with private schemes liable to exploit residents by raising service charges. Controversy over sheltered housing is likely to continue because it can be argued that scarce resources should not go on those who do not 'need' them, in other words to elders who are neither helpless nor bereft of carers (Middleton, 1987). However, if quality of life is the aim and choice the watchword, it can equally be argued that elders should be encouraged to opt for a type of housing that allows them peace of mind, freedom from the fear of dying alone, and the chance of making new friendships in a supportive community. Sheltered housing will never suit those who abhor the company of other older people, but for the more socially minded it can be far better than struggling on in unsuitable accommodation with growing disability (Hochschild, 1973).

There are still large parts of the world where *residential care* is indeed the last refuge and if there is none, the only alternative for destitute elders (mainly women) is death. Institutions are provided by charities or co-operatives and in parts of Latin America, for example, each town prides itself on having an orphanage and an old people's home (Tout, 1989). Other countries increasingly recognize the need for more residential care but often there are strong ideological as well as economic reasons why governments do not divert scarce funds to building institutions for old people. Guilt and shame can spread from those who enter care and their relatives, to staff and all connected with care provision. In Islamic countries and others where it is believed that elders have always been cared for by their families, the stigma appears to be even worse than in Europe. In South Korea, where only those completely without relatives were expected to enter a home, the social devaluation may be intense and revealed in the low quality of the facilities provided. Homes run by charities or religious bodies are traditionally highly regimented and may also be part of a stigmatizing system where those without family support are deemed to have failed. Nyanguru (1987), for example, contrasts two homes in Zimbabwe, one run by a religious order and the other a co-operative of older men and women. Despite the very much better material conditions provided by the religious order, autonomy and life satisfaction were far greater in the co-operative.

In the UK Peter Townsend (1962) presented life in post-Second World War residential homes, which were mostly former workhouses, as bleak, regimented, dehumanizing and in every way unpleasant. His photographs show very clearly why early campaigners fought against residential care. Since then the picture of residential life as depersonalizing and degrading has rarely been challenged. Powerful classic texts such as Goffman's *Asylums* (1961) simply reinforced existing beliefs. The Wagner Report, optimistically titled *A Positive Choice* (1988; Sinclair, 1988), attempted to improve the image of all types of residential care in the UK but had little impact on homes for older people. It appears that only the Netherlands and Denmark have been able to give institutions a halfway decent image. In the Netherlands forms of group living for older people expanded greatly after the Second World War, when it was a patriotic act in the post-war housing shortage for elders to move to some form of co-operative living and free up homes for young families. The result was a higher rate of institutional living than any other country in Europe, and a tradition of better quality provision. In Denmark, high-quality residential care is just one of a comprehensive range of services developed for elders.

Acceptable residential care involves as much choice and control by residents as possible, probably more than most managements wish to allow, or feel is economic (Booth, 1985; Peace et al., 1997; Youll and McCourt-Perring, 1993). Keith (1982), for example, describes the politics of a successful example of a single-room residential care scheme run by a trade union in France. The residents were used to an active political life and continued to make demands on management. They apparently felt united by their poverty rather than disempowered. Such a finding is important because one of the biggest disadvantages of residential care is that the high cost means that few can enter without giving up virtually all their income or pension. To be reduced to pocket money of £15 a week is degrading and disempowering at any age. Like sheltered housing, residential homes rarely guarantee a place for life and an older man or woman who becomes incontinent or demented will probably be moved on.

Nursing homes are the normal form of institutional care in the USA and this pattern is likely to spread. Like residential homes, nursing homes get a bad press, for example in *Negotiating a Good Old Age* (Schmidt, 1990; see also Castle et al., 1997). Stereotypically, they lack qualified staff, pay low wages and offer little stimulation to residents beyond the occasional trip in a disabled persons' bus. Medical support from visiting doctors can also be limited and even inadequate. Another major problem with nursing homes is size. It appears that homes need between 30 and 50 beds to be economically efficient, but this means drawing from a wide catchment area, so most patients are going to be far from friends and maybe relatives. There is a case for subsidizing smaller homes in rural areas where the employment possibilities that they offer can be important to the local economy. Even nursing homes do not offer a place for life, and residents may still find themselves moved on to another, more specialized, nursing home or a hospital. In future more nursing homes may offer short-term stays but profits from this type of patient are not usually so high.

The mainstream nursing home industry is a growing business area with listed companies on the stock exchange, take over bids and international links. For example, the *Independent* (28 October 1997) reported that Tamaris, the UK's fourth largest provider, was about to link up with a Far Eastern health care group to run nursing homes in Singapore. Mergers, takeovers and boardroom disputes figure in the financial pages. The Australian government has financed exploratory work on the possibilities of exporting Australian expertise in nursing home management to the southeast Asian NICs (Health Solutions Pty. Ltd, 1994; McCallum and Geiselhart, 1996).

Geriatric, or *Elderly Care* hospitals as they are now called in the UK, have the worst reputation in many countries. Various scandals (Howe,

1990; Southwark, 1988) expose dehumanizing environments, poor food, inadequate medical input and poorly trained, unmotivated or abusive nurses (Dissenbacher, 1989). Costs are lower than in acute hospitals and patients often suffer from malnutrition (*Le Monde*, 8 April 1999).

Demand for institutional care

Despite all the problems outlined above, there is a strong and almost certainly growing demand for residential care that is not going to go away. While it is untrue that all frail elders were cared for by their families in the past (many died and some were abandoned in more or less subtle ways), the modern ability to buy care, rather than deliver it hands on, is a welcome choice for many women. It is also welcome to older people in Western countries where the tradition of independence is very strong. Older women, in particular, seem unwilling to become a burden on their children if they can avoid it (Qureshi and Walker, 1989). There is no reason to believe that this trend will not be repeated as incomes rise in other parts of the world.

Demand from older people

A move into any communal setting involves some loss of autonomy and control. Evidence, such as it is, indicates that older people are usually willing to move if there is a good reason to do so. It is enforced moves that create most misery (or even death) – whether they are forced by frailty, or by relatives or professionals. Prime reasons for moving in developed countries are: loneliness (which is often not relieved by residential or nursing care); fear of crime; fear of falling or other emergency; inability to manage activities of daily living (including garden) without help; and to be nearer relatives or friends (Department of Health, 1994).

In the inner cities insecurity and loneliness may be the main push factors which make older people willing to move into some form of institution. In rural areas they can be poorly housed, hopelessly isolated and unable to get to shops. Isolated elders can be grouped in sheltered housing or residential homes in small towns or even villages, as in rural France. In developing countries the choice is likely to be between starvation and a poor quality institution.

Demand from relatives

In developing countries or NICs it is rarely possible for relatives to *openly* pressurize elders to go into institutions, but in Western societies there is often very great pressure from relatives for people to be institutionalized. Relatives want to sleep easily at night and if a dementing elder is wandering, leaving the gas unlit or simply not eating well, the chances are that there will be pressure for institutionalization from relatives or neighbours. Sometimes this is completely understandable. An elder who is a fire risk is not a good neighbour, but in other cases a person with dementia will be much better off in familiar surroundings and will have a better, if more risky, quality of life.

Demand from professionals

Many professionals see institutional care as a way of reducing risk or containing costs. Different types of long-term care have become more essential as the priority given to cost containment has risen. Hospital doctors and, in the UK, hospital managers or accountants, may want beds unblocked. Social workers or home helps may find the risks of allowing an older person to stay at home unacceptable or the behaviour problems of mentally-ill or dementing elders can become unmanageable. Wardens in sheltered housing may want difficult residents moved on (so may elderly neighbours and other tenants). Managers of residential homes may find the nursing burden too high and want residents moved to nursing homes. Nursing homes send those in crisis to hospital. In theory, elders are citizens and can only be moved with their consent. In practice, it is remarkably easy to railroad a frail elder into long-term care and very difficult for them to get out again. Violent elders can be sedated.

Issues

Culture

As far as can be seen, the temptation to exploit frail elders is very widespread. Older women, widows and others who lack social status are particularly at risk. In cultures where failure to care for parents can be a bar to a good afterlife, it appears that guilt and shame can easily shift from non-existent or unwilling relatives to the elder herself. A life of destitution in crowded dormitories or bamboo bunks stacked one on top of another is always a possible outcome for those without family. Governments may prefer to leave long-term care to charity on the grounds of ideology or cost. Certainly popular movements for more old age homes seem highly unlikely, even in Western countries where numbers of potential users are high.

Minorities

In countries with resident minority ethnic groups there may be well-developed NGOs that provide residential care for specific groups. Alternatively, there may be de facto area segregation that leads to provision on ethnic lines. Mainstream services may or may not provide culturally sensitive institutional care. The problem of institutionalization across cultures is most acute for older migrants, who may not speak the dominant language well and who may not have embraced the dominant culture. Unless they can go to a culturally appropriate home or long-term care ward, they are likely to be very unhappy and isolated. In the terms used in Chapter 6, assimilation means there will be ethnospecific residential or nursing homes. If mainstream services fail to provide, as they often do, voluntary sector homes (integration of ethnic groups) will have to be set up. Much depends on how finance can be provided by central and local governments (see Ethnic Affairs Commission of NSW, 1992, for examples of successful integration).

Costs

To quote Rivlin and Wiener, long-term care is a solvable problem in advanced countries:

> Although financing long term care has traditionally been viewed as an insoluble issue, it is actually one of the more tractable problems facing the United States. Indeed, unlike crime, poverty, racism, and teenage pregnancy, financing long term care has a range of known and feasible solutions. The question is whether we as a society have enough political will and ingenuity to choose among them and to put an improved system in place. (1988: 247).

However, as noted in Chapter 3, it is in the interests of governments to present long-term care as a crisis issue. Few votes have so far been involved, and there is always a strong lobby in favour of non-institutional care. Those who say care in the community is cheaper join forces with those who say it is better. Neither need be true. In cost terms there is a gradient:

self-care and care by unpaid (mainly women) relatives or neighbours is cheaper (because it is not costed) than:
care in the community for a restricted number of hours per week by low-paid care workers, which is cheaper than:
24-hour residential care employing staff with little training, which is cheaper than:

24-hour nursing home care where some staff have to have professional
   qualifications which is cheaper than:
hospital care where many staff will be professionally qualified and the
   capital investment is greater.

It follows that there are incentives for governments to shift service users
from the most expensive settings and to make them, or their relatives,
pay whatever they can afford. Such tendencies can be seen in OECD
countries. Compulsory long-term care insurance appears to be the
best method of finance at present. Any long-term care scheme has to be
compulsory or premiums will be impossible to pay except for the very
rich. Wiener et al. (1994) state that half of all insured people (for private
long-term care in the USA) lapse within five years of starting and 75 per
cent within 15 years (excluding those who die). This means that most of
those who take out long-term care insurance lose their money, but if the
companies allowed even partial benefit on withdrawal for those who
leave, it would raise premiums still further. Germany and Japan have
already legislated for compulsory long-term care insurance. In Germany,
insurance has covered home care, which includes shopping, cooking and
cleaning since 1995 and institutional care since 1996.
    The German division between long-term care at home and in an
institution highlights the economic limits to home care. People with high
needs are very expensive to care for in their own homes, though if
they can be grouped in high care sheltered housing the costs may be
more favourable. There is also a quality issue as long as home carers are
specialized into professions and are limited in the various tasks and
levels of care that they are willing or able to perform. An older person
with complex needs may find that three or four different professionals
or carers are coming in each day. If they are also changing the strain may
be too much and the relative stability of a nursing home may be more
attractive.

Quality and rationing

The easiest way to ration institutional care is to make it stigmatizing
and poor quality. There are long traditions of rationing charity in this
way in most countries. There is also plenty of evidence to suggest that it
is very difficult to change institutional practices that have developed in
such a political climate. Experience in the Netherlands and Denmark
shows that improvement is possible but not easy. This type of rationing
is in obvious conflict with quality.
    Rationing by assessment or the empowerment of professionals (or
less highly trained staff) to decide who 'needs' expensive care is an
alternative to direct deterrence. In the USA and UK it may be called 'case

management' or 'care management'. It can be combined with assessment of finances to fix a level of co-payment. In a few countries, such as Germany and Japan, children are still liable to be asked to pay for their parents (a family means test). The impact of assessment on quality can be complex. In theory, when assessment is sensitive to changing needs and therefore takes place at regular intervals, it offers the chance to monitor care as it is received. Assessors may also influence the mix of clients and so affect the work load of staff in institutions and possibly the service they are able to provide. Hunter et al. (1988) give instances of GP assessors deciding whether or not to allocate a new patient to a home on the basis of the existing case mix in the home rather than on the state of the patient.

Regulation and inspection

Inspection of homes and hospitals is difficult to do well, especially if any measure of quality of care (as opposed to quality of facilities) is involved. Governments, who may be blamed for scandals in institutions, still lack the technology to control for quality. Buildings can be evaluated, numbers and qualifications of staff can be checked and various procedures or systems can be put in place, such as ways of recording accidents, medication and individual care plans, but these do not add up to quality of care. However, even if care is known to be low quality, the remedies are not always clear. At the simplest a home that is closed means relocating frail elders who may die in the move, and facing angry relatives demanding explanations. There are always tensions between maintaining adequate records (unusual, as anyone who has looked at care plans will testify) and looking after the residents.

Autonomy and control

All institutions raise issues of autonomy and control for their residents. In sheltered housing they arise from communal living – the inevitable surveillance by other residents and by the warden(s). Regimentation tends to increase as more services are provided, and in nursing homes there is the dominance of the medical model which further disempowers patients. Loss of autonomy and control are not inevitable with greater age or greater frailty but they are likely, and poor quality institutions are distressingly common in all countries. Clough (1981: 187) sums up one pervasive dilemma: on the basis of a British study he says, 'staff, residents and outsiders predominantly believed in keeping active, in finding things to do. However, only a few believed that there were worthwhile tasks for the very old to perform'. As a result staff did most things for the residents and they were not active and had very little autonomy. Being forced to choose which dress to wear in the morning is not choice in the normal meaning of the term, but it may be the experience of institutionalized elders, and may be presented as choice by staff.

Management

Management theory and practice which encourage high quality institutional care of frail older men and women is virtually non-existent. Devalued, low-paid and usually poorly trained staff, often from another culture, attend devalued people. Residents are vulnerable to exploitation, often discontented and may die. The characteristics of residential services add up to a management nightmare if quality is the aim. When staff turnover is high there is one set of problems. No one gets to know the residents, and continuity of care is hard to build up. When staff turnover is low there is a chance to develop an institutional culture which may be good or bad. Long-run scandals are usually the product of a vicious culture of abuse developing among staff. Those who do not conform are driven out and those who do conform either stay or are too compromised to whistleblow when they leave.

Abuse

Much research on elder abuse has concentrated on abuse in the community and usually by carers. This presented a biased picture of family abuse that is more gendered than carer oriented. Since around 95 per cent of elders are living in the community in virtually all countries it is not surprising that most elder abuse is found outside institutions. However, the risk of abuse in an institution may be very much higher than in the community. Institutional abuse can be divided into two main types: routine institutionalized abuse which passes unnoticed for most of the time, and deliberate abuse which is part of a culture of cruelty or individual victimization of residents. Institutional abuse is extremely widespread, especially in nursing homes and elderly care wards. Its extent depends on definition. Methods of restraint vary but tying patients to their chairs, using chairs which lock them into an uncomfortable position, leaving them on the toilet for longer than necessary and various bathing procedures can all be defined as abusive.

A nurse who trained in the 1970s recalled a placement where bath time was a tub of water in the middle of the ward with each patient publicly stripped in turn and washed down with the same rag. In this case the ward managers did not feel they had anything to hide. They were only doing what had always been done. In another example dating from 1993, an elderly woman was admitted to a council home for two nights of respite care in a London borough. Suddenly, in the middle of her first night, two care staff rushed into her room, pulled off the bed clothes and changed her sheet. They pushed her back into bed and rushed out without a word. The staff were completely amazed to find themselves the subject of a complaint which led to disciplinary action. Both were very experienced and had been changing incontinent or potentially incontinent residents in that way for years. The disciplinary panel took the view that if staff had never been adequately trained or had their procedures questioned they could not be disciplined. In such a case it is the local management that is at fault in not monitoring night time care practices and not providing essential training. It is unfortunately impossible to imagine that these are isolated cases.

Many other types of institutionalized abuse fall into Bennett and Kingston's (1993) definition of elder abuse as 'inadequate care.' For example, failure to prevent bedsores must now be so widespread in British hospitals that it might even be a normal hazard of elder care in hospital – even though Florence Nightingale showed how bedsores could be eliminated in the 19th century. Oversedation and the use of drugs to control patients can be straightforward abuse or may be verging on the medically necessary (Castle et al., 1997; Dissenbacher, 1989).

Deliberate abuse is a less common problem but usually more serious for the victims. Most countries can produce a string of reports showing how a ward, home or hospital can be captured by a dominant culture of abuse which becomes almost impossible to change. Those who fail to conform are driven out and such authorities as there are consistently refuse to act. Legislation to protect staff or inmates who try to get action (whistleblower protection) is essential, but few countries have yet passed such laws and even when they have been passed they are hard to implement (see Martin, 1999 for a useful handbook).

Conclusion

The numbers, if not the proportion of elders in residential care of some sort, seem certain to grow. The question is not so much will there be institutional care in the future, but will there be enough residential care, and will it be good enough. The minority of older people who do want to move to some form of institution are liable to find it very difficult to get a place, and even more difficult to get a *good quality* place in a home or hospital. As things stand, the greatest problems will arise in developing countries and NICs unless more beds are provided. Many of these governments have strong ideological objections to residential care and will give no priority to financing good quality provision.

> These countries have only one important misgiving about health and care services targeted for the elderly. . . . That exception is nursing home care . . . analysts frequently state that individuals should be allowed to die in a state of activity in their own home, rather than meeting death in a public or private institution. (Tracy, 1991: 146)

It is not unreasonable to see continuing poor quality of residential care as partly a method of rationing and partly a method of maintaining unpaid care by women and other family members. Religious bodies, whether temples or monasteries, have always financed elder care for a few. In the future they are likely to be joined by a wider range of NGOs and profit-making enterprises that will look after a small minority of rich elders. The role of government will be to attempt to regulate quality and avoid scandals, whoever provides the service and however it is financed.

If 'the old' are defined as those of retirement age, the vast majority will always be able bodied and will choose to live and work in their own homes and not in institutions. It is hard to imagine a country where this was not true. Equally it is hard to imagine a country where some older men and women did not need residential care. Some form of institutionalization appears to be essential in all cultures unless elders are simply left to die. Institutional care covers a range of grouped living models. Diversity is essential to meet the varied needs of older men and women who go into institutional care. Some are more in need of company and security, while others have very high intensity nursing needs. In the future variations of sheltered housing are likely to be the best quality and most acceptable form of institution, with nursing homes available for special cases (OECD, 1996). However, if cost imperatives triumph over quality, nursing homes may become the standard as they appear to be in the USA. A few better off elders, or their children, will be able to avoid the stigma of institutionalization by employing live-in carers but this is not always a happy or high quality solution, even for the rich.

Life in institutions need not be bad, but it commonly is. This holds everywhere in the world. People go into institutions because they have no relatives to care for them, no way of earning a living and cannot, through poverty or disability, look after themselves. Cultures vary in how strongly they devalue those who lack relatives or resources, or who are disabled, but nearly all cultures appear to devalue older people on these grounds. In Europe lack of relatives is more a matter for sympathy than shame, but perceptions of low esteem spread from residents to staff of institutions who are usually poorly paid and barely trained. Management is commonly a problem, with poor management leading to low quality care and even abuse. Exceptions exist, especially when elders are fit and well and when they have built up supportive communities within an institution (hence mainly in sheltered housing). Advocacy is increasingly recognized as an essential part of institutional services. In future it is to be hoped that new forms of residential care will be developed that have advocacy as an integral aspect.

Policies which make it more difficult to enter residential or nursing care help to ensure that residents and patients who finally enter institutions are frailer, physically and mentally, than they were before cost controls were so carefully applied. They may be easier to look after in terms of being inactive and unable to move far from bed, and unlikely to protest if ill treated, but streamlined care is not necessarily good quality care. Regulation and quality control are slightly easier in institutions than in domiciliary care. Staff and residents are on view in the place where they live and work, and abuses are more difficult to hide. However, a culture of abuse (or poor care practice) can grow and be hard to detect, and very hard to change. The only way may be to close the institution and sack all staff – an approach that is not favoured by the unions and one that may even be strongly resisted by residents and relatives.

Finally, the employment opportunities generated by institutional care (as with domiciliary care) in developed countries cannot be under-estimated. In rural areas with ageing populations there are often few openings for young workers and residential care has a contribution to make along with services for elders still living in their own homes.

Further reading

http://research.aarp.org/ppi/publist.html – good for elders as consumers and for long-term care in America.
http://www.eurolinkage.org/euro – Europe.

CHAPTER 12

AGEING IN CONTEXT

In the West, the 'burdens' of pensions, caregiving and intergenerational equity dominate the debate on the problems of an ageing world. These are normally presented as aspects of 'the old age crisis' and very often deemed to be world wide. In contrast, in the developing world there is very little debate, but there are basic assumptions that older people will work unless pension schemes become viable, and that care will be given by the family if it is needed. The argument of this book has been that power relations structure the ways that such stereotypical knowledge about old age is presented, so that some aspects are given prominence and others are suppressed. For example in the West there are many academic and practitioner texts on the *problems* of old age but very few on the *benefits*, which can be related to the way that dominant age groups wish to present old age. Faced with such 'knowledge', it becomes easy to think of old age as 'naturally' problematic, and mainstream social science in developed countries has taken this line without much question. Alternatively in other countries there are widespread beliefs that old age is revered and frail elders are cared for by their families (women), and it has been just as easy to assert that there is no ageing problem. Such beliefs can be described as dominant ideologies and they are widely taken for granted in the societies concerned.

These dominant ideologies and the power relations that sustain them can influence whose voices are heard and whose experiences are the subject of research. So for example the 'knowledge' that 'elders are a burden' to be cared for either at home or in institutions has been far more widely spread than information on the experience of the older men and women who are being cared for. Their experiences of elder abuse, in the family or in institutions, were virtually unknown (unmentioned or invisible) twenty years ago in America and ten years ago in the UK and are still unrecognized in many countries. The gendered aspects of elder abuse (men are more likely to abuse women, than vice versa) have taken even longer to surface (Whittaker, 1995). The contribution of older men and women to economic and social development is a similarly blank area in Western knowledge, although this too is changing:

> Older people play valuable roles as carers and resource managers, while the knowledge they hold – of traditional survival systems, appropriate technologies, and alternative medicines – can be central to the development of community coping strategies in and after crises. Their sense of history can

help preserve communities' cultural and social identity, even in situations such as refugee camps, where corrosive 'camp culture' can predominate. (http://www.helpage.org/members/ 29.9.99.)

At present such a positive approach must be defined as an alternative or oppositional ideology but it is an indication that dominant ideologies are increasingly being challenged in the public sphere. In private life elders who have the resources are challenging many stereotypes and forging new lifestyles (see below).

Cross-cultural comparisons and dominant ideologies

The strength of a cross-cultural approach is that it contrasts dominant ideologies in different cultures, makes the power relations involved more visible and so allows us to question what appears to be 'natural' in any society. Comparison between cultures also highlights the diversity within cultures by showing that ideologies that are dominant in one culture are present in others, but very often in muted form, or in ways that are modified to suit the different cultural and environmental constraints (see below and Chapters 2 and 9). Some of the key components of dominant ideologies and their alternatives are outlined below.

Ageism

Previous chapters have argued that in Western countries there is a strong tendency to equate old age with incapacity – mental and physical. Many things follow from this cultural prejudice against old age and older people. In the first place, such beliefs are so strong that even older men and women themselves commonly hold negative views of each other or themselves in later life. Here is an extract from an interview:

> I did try going once to bingo and, I'm sorry to say this, I'm 75 and I don't like old people, I don't, I'm sorry. I sat there and I looked at this bingo hall, and [she took me next door], and every woman there's got grey hair and they all had the same hairstyle – if they all had their backs to you, you could never sort out who was who. Now some Wednesdays, there is an organ club and they're mostly middle aged people that get there and it's good. (author's interview , 1993)

Such a negative view of old age can be disabling in political terms since it discourages elders from banding together as a recognized group (see Chapter 4.) It also reflects a deep seated cultural fear of old age and death, and further encourages the feeling that older people are 'the other' – not like younger people, not very diverse and not necessarily worthy of full citizenship rights.

When this ageism is combined with the Enlightenment view of Western knowledge as scientific and universal, it produces a certain type of knowledge which passes as culture-free and unbiased, but in fact is limited by the power relations and the cultures that produce it. A problem for critical gerontologists and others who oppose dominant ideologies from within ageist cultures, is that even as they campaign against the denigration of later life and the presentation of elders as burdens on the rest of society, they have to speak of elders as a disadvantaged group and so reinforce the idea of elders as victims. A better knowledge base would give a voice to those older men and women whose later lives are not simply problem free, but are marked by positive aspects or are even highly enjoyable. It would also give more prominence to advocacy and self-advocacy for elders (Dunning, 1998) since these voices are essential to counteract professional power and ensure that the views of older men and women are incorporated into national policies.

Opposition to mainstream ageist and biased knowledge is already present in Western culture. One form of anti-ageism refuses to acknowledge that old age exists (see Gullette, 1997, for example). Such a stance is justified by a range of Western research on the views of older people themselves, for example *I Don't Feel Old* (Thompson et al., 1990), which stressed continuity not change over the life course. It also has wide support in other cultures where seniority is more important than chronological age, and where people may not be seen as old until serious disability stops them looking after themselves. As a campaigning position it is reasonable to say that old age is no different from the rest of the adult life course, and even in some circumstances to deny that it exists at all. However there is the problem of the ageing body. Biological ageing is linked to the passage of time and cannot be avoided in some form or other. It is not necessarily linked to chronological age and a person is not automatically physically old because they are 70, even though they may feel a bit slower and a bit less energetic.

The family

The major divide in understanding of the family is between societies where the dominant ideology sees *individuals* as the basic units of society and societies where *families* are seen as the basic unit (see Chapter 9). In the first case families are assumed to be composed of individuals. In the second it may be extreme to say that individuals only exist in so far as they are members of families – but that is the traditional position. Family dominance over individuals has been modified by the processes of individualization associated with modernization in traditional societies, but the taken-for-granted approach to life may still be that the needs of individual members (especially women) come second to the needs of the family.

An intellectual consequence of this divide is that in cultures where the family is defined as a collection of individuals it is easy to see some members as a burden on others. It is then a short intellectual step to debates about intergenerational equity. Workers are deemed to be supporting those who do not work. Pensions are not seen as deferred earnings or enforced savings made by elders during their working lives, but simply as a burden on the young. It is further assumed that the situation must be unfair since there is no way of knowing whether the next generation will give today's workers as much as they are deemed to be giving today's elders. Minkler (1991) noted that even in America, where individualism and intergenerational competition are highly developed, this way of thinking did not seem very relevant to ordinary people. The argument of this book is that the costs of ageing populations are likely to be entirely sustainable in Western countries and hence that debates about intergenerational equity are of academic rather than practical interest. Their political attraction is however undeniable and as such they can be opposed on ethical or political grounds.

In those countries where the family is seen as the main building block of society, the concept of intergenerational equity is not a home grown discourse, but it is available via international economic policy documents. Elders are assumed to contribute to family resource strategies in different ways over the life course. They are integral members of their families and so cannot be separated out as specific burdens in a dominant discourse. This does not mean that individual elders are not *experienced* as a burden within individual low income families, or as a care burden on individual daughters-in-law, only that the public discourse is likely to be different.

The free market consensus

Globalization, economic development and the increase in average living standards, combined with the collapse of communism has greatly accentuated the dominance of what has come to be known as the 'Washington consensus', the conventional market individualist model of the world. It is a world in which older men and women have no place, though they may figure as 'burden' or a cause of 'crisis' in terms of pensions. The World Bank (1994) has published *Averting the Old Age Crisis*, which used conventional western demographic concepts to arrive at predictions of disaster. The doctrinaire solution proposed was a market model of private funded pensions for the majority, despite the fact that there is no evidence that such pension systems can provide *adequate* support in later life for more than a minority of elders. Elders also figure occasionally in World Bank and International Monetary Fund documents as in need of very limited safety netting when structural adjustment policies produce poor outcomes for the old (Ahmad, 1994; Ahmad and Chalk, 1993), but this is only a version of elders as burden. The World Trade Organization is another international agency that takes little account of the effects of the free market (a market that is rigged in favour of the economically powerful) on the poorest people. Countries that are forced to lower tariff barriers and end preferential trade agreements are liable to widespread loss of jobs or the collapse of farming as their markets disappear. Such policies dislocate family support systems and cut the opportunities for elders to support themselves. It appears that an increase in old age poverty is inevitable since markets discriminate against those with inadequate market power.

Despite the dominance of market ideology in world economic institutions others such as the World Health Organization and some subsidiaries of the United Nations take a much more positive view of an ageing world. These policies are a reflection of the views of user groups, activists and advocates for older peoples' rights and citizenship (hence the Internet references at the end of each chapter in this book.) UN policies such as the International Year of Older Persons 1999 and its International Plan of Action on Ageing are far ahead of normal Western discourse in terms of anti-ageism and a positive approach to later life. When they are combined with international policies on gender and women in development they offer a wide reaching set of exhortations to empowerment, co-operative development and a better quality of life. The OECD is another organization that has been able to use a strong cross-national statistical base to present evidence that health and pensions crises are politically manufactured rather than based on the best available data.

The dominance of free market ideology is also evident in the widespread adoption of the idea of 'consumer choice' as a way of improving needs related services for older people. The technical knowledge needed to run good quality services in the community and in long term health and social care institutions, is still very under-developed. The globally fashionable solution in the 1990s was to privatize services, but relying on the profit motive when those being served are frail and disempowered and cannot exercise consumer power is unlikely to be a recipe for quality services.

Lumpen elders – homogenization of old age

Despite the very widespread use of demographic data counting everyone over 65 as old, ageing is not 'the great leveller' making all older men and women the same. This is true of international differences between countries but also applies to individuals. In a very wide range of cultures (see Chapter 2) boundaries that admit an older man or woman to *senior status* are not necessarily the same as the boundaries of old age that are assumed in Western societies. Within societies the outcomes of old age are related to experiences over the life course for cohorts and individuals, with only death as a constant. Migrants and minority ethnic groups experience ageing differently from dominant ethnic groups (see Chapter 6). They have to combat prejudice and racism over the life course and they may also have distinctive cultural strengths or needs. In addition previous chapters have often referred to older men and women, rather than older people, in order to highlight the different experiences of later life that flow from a gendered life course. At an individual level, the spread of pensions (a retirement wage) to produce a later life which is free from the need to work to survive, has opened up enormous opportunities for large numbers of men and women. Ageing identities are becoming more fluid in a postmodern world and there is greater scope for self-expression in later life. It may upset the children who want their parents to remain conventional, but friends will probably approve. Take Enid (not her real name): she is divorced and retired from the National Health Service, but still able to do locum and private agency work. Life in the UK can be a little dull so she visits her son in New Zealand on extended trips of six to nine months. Her son is at work but acts as a base while Enid tours New Zealand, staying at backpackers lodges and talking to the people she meets. She is never bored and in due course she returns to England to save up money for her next trip. Such a life cannot continue for ever but can be viable for many years after the age of 55. The chances are that even if her later years get more restricted Enid will be able to look back on many years of life lived to the full.

The 'burden' of health care

The simple assumption that an ageing population is a burden on health services colours most research, discourse and policy on health care (see Chapter 8). Health care costs are rising in most countries and ageing populations are usually blamed. However Robinson and Judge (1987) showed that in the UK only one fifth (20 per cent) of observed increases in costs could be put down to an ageing population, and technological change accounted for most of the rest. There is no reason to think that the situation has changed. In developed countries health care is technically available to all, but the highest costs per patient occur in the last two years of life (OECD, 1998). As lives lengthen, there is a slower increase in death rates or they may even fall in the short term, so the rate at which heavy health care costs are incurred also increases more slowly than the number of older people. Such a situation cannot last, but it does put off the time when a big rise in health care costs might be expected.

There is also much that is hidden in terms of the way that health services for older patients are rationed in all countries. For example Ahenkora (1999) in Ghana reported that older people found it hard to be taken seriously by health service personnel. In South Africa, HelpAge International (1999) quotes: 'At times we are abused by nurses who say "Why are you coming to the clinic? You are old. Are you afraid of dying?"' In India, Cohen (1998) was unable to recruit patients with dementia because the right age group was not brought to the hospital where he was working. In developed countries informal rationing has long been the norm. It is very easy to ration health care for elders by making access more difficult, offering poor quality or inappropriate treatment, or simply stating that medical opinion does not think a treatment is advisable after a certain age. In pharmaceuticals, rationing may prove more difficult, not so much because doctors are unwilling to reduce costs, but because there is great pressure from the industry to prescribe. The ideal market for pharmaceuticals is an expanding customer group with a long run need for high cost drugs and no prospect of a cure. The elderly fit the bill nicely. In developing countries the elite are the main market. Cohen (1998) includes interviews with pharmaceuticals managers intent on pushing an anti-Alzheimer's drug in India, despite the fact that Alzheimer's had not been identified as a scourge (Gubrium, 1986) in India, and still more important, despite the fact that the drug was known to have little effect. Other cost pressures come from expensive treatments to keep dying people alive. Apart from pharmaceuticals, the future of health costs for ageing populations is therefore unclear in detail, but the technical means to keep costs within manageable bounds are easily available. Short of an unforeseen catastrophe, population ageing is not a reason for health finance systems to collapse.

Intergenerational inequity and the pensions burden

It can be argued that all the problems of biased knowledge produced by Western dominant ideologies come together in the debate over pensions and intergenerational equity. First, pensions are not universal. For most of the population in developing countries a pension is not a retirement wage (the army and civil servants are the main exceptions) and older men and women work until they die or until they become too ill to manage. Then there is the common practice of lumping together all over 65s or over 55s (two common demographic boundaries of old age) as a percentage of the working age population (say 15–64) to calculate dependency rates. This type of knowledge has its uses, but in much of the world it is normal to work from the age of four till death (Caldwell and Caldwell, 1992), so dependency rates are largely fictitious and a rise in the number of people over 65 merely increases the available (unpaid) work force (see Chapters 5, 7 and 8). Another problem is that the dominant ideology of dependency ratios assumes that current patterns of gendered involvement in the labour force can be projected forward without change. This ability to ignore changes in women's participation in the labour market (pointed out by Johnson and Falkingham, 1992) has been one component of the apocalyptic demography that presents the numerical burden of elders as too much for the young to bear (Robertson, 1997).

In developing countries pensions are not yet a problem, but it is to be hoped that the practice in India of providing near universal pensions at very low levels will be widely followed. A very low level pension is a token of national recognition and a small bargaining counter in family resource negotiations. In the newly industrializing countries of the Pacific rim many pension funds are in surplus while families are still supporting older relatives. As a result, low income families and elders who have no family or no functioning family, face hardship, but there is no pensions crisis (Kwon, 1999a). Problems exist in the older schemes in Japan and Singapore but solutions are possible.

Pensions are financed out of current economic surplus regardless of the system, and long run economic activity is therefore the main determinant of the success or failure of pension systems. An ageing population is a minor problem compared with a collapse in the formal labour market or serious inflation. Both these disasters have occurred in some former communist states and the pensions crises there are very real (see *http://www.undp.org:80/rbec/nhdr/tajikistan/chapter5.htm* for a graphic description of the pensions crisis in Tajikistan). In the unlikely event that such economic collapse becomes widespread older people will be exposed to serious hardship but they will not be a cause of the problem.

As pension systems mature, controversy over the balance between the years spent contributing to a scheme and the years spent as a beneficiary, seems likely to intensify. However policies that can reverse current trends and keep older men and women in paid work have yet to be developed. Among the exceptions are the Silver Centres in Japan (Bass and Oka, 1995; Campbell, 1992) which provide low paid work for retired people to supplement their incomes, but it is not clear how easily this policy could transfer to other countries where the work ethic is less developed. There are also technical and political difficulties in reforming existing pension schemes. On the technical side there is no perfect pension system that will simultaneously ensure good pensions for current and future pensioners, a viable level of current contributions, and have positive effects on macro level measures of public expenditure, personal savings and national investment. Economic performance, political pressures and the historical and cultural attitudes to older people, combine to produce compromises that benefit elders to a varying degree (see Figure 1.1, p. 10). The political unwillingness to increase the retirement wage can be contrasted with the failure of attempts to cut benefits to elders in a number of countries. It appears very much easier to unite older voters and their allies in defence of existing benefits than to get them to campaign for a better deal (see Chapter 4). Pension systems are therefore more likely to be changed at the margins than wholly restructured.

It is fair to say that pensions offer some prime examples of bad policy-making for an ageing world. The spread of early retirement reduces pension contributions at the same time as it increases payouts. In Europe where the official retirement age is generally 65 for men, the spread of early retirement has resulted in a *de facto* retirement age of 60 in many occupations. Early retirement for reasons of ill health has been widely used as a way of leaving the workforce. Policies have encouraged early retirement rather than attempted to keep older workers in the labour force. This has sometimes been justified on the grounds that older workers make way for younger, but there is little evidence that this is so. Private pension schemes for the better off are even structured to make it uneconomic to retain older workers. As a result the very rich take large pensions in their fifties while the poor struggle on with social assistance until they reach the age of 65 and claim a reduced pension.

Emancipatory values

The emphasis that has been placed on family solidarity and social cohesion throughout the preceding chapters is only justifiable if it is accompanied by a similar or even greater emphasis on emancipatory policies for women and older people. In future older men and women who have families will almost certainly continue to rely on them. There is no evidence of a breakdown in family care on a worldwide scale. However if family care is defined as care by unpaid and invisible women, its days appear to be limited. Countries which see no need to support family caregivers or to provide services to enhance the quality of life for those who do not have families, or to provide residential care of high enough quality to be a real choice, are likely to face problems. The education of women, the chance for some to take paid work or to migrate, and reductions in family size are likely to change the gender balance of power within household and family (Moser, 1996). New ways of producing family care and social cohesion that do not rely on the exploitation of women are urgently needed, but neither of the dominant discourses on ageing and caregiving is helpful. In the developing world and emerging economies the certainty that the family (the invisible women) will care is shortsighted. A straightforward recogniton that traditional values need support would be more positive. A discourse of this type is emerging in Japan (Economic Planning Agency, Government of Japan 1994). In Western countries the discourses of elders as a 'burden' are also unhelpful. As the previous chapters have shown, this encourages the presentation of very partial knowledge and allows popular politics to blame population ageing for rising taxes, rising health care costs and possibly even for a failure to develop quality care services for older people.

Future policies

As far as can be seen at present, there are no demographic, economic or health related old age crises that are not manageable, though this is not to say that they will be managed in a way that is acceptable to older people or their advocates. All the changes in ageing populations are potentially sustainable (with more or less difficulty) in the foreseeable future. This was clear as early as 1978 (Maddox, 1978) but it is easier to speak of ageing as a crisis issue than to take action to solve it. For a start there are large gaps in our understanding of how to formulate policies and at a practical level, how to make them work well. We do not know how to make and implement policy that will allow elders to participate fully in modern communities and to have much greater control over their lives. Nor do we know how to support individuals, families and civil society so that they can provide care for those who need it in later life. Even for something as basic as pensions, there is no perfect scheme. The problems of providing quality services in the complex and stigmatized areas of institutional care and home support are even greater, although the cost of improvements is so much less. Scandinavian countries have insisted on more training and legislation but the politics of increasing expenditure on such a devalued area as long-term care are problematic everywhere. So far it has proved very difficult to monitor quality in services and institutions and this is another technical problem that has not been solved.

Since very few men and even fewer women can provide for themselves in later life, ageing societies will face great difficulties if they do not choose polices that encourage social cohesion by collectivizing social needs at family, community (local), national and global levels. Pensions and health are the two outstanding areas of collective activity. State provision is not essential but the systems chosen need to unite as many of the population as possible in sharing risks and using collectively provided services. It can easily be forgotten that pensions and accessible health care are social successes that have changed the quality of life of very large numbers of older people. They rarely receive the same level of publicity as the dubious projections of system collapse. The success of the retirement wage in raising the quality of later life is almost totally obscured by the discourse of 'burden' (Scherer, 1996). The policy challenge is to maintain social cohesion and to strengthen families but not at the expense of women. Global tendencies working for an improvement in the status of women appear to be unstoppable so any future that relies on the continued invisibility of women's labour and love will not work.

There are major and varying political issues in terms of the will to sustain new policies that combat market individualism and strengthen social solidarity. The impact of older voters in Japan and the West, where one voter in two may be over 50 in the coming century, may well be greater than any so-called crises in health and pension systems. In global terms pensions are for the privileged few and the danger is not that the young will be overburdened, but that no solutions will be found to the political and technical problems of raising the level of pensions where they are low, and expanding the coverage. The problem will then be a matter of maintaining very large numbers of destitute elders. Health care problems likewise appear more manufactured than real. There are solutions for the minority of elders who are frail and need some form of care but they are not easy to convert into working policies that deliver high quality services for those who need them most.

And finally, social policies are not simply transferable from country to country. Poor understanding of different cultures and conditions can lead to implementation failure at national and local level. In a globalizing world where policy transfer appears increasingly attractive, it is easy to homogenize older people, and so to make policy failure more likely. A better understanding of different cultures and different values is a first step to identifying policies that work for ageing populations and finding ways to implement them sensitively across cultures.

REFERENCES

Abel, E.K. and Nelson, M.K. (eds) (1990) 'Circles of care: an introductory essay', in *Circles of Care: Work and Identity in Women's Lives*. Albany: State University of New York Press. pp.4–34.

Achenbaum, W.A (1983) *Shades of Gray: Old Age, American Values, and Federal Policies Since 1920*. Boston: Little Brown.

Agarwal, B. (1998) 'Widows versus daughters or widows as daughters? Property, land and economic security in rural India', in M.A. Chen (ed.) *Widows in India: Social Neglect and Public Action*. New Delhi, Thousand Oaks: Sage Publications. pp. 124–69.

Ahenkora, K. (1999) *The Contribution of Older People to Development: The Ghana Study*. London: HelpAge International and HelpAge Ghana.

Ahmad, E. and Chalk, N. (1993) *On Improving Public Expenditure Policies for the Poor: Major Informational Requirements*. Washington, DC: International Monetary Fund.

Ahmad, E., (1994) *Pensions, Price Shocks, and Macroeconomic Stability in Transition Economies: Illustrations from Belarus*. Washington, DC: International Monetary Fund.

Ahmad, W.I.U. and Atkin, K. (eds) (1996) *Race and Community Care*. Buckingham: Open University Press.

Alwin, D.F. (1997), 'Aging, social change and conservatism: the link between historical and biographical time in the study of political identities', in M.A. Hardy (ed.) *Studying Aging and Social Change*. Thousand Oaks: Sage.

Andrews, K. and Brocklehurst, J. (1987) *British Geriatric Medicine in the 1980s*. London: King Edward's Hospital Fund for London.

Andrews, M. (1991) *Lifetimes of Commitment*. Cambridge: Cambridge University Press.

Arber, S. and Gilbert, J. (1989) 'Men the forgotten carers', *Sociology*, 23(1): 111–18.

Arber, S. and Ginn, J. (eds) (1991) *Gender and Later Life*. London: Sage.

Arasse, L., (1992), L'Example des Portugais de N', *Le Vieillissement des Immigrés en Région Parisienne*. Paris: Fonds d'Action Sociale. pp. 476–556.

Atcherly, R.C. (1987) *Aging: Continuity and Change*. Belmont, CA: Wadsworth.

Baldock, J. and Ely, P. (1996) 'Social-care for elderly people in Europe', in B. Munday and P. Ely (eds) *Social Care in Europe*. London: Prentice Hall. pp. 195–225.

Barr, N. (1994) *Labor Markets and Social Policy in Central and Eastern Europe: The Transition and Beyond*. Oxford: Oxford University Press (for the World Bank).

Barr, N. (1995) 'Safety nets for the rural poor: an overview', in D. Umali-Deininger and C. Maguire (eds) *Agriculture in Liberalizing Economies : Changing Roles for Governments: Proceedings of the Fourteenth Agricultural Sector Symposium*. Washington, DC: World Bank. pp. 331–44.

Basham, A.L. (1954) *The Wonder that was India*. London: Sidgwick and Jackson.

Bass, S.A. and Oka, M., (1995), 'An older worker employment model: Japan's Silver Human Resource Centres', *Gerontologist*, 35(5): 679–82.

Bengtson, V.L. and Achenbaum, W.A. (eds) (1993) *The Changing Contract Across Generations*. New York: Aldine de Gruyter.

Bennett, G. and Kingston, P. (1993) *Elder Abuse*. London: Chapman and Hall.

Besnard, J.-L. (1993) 'La novation sociale introduite par la loi sur le RMI', in *Vieillir et mourir en exil: immigration maghrébine et vieillissement.* Lyon: Presses universitaires de Lyon. pp. 25–9.

Bevölkerung und Erwerbstätigkeit (1995) *Germany (Federal Republic).* Wiesbaden: Statistisches Bundesamt.

Bialik, R. (1989) 'Profile of Mexican elderly women: a comparative study', in PAHO *Mid-Life and Older women in Latin America and the Caribbean,* Washington, DC: PAHO. pp. 242–52.

Biggs, S., Philipson, C., and Kingston, P. (1995) *Elder Abuse in Perspective.* Buckingham: Open University Press.

Binstock, R.H., (1997), 'The 1996 election: older voters and implications for policies on aging', *Gerontologist,* 37 (1) 15–19.

Binstock, R.H. and Day, C.L. (1995) 'Aging and politics', in R.H. Binstock and L.K. George (eds) *Handbook of Aging and the Social Sciences,* 4th edition. San Diego: Academic Press.

Black, D., Townsend, P., Davidson, N. and Whitehead, M. (eds) (1988) *Inequalities in Health: The Black Report The Health Divide.* London: Penguin.

Booth, C. (1892) *Pauperism, a Picture and the Endowment of Old Age, an Argument.* London: Macmillan.

Booth, T. (1985) *Home Truths: Old People's Homes and the Outcome of Care.* Aldershot: Gower.

Bornat, J. (1998) 'Pensioners organise: hearing the voice of older people', in M. Bernard and J. Phillips (eds) *The Social Policy of Old Age.* London: Centre for Policy on Ageing. pp. 183–99.

Bos, E. (1994) *World Population Projections, 1994–95 Edition: Estimates and Projections with Related Demographic Statistics.* Baltimore: Johns Hopkins University Press (published for the World Bank).

Bosanquet, N., Laing, W. and Propper, C. (1990) *Elderly Consumers in Britain: Europe's Poor Relations? Charting the Grey Economy in the 1990s.* London: Laing and Buisson.

Bourdelais, P. (1998) 'The ageing population: relevant question or obsolete notion?', in P. Johnson and P. Thane (eds) *Old Age from Antiquity to Post-Modernity.* London: Routledge. pp. 110–31.

Brathwaite, F.S. (1989) 'Social life among females aged 75 and over in Barbados', in PAHO *Mid-Life and Older women in Latin America and the Caribbean.* Washington, DC: PAHO. pp. 253–64.

Bulmer, M. (1986) *Neighbours: The Work of Philip Abrams.* Cambridge: Cambridge University Press.

Burman, S. (1989) 'Law versus reality: the interaction of community obligations to and by the black elderly in South Africa', in J. Eekelaar and D. Pearl (eds) *An Aging World: Dilemmas and Challenges for Law and Social Policy.* Oxford: Clarendon Press. pp. 211–25.

Burnley, I.H., Encel, S. and McCall, G. (eds) (1985) *Immigration and Ethnicity in the 1980s.* Melbourne: Longman Cheshire.

Butler, D. and Stokes, D. (1974) *Political Change in Britain: The Evolution of Electoral Choice.* London: Macmillan.

Buton, F. (1992) 'La Production Sociale d'une Présence Illégitime', *Le Vieillissement des Immigrés en Région Parisienne.* Paris: Fonds d'Action Sociale. pp. 313–90.

Bytheway, B. (1995) *Ageism.* Buckingham: Open University Press.

Cain, M. (1986a) 'Risk and fertility: a reply to Robinson', *Population Studies* 40(2): 299–304.

Cain, M. (1986b) 'The consequences of reproductive failure', *Population Studies* 40(3): 375–88.

Calasanti, T.M. and Zajicek, A.M. (1997) 'Gender, the state, and constructing the old as dependent: lessons from the economic transition of Poland', *Gerontologist* 37(4): 452–61.

Caldwell, J.C. and Caldwell, P. (1992) 'Family systems: their viability and vulnerability', in E.

Berquó and P. Xenos (eds) *Family Systems and Cultural Change*. Oxford: Oxford University Press. pp. 46–66.

Callahan, D. (1995) 'Aging and the life cycle: a moral norm', in D. Callahan, R.H.J. ter Meulen and E. Topinková (eds) *A World Growing Old: the Coming Health Care Challenges*. Washington, DC: Georgetown University Press. pp. 20–7.

Campani, G. (1995) 'Women migrants: from marginal subjects to social actors', in R. Cohen (ed.) *The Cambridge Survey of World Migration*. Cambridge: Cambridge University Press. pp. 546–50.

Campbell, J.C. (1992) *How Policies Change: The Japanese Government and the Aging Society*. Princeton, NJ: Princeton University Press.

Case, A. and Deaton, A. (1996) *Large Cash Transfers to the Elderly in South Africa*. Cambridge, MA: National Bureau of Economic Research.

Castle, N.G., Fogel, B. and Mor, V. (1997) 'Risk factors for physical restraint in nursing homes: pre- and post-implementation of the Nursing Home Reform Act', *Gerontologist* 37(6): 737–47.

Castles, S. and Miller, M.J. (1998) *The Age of Migration*. Basingstoke: Macmillan.

Cayley, A.C.D. (1987) *Hospital Geriatric Medicine*. London: Edward Arnold.

Chaney, E.M. (1989) 'The empowerment of old women: a cross-cultural view', paper presented at the Conference 'Coping with Social Change'. Acapulco, Mexico.

Chant, S. (1990) *Women and Survival in Mexican Cities: Perspectives on Gender, Labour Markets and Low-Income Households*. Manchester: Manchester University Press.

Chant, S. (1997) *Gender Aspects of Urban Economic Growth and Development*. Helsinki: UNU World Institute for Development Economics Research.

Chantreaux, A. and Marcoux-Moumen, R. (1991) 'Entre ici et là-bas', *Mutations* 124: 185–91.

Chelala, C.A. (1992) *Health of the Elderly: A Concern for All*. Washington, DC: Pan American Health Organization.

Chen, A.J. and Jones, G.W. (1989) *Ageing in ASEAN: Its Socio-Economic Consequences*. Singapore: Institute of Southeast Asian Studies.

Cheung, P. and Vasoo, S. (1992) 'Ageing population in Singapore: a case study', in D.R. Phillips (ed.) *Ageing in East and Southeast Asia*. London: Arnold. pp. 77–104.

Clough, R. (1981) *Old Age Homes*. London: Allen and Unwin.

Cm 4192-I (1999) *With Respect to Old Age: Long Term Care – Rights and Responsibilities: A Report by the Royal Commission on Long Term Care*. London: HMSO.

Cohen, L. (1992) 'No aging in India: the uses of gerontology', *Culture, Medicine and Psychiatry*, 16 (2): 123–62.

Cohen, L. (1998) *No Aging in India: Alzheimer's, the Bad Family, and Other Modern Things*. Berkeley: University of California Press.

Coolen, J.A.I. (ed.) (1993) *Changing Care for the Elderly in the Netherlands*. Assen/Maastricht: Van Gorcum.

Cowgill, D.O. and Holmes, L.D. (1972) *Aging and Modernization*. New York: Appleton.

Cribier, F. (1990) 'Mobilité résidentielle et stratégie sociale dans les 15 ans qui suvient la retraite: suivi d'une génération de Parisiens', in C. Bonvalet and A.-M. Fribourg (eds) *Stratégies Résidentielles*. Paris: Institut National d'études Démographiques.

Cribier, F. and Kych, A. (1992) 'The migration of retired Parisians – an analysis of a propensity toward departure', *Population*, 47(3): 677–717.

Cumming, E. and Henry, W.E. (1961) *Growing Old: The Process of Disengagement*. New York: Basic Books.

Cylwik, H. and Wilson, G. (1996) 'Cypriot elders and their carers', Report to Enfield Council, Enfield.

DaneAge Foundation (1990) *New Horizons – New Elderly DaneAge Foundation's Study on the Future Elderly.* Copenhagen: Senior Forlaget.

Davies, G. (1998) 'The real cost of IMF rescue deals', *The Independent,* 16 November.

Day, A.T. (1985) *We Can Manage: Expectations about Care and Varieties of Family Support among People 75 Years and Over.* Melbourne: Institute of Family Studies.

Day, L. (1992) *The Future of Low-Birthrate Populations.* London: Routledge.

Day, P., Klein, R.A., and Redmayne, S. (1996) *Why Regulate? Regulating Residential Care for Elderly People.* Bristol: The Policy Press.

Department of Health (1994) *Reasons Why Some Older People Choose Residential Care: The F Factor.* London: Department of Health.

Deven, F., Inglis, S., Moss, P. and Petrie, P. (1998) *State of the Art Review on the Reconciliation of Work and Family Life for Men and Women and the Quality of Care Services,* Research Report No 44. London: Department for Education and Employment.

Disney, R. (1996) *Can We Afford to Grow Older.* Cambridge, MA: MIT Press.

Disney, R., Grundy, E. and Johnson, P. (1997) *The Dynamics of Retirement: Analyses of the Retirement Surveys.* London: HMSO.

Dissenbacher, H. (1989) 'Neglect, abuse and the taking of life in old people's homes', *Ageing and Society* 9(1): 61–71.

Dixon, J. and Kim, H.S. (eds) (1985) *Social Welfare in Asia.* London: Croom Helm.

Dunleavy, P. and Husbands, C.T. (1985) *British Democracy at the Crossroads: Voting and Party Competition in the 1980s.* London: Allen and Unwin.

Dunning, A. (1998) 'Advocacy, empowerment and older people', in M. Bernard and J. Phillips (eds) *The Social Policy of Old Age.* London: Centre for Policy on Ageing. pp. 200–21.

du Toit, B.M. (1994) 'Does the road get lonelier? Aging in a Coloured community in South Africa', *Journal of Aging Studies* 8(4): 357–74.

Ebrahim, S. and Kalache, A. (1996) *Epidemiology in Old Age.* London: British Medical Journal Publishers.

Economic Planning Agency Government of Japan (no date) White paper on the national lifestyle towards a society of fulfilled longevity fiscal year 1994, Economic Planning Agency Government of Japan.

Eisenhandler, S.A. (1993) 'The asphalt indentikit: old age and the driver's licence', in B.B. Hess and E.W. Markson (eds) *Growing Old in America.* New Brunswick, NJ: Transaction. pp. 107–20.

Ekongot, J.R. (1993) 'Fuelling a small enterprise', in K. Tout (ed.) *Elderly Care: A World Perspective.* London: Chapman and Hall. pp. 135–9.

Ekpenyong, S. (1995) 'Structural adjustment programme and the elderly in Nigeria', *International Journal of Aging and Human Development* 41(4): 267–80.

Elman, C. (1995) 'Age-based mobilisation: the emergence of old age in American politics', *Ageing and Society,* 15(3): 299–324.

Estes, C. (1979) *The Aging Enterprise.* San Francisco, CA: Jossey Bass.

Estes, C.L., Swan, J.H. and Gerard, L.E. (1984) 'Dominant and competing paradigms in gerontology', in M. Minkler and C.L. Estes (eds) *Readings in the Political Economy of Aging.* Farmingdale, NY: Baywood. pp. 25–36.

Estes, C.L. and Binney, E.A. (1991) 'The biomedicalising of aging: dangers and dilemmas', in

M. Minkler and C.L. Estes (eds) *Critical Perspectives on Aging: The Political and Moral Economy of Growing Old*, Amityville, NY: Baywood. pp. 117–34.

Ethnic Affairs Commission of New South Wales (1992) *Ageing People of Non-English Speaking Background: A Policy Perspective*. Ashfield: Marketing and Public Affairs Division, Ethnic Affairs Commission of NSW.

Evans, L. and Williamson, J.B. (1984) 'Social control of the elderly', in M. Minkler and C.L. Estes (eds) *Readings in the Political Economy of Aging*. Farmingdale, NY: Baywood. 47–72.

Fagan, M. and Longino, C.F. (1993) 'Migrating retirees: a source for economic development', *Economic Development Quarterly* 7(1): 98–106.

Featherstone, M. and Hepworth, M. (1991) 'The mask of ageing and the postmodern life course', in M. Featherstone, M. Hepworth and B.S. Turner (eds) *The Body: Social Process and Cultural Theory*. London: Sage. pp. 371–89.

Featherstone, M. and Wernick, A. (eds) (1995) *Images of Ageing: Cultural Representations of Later Life*. London: Routledge.

Ferjani C. (1993) 'Vieillissement des immigrés maghrébins et demande de religion', in *Vieillir et Mourir en Exil: Immigration Maghrébine et Vieillissement*. Lyon: Presses Universitaires de Lyon.

Fishman, W.J. (1988) *East End 1888: A Year in a London Borough among the Labouring Poor*. London: Duckworth.

Foner, N. (1984) *Ages in Conflict*. New York: Columbia University Press.

Foner, N. (1994) 'Endnote: the reach of an idea', in M.W. Riley, R.L. Kahn and A. Foner (eds) *Age and Structural Lag*. New York: John Wiley. pp. 263–80.

Forster, M. (1989) *Have the Men Had Enough? A Novel*. London: Chatto and Windus.

Fortes, M. (1949) *The Web of Kinship Among the Tallensi*. London: Oxford University Press.

Foster, C. and Kendig, H. (eds) (1987) *Who Pays? Financing Services for Older People*. Canberra: Australian National University Press.

Foucault, M. (1980) *Power/Knowledge: Selected Interviews and other Writings 1972–1977*, ed. Colin Gordon. Brighton: Harvester Press.

Gavilan, H. (1992) 'Care in the community: issues of dependency and control – the similarities between institution and home', *Generations Review* 2 (4): 9–14.

Geddes, A. and Tonge, J. (eds) (1997) *Labour's Landslide: The British General Election 1997*. Manchester: Manchester University Press.

Ghai, D. (1992) *Structural Adjustment, Global Integration and Social Democracy*, United Nations Development Research Institute for Social Development, Discussion Paper No 37. Geneva: UNRISD.

Ghai, D. (1997) *Economic Globalisation, Institutional Change and Human Security*, United Nations Development Research Institute for Social Development, Discussion Paper No 91. Geneva: UNRISD.

Giarchi, G.G. (1996) *Caring for Older Europeans*. Aldershot: Avebury.

Gibson, D. (1996) 'Broken down by age and gender: "The Problem of Old Women" Redefined', *Gender and Society* 10(4): 433–48.

Gibson, D. (1998) *Aged Care: Old Policies, New Problems*. Cambridge: Cambridge University Press.

Giddens, A. (1991) *Modernity and Self-Identity: Self and Society in the Late Modern Age*. Cambridge: Polity.

Gifford, C.G. (1990) *Canada's Fighting Seniors*. Toronto: J. Lorimer.

Gilleard, C. (1996) 'Consumption and identity in later life: toward a cultural gerontology', *Ageing and Society* 16(4): 489–98.

Gillion, C. (1993) 'Structural adjustment and social security: the interaction', in *The Implications for Social Security of Structural Adjustment Policies*. Geneva: International Social Security Association. pp. 83–102.

Goffman, E. (1961) *Asylums: Essays on the Social Situation of Mental Patients and other Inmates*. Harmondsworth: Penguin.

Goldberg, A. (1996) 'The status and specific problems of elderly foreigners in the Federal Republic of Germany', *Journal of Comparative Family Studies* 27(1): 129–46.

Goodman, R., White, G. and Kwon, H.-J. (1998) *The East Asian Welfare Model*. London: Routledge.

Government of Canada, Health and Welfare Canada (1993) *Age and Independence: Overview of a National Survey*. Ottawa: Health and Welfare Canada.

Green, H. (1988) *Informal Carers: A Study Carried out on Behalf of the Department of Health and Social Security as Part of the 1985 General Household Survey*. London: HMSO.

Guardian (19 February 1999) 'Tanzania was paying more per head on debt servicing than its entire social expenditure on education and health'.

Gubrium, J.F. (1986) *Oldtimers and Alzheimer's: The Descriptive Organization of Senility*. Greenwich, CT: JAI Press.

Guillemard, A-M. (1980) *La vieillesse et l'Etat*. Paris: PUF.

Gullette, M.M. (1997) *Declining to Decline: Cultural Combat and the Politics of the Midlife*. Charlottesville: University of Virginia Press.

Gutmann, D. (1988) 'Age and leadership: cross cultural observations', in A. McIntyre (ed.) *Aging and Political Leadership*. Melbourne: Oxford University Press. pp. 89–101.

Gylfason, T. (1994) *The Path of Output from Plan to Market*, IMF working paper; WP/94/71. Washington, DC: International Monetary Fund.

Hardy, M.A. (ed.) (1997) *Studying Aging and Social Change*. Thousand Oaks, CA: Sage.

Harper, S. (1997) 'Constructing later life/constructing the body: some thoughts from feminist theory', in A. Jamieson, S. Harper and C. Victor (eds) *Critical Approaches to Ageing and Later Life*. Buckingham: Open University Press. pp. 160–72.

Harris, C.C. (1983) *The Family and Industrial Society*. London: Allen and Unwin.

Harriss, B. (1995) 'The intrafamily distribution of hunger in South Asia', in J. Drèze, A. Sen and A. Hussain (eds) *The Political Economy of Hunger: Selected Essays*. Oxford: Clarendon Press. pp. 224–97.

Hazan, H. (1980) *The Limbo People: A Study of the Constitution of the Time Universe among the Aged*. London: Routledge and Kegan Paul.

Health Advisory Service (1983) *The Rising Tide: Developing Services for Mental Illness in Old Age*. London: HMSO.

Health and Welfare Bureau for the Elderly, Ministry of Health and Welfare of Japan (1998) *New Gold Plan*. Ministry of Health and Welfare of Japan.

Health Solutions Pty. Ltd (1994) *Exporting Australia's Aged Care Services to Asia: Report*. Canberra: Australian Government Publishing Service.

Hedin, B. (1993) *Growing Old in Sweden*. Stockholm: Swedish Institute.

Heller, P.S., Hemming, R. and Kohnert, P.W. (1986) *Aging and Social Expenditure in the Major Industrial Countries 1980–2025*. Washington, DC: International Monetary Fund.

HelpAge International South Africa (1999) ' The contribution of older people to development:

the South Africa study', research dissemination workshop. Johannesburg: Kempton Park Conference Centre.

Hendricks, J. (1995) 'Older women in social and economic development', *Ageing International* 22(2): 55–8.

Henwood, M. (1993) 'Age discrimination in health care', in J. Johnson and R. Slater (eds) *Ageing and Later Life*. London: Sage. pp. 112–19.

Heycox, K. (1997) 'Older women: issues of gender', in A. Borowski, S. Encel and E. Ozanne (eds) *Ageing and Social Policy in Australia*. Cambridge: Cambridge University Press. pp. 94–118.

Hill, M.N. (1961) *An Approach to Old Age and its Problems*. Edinburgh: Oliver and Boyd.

Hills, J. (1993) *The Future of Welfare: A Guide to the Debate*. York: Joseph Rowntree Foundation.

Hochschild, A.R. (1973) *The Unexpected Community*. Englewood Cliffs, NJ: Prentice-Hall.

Howe, A.L. (1990) 'Nursing home care policy: from laissez faire to restructuring', in H. Kendig and J. McCallum (eds) *Grey Policy: Australian Policies for an Ageing Society*. Sydney: Allen and Unwin. pp. 150–69.

Howe, N. (1997) 'Why the graying of the welfare state threatens to flatten the American dream – or worse', in R.B. Hudson (ed.) *The Future of Age-Based Public Policy*. Baltimore, MD: The Johns Hopkins University Press. pp. 36–45.

Hunt, M.E., Feldt, A.G., Marans, R.W., Pastalan, L.A. and Vakalo, K.L. (1988) 'Retirement communities: an American original', *Journal of Housing for the Elderly* 1(3–4): 1–278.

Hunter, D., McKeganey, N.P. and MacPherson, I.A. (1988) *Care of the Elderly: Policy and Practice*. Aberdeen: University of Aberdeen Press.

Ignatieff, M. (1984) *The Needs of Strangers*. London: Chatto and Windus.

Ihromi, T.O. (1989) 'Social support systems in transition in Indonesia', in J.M. Eekelaar and D. Pearl (eds) *An Aging World: Dilemmas and Challenges for Law and Social Policy*. Oxford: Clarendon. pp, 133–44.

Iliffe, S., Mitchley, S., Gould, M. and Haines, A. (1994) 'Evaluation of the use of brief screening instruments for dementia, depression and problem drinking among elderly people in general practice', *British Journal of General Practice* 44(388): 503–7.

ILO (1986) *Economically Active Population Estimates and Projections, 1950–2025*. Geneva: International Labour Organization.

Jacobs, D. (1998) *Social Welfare Systems in East Asia: A Comparative Analysis Including Private Welfare*. London: Centre for the Analysis of Social Exclusion, London School of Economics.

Jacobs, R.H. (1980) 'Portrait of a phenomenon: the Gray Panthers: do they have a long-run future?', in E.W. Markson and G.R. Batra (eds) *Public Policies for Aging Populations*. Lexington, MA: Lexington. pp. 93–104.

Japan Research Institute on Child Welfare (1993) *Child Welfare Quarterly News from Japan* 14(2): 13–14.

Jeffery, P. and Jeffery, R. (1996) *Don't Marry Me to a Plowman*. Boulder, CO: Westview Press.

Jerrome, D. (1992) *Good Company: An Anthropological Study of Old People in Groups*. Edinburgh: Edinburgh University Press.

Johnson, M. (1993) 'Dependency and Interdependency', in J. Bond, P. Coleman and S. Peace (eds) *Ageing in Society: An Introduction to Social Gerontology*. London: Sage. pp. 255–79.

Johnson, P. (1988) 'The structured dependency of the elderly: a critical note', Centre for Economic Policy Research, Discussion Paper No. 202. London.

Johnson, P., Conrad, C. and Thomson, D. (1989) *Workers versus Pensioners: Intergenerational Justice in an Aging World.* Manchester: Manchester University Press.

Johnson, P. and Falkingham, J. (1992) *Ageing and Economic Welfare.* London: Sage.

Kalache, A. (1988) *Promoting Health among Elderly People: A Statement from a Working Group.* London: King Edward's Hospital Fund for London.

Kalache, A. (1993) 'Ageing in developing countries: has it got anything to do with us?', in J. Johnson and R. Slater (eds) *Ageing and Later Life.* London: Sage. pp. 339–43.

Kane, R. (1996) 'The future of group residential care', in OECD *Caring for Frail Elderly People, Social Policy Studies* OECD, No. 19. Paris: OECD. pp. 93–105.

Kaplan, K. M. and Longino, C.F. (1993) 'Gray in gold: a public-private conundrum', in B.B. Hess and E.W. Markson (eds) *Growing Old in America.* New Brunswick, NJ: Transaction. pp. 389–97.

Kastenbaum, R. (1993) 'Encrusted elders: Arizona and the political spirit of postmodern aging', in T.R. Cole, W.A. Achenbaum, P.L. Jakobi and R. Kastenbaum (eds) *Voices and Visions of Aging: Toward a Critical Gerontology.* New York: Springer. pp. 160–83.

Katz, S. (1996) *Disciplining Old Age: The Formation of Gerontological Knowledge.* Charlottesville: University Press of Virginia.

Kaul, I. (1997) 'Foreword', in L. Taylor and U. Pieper (eds) *Reconciling Economic Reform and Sustainable Human Development: Social Consequences of Neo-Liberalism.* New York: United Nations Development Programme.

Keith, J. (1982) *Old People, New Lives: Community Creation in a Retirement Residence.* Chicago: University of Chicago Press.

Keith, J. (1994a) *The Aging Experience: Diversity and Commonality across Cultures.* Thousand Oaks, CA: Sage.

Keith, J. (1994b) 'Old age and age integration: an anthropological perspective', in M.W. Riley, R.L. Kahn and A. Foner (eds) *Age and Structural Lag.* New York: John Wiley. pp. 197–216.

Kendig, H.L., Hashimoto, A. and Coppard, L.C. (eds) (1991) *Family Support for the Elderly: the International Experience.* Oxford: Oxford University Press.

King, R., Warnes, A.M. and Williams, A.M. (1998) 'International retirement migration in Europe', *International Journal of Population Geography,* 4(2): 91–111.

Knodel, J. and Chanpen, S. (1998) 'Studying living arrangements of the elderly: lessons from a quasi-qualitative case study approach in Thailand', Elderly in Asia Research Report no. 98–48. Ann Arbor: University of Michigan Population Studies Center.

Kobayashi, R. (1997) 'Developing health and long-term care for a more aged society', in OECD *Family, Market and Community: Equity and Efficiency in Social Policy.* Paris: OECD. pp. 189–205.

Koo, J. (1987) 'Widows in Seoul, Korea' in H. Lopata, (ed.) *Widows, Vol. 1: The Middle East, Asia, and the Pacific.* Durham, NC: Duke University Press. pp. 56–78.

Kovalainen, A. (1999) 'The welfare state, gender system and public sector employment in Finland', in A. Kovalainen, J. Christiansen and P. Koistinen (eds) *Working Europe: Reshaping European Employment Systems.* Aldershot: Ashgate. pp. 137–54.

Kovalainen, A. and Simonen, L. (1998) 'Paradoxes of social care: the Finnish case', in J. Lewis (ed.) *Gender, Social Care and Welfare State Restructuring in Europe.* Aldershot: Ashgate. pp. 229–56.

Koyana, W. (1996) 'Filial piety and intergenerational solidarity in Japan', *Australian Journal of Ageing,* 15(2): 51–6.

Krugman, P. (1996) 'The future of global growth', *Centrepiece* 1(3): 8–11.

Krugman, P. (1999) *The Return of Depression Economics.* Harmondsworth: Penguin.

Kwon, H.-J. (1999a) *Income Transfers to the Elderly in East Asia: Testing Asian Values*, Case Paper 27. London: Centre for the Analysis of Social Exclusion, London School of Economics.

Kwon, H.-J. (1999b) *The Welfare State in Korea: The Politics of Legitimation.* Basingstoke: Macmillan.

Kwong, P. and Guoxuan, C. (1992) 'Ageing in China: trends, problems and strategies', in D.R. Phillips (ed.) *Ageing in East and Southeast Asia.* London: Arnold. pp. 105–27.

Laing, W. (1991) *Empowering the Elderly: Direct Consumer Funding of Care Services.* London: Institute of Economic Affairs.

Latimer, J. (1997) 'Figuring identities: older people, medicine and time', in A. Jamieson, S. Harper and C. Victor (eds) *Critical Approaches to Ageing and Later Life.* Buckingham: Open University Press. pp. 143–59.

Laslett, P. (1989) *A Fresh Map of Life.* London: Weidenfeld and Nicolson.

Laslett, P. and Fishkin, J.S. (1992) *Philosophy, Politics and Society, 6th Series, Justice between Age Groups and Generations.* New Haven, CT: Yale University Press.

Lee, J.J. (1997) 'The policy of developing elderly services in Hong Kong: look back and look forward', in J.S. Ismael and E. Hill (eds) *Social Welfare and Social Development: Asian Experiences.* Calgary: Detselig Enterprises.

Leichsenring, K., Barh, C. and Strumpel, C. (1999) 'The politics of old age in Austria', in A. Walker and G. Naegele (eds) *The Politics of Old Age in Europe.* Buckingham: Open University Press. pp. 65–82.

Libercier, M.-H. and Schneider, H. (1996) *Migrants: Partners in Development Co-Operation.* Paris: Development Centre, OECD.

Liu, Z. (1996) *Length of Stay in Australian Nursing Homes.* Canberra: Australian Institute of Health and Welfare.

Lloyd-Sherlock, P. (1997) *Old Age and Urban Poverty in the Developing World: The Shanty Towns of Buenos Aires.* Basingstoke: Macmillan.

Lloyd-Sherlock, P. (1999) 'Old age, migration, and poverty in the shantytowns of São Paulo, Brazil', *The Journal of Developing Areas* 32(4): 491–514.

Lloyd-Sherlock, P. and Johnson, P. (1996) *Ageing and Social Policy: Global Comparisons.* London: Suntory Toyota International Centres for Economics and Related Disciplines, London School of Economics and Political Science.

Longino, C.F. (1990) 'Geographical distribution and migration', in R.H. Binstock and L.K. George (eds) *Handbook of Aging and the Social Sciences*, 3rd edn. San Diego, CA: Academic Press. pp. 45–63.

Longino, C.F., and Marshall, V.W. (1990) 'North American research on seasonal migration', *Ageing and Society* 10(2): 229–35.

Longman, P. (1987) *Born to Pay: The New Politics of Aging in America.* Boston, MA: Houghton Mifflin.

Lorenz-Meyer, D. (1996) 'The other side of the generational contract', LSE Discussion Papers, Issue 1. London: Gender Institute, London School of Economics.

Lorenz-Meyer, D. (1999) 'The gendered politics of generational contracts. Changing discourses and practices of intergenerational commitments in West Germany'. Unpublished PhD thesis, University of London.

Mackintosh, S., Means, R. and Leather, P. (1990) *Housing in Later Life.* Bristol: School of Advanced Urban Studies.

Maddox, G. (1978) 'Social and cultural context of aging', in G. Usdin and C.K. Hofling (eds) *Aging: The Process and the People.* New York: Brunner/Mazel. pp. 20–46.

Maddox, G. (1992) 'Long-term Care Policies in Comparative Perspective', *Ageing and Society* 12(3): 355–68.

Maria, P. (1993) 'Vieillir en foyer', in *Vieillir et mourir en exil: immigration maghrébine et vieillissement.* Lyon: Presses Universitaires de Lyon. pp. 123–9.

Markides, K.S., Liang, J. and Jackson, J.S. (1990) 'Race, ethnicity, and aging: conceptual and methodological issues', in R.H. Binstock and L.K. George (eds) *Handbook of Aging and the Social Sciences.* San Diego, CA: Academic Press. pp. 112–29.

Markides, K.S. and Mindel, C.H. (1987) *Age and Ethnicity.* Newbury Park, CA: Sage.

Markides, K.S. and Miranda, M.R. (eds) (1997) *Minorities, Aging, and Health.* Thousand Oaks, CA: Sage.

Martin, B. (1999) *The Whistle Blower's Handbook: How to be an Effective Resister.* Chipping Norton: Jon Carpenter.

Matthews, S. (1979) *The Social World of Old Women: Management of Self-Identity.* Beverly Hills, CA: Sage.

McCallum, J. (1990) 'Winners and losers in retirement income', in H. Kendig and J. McCallum (eds) *Grey Policy: Australian Policies for an Ageing Society.* Sydney: Allen and Unwin. pp. 55–73.

McCallum, J. and Geiselhart, K. (1996) *Australia's New Aged.* Sydney: Allen and Unwin.

McCreadie, C. (1996) *Elder Abuse: Update on Research.* London: Age Concern Institute of Gerontology.

McHugh, K.E. and Mings, R.C. (1994) 'Seasonal migration and health care', *Journal of Aging and Health* 6(1): 111–32.

McKeown, T. (1976) *The Modern Rise of Population.* London: Edward Arnold.

McMurdo, M.E.T. and Burnett, L. (1992) 'Randomised controlled trial of exercise in the elderly', *Gerontology,* 38: 292–8.

McNeely, R.L. and Cohen, J.L. (eds) (1983) *Aging in Minority Groups.* Beverly Hills, CA: Sage.

Means, R. (1988) 'Council housing, tenure polarisation and older people in two contrasting localities', *Ageing and Society* 8(4): 395–421.

Meyer, M.H. (1993) 'Organising the frail elderly', in B.B. Hess and E.W. Markson (eds) *Growing Old in America.* New Brunswick, NJ: Transaction. pp. 363–76.

Middleton, L. (1987) *So Much for So Few: A View of Sheltered Housing.* Liverpool: Liverpool University Press.

Millar, J. and Warman, A. (1996) *Family Obligations in Europe.* London: Family Policy Studies Centre.

Minkler, M. (1991) '"Generational equity" and the new victim blaming', in M. Minkler and C.L. Estes (eds) *Critical Perspectives on Aging: The Political and Moral Economy of Growing Old.* Amityville, NY: Baywood. pp. 67–80.

Morris, J. (1993) *Independent Lives? Community Care and Disabled People.* Basingstoke: Macmillan.

Moser, C.O.N. (1996) *Household Responses to Poverty and Vulnerability.* Washington, DC: World Bank.

Murgatroyd, L. and Neuburger, H. (1997) 'A household satellite account for the UK', *Economic Trends* 527(October): pp. 63–9.

Murphy, E. (1986) *Dementia and Mental Illness in the Old.* London: Papermac.

Myerhoff, B. (1992) 'Surviving stories: reflections on *Number Our Days*', in B. Myerhoff, (ed.) *Remembered Lives.* Ann Arbor: University of Michigan Press. pp. 277–304.

Myers, G.C. (1990) 'Demography of aging', in R.H. Binstock and L.K. George (eds) *Handbook of Aging and the Social Sciences,* 3rd edn. San Diego, CA: Academic Press. pp. 19–44.

Myles, J. (1991) 'Postwar capitalism and the extension of social security into a retirement wage', in M. Minkler and C.L. Estes (eds) *Critical Perspectives on Aging: The Political and Moral Economy of Growing Old*. Amityville, NY: Baywood. pp. 293–309.

Naegele, G. (1999) 'The politics of old age in Germany', in A. Walker and G. Naegele (eds) *The Politics of Old Age in Europe*. Buckingham: Open University Press. pp. 93–109.

Nana Apt, A. (1996) *Coping with Old Age in a Changing Africa: Social Change and the Elderly Ghanaian*. Aldershot: Avebury.

Newell, C. (1988) *Methods and Models in Demography*. London: Bellhaven.

Newbold, K.B. (1996) Determinants of elderly interstate migration in the United States, 1985–1990', *Research on Aging*, 18(4): 451–76.

Neysmith, S.M. and Edwardh, J. (1984) 'Economic dependency in the 1980s: its impact on third world elderly', *Ageing and Society* 4(1): 21–44.

Nolan, M., Grant, G. and Keady, J. (1996) *Understanding Family Care: A Multidimensional Model of Caring and Coping*. Buckingham: Open University Press.

Noiriel, G. (1992) *Le Vieillissement des Immigrés en Région Parisienne*. Paris: Fonds d'Action Sociale.

Norman, A. (1985) *Triple Jeopardy: Growing Old in a Second Homeland*. London: Centre for Policy on Ageing.

Normann, R. (1991) *Service Management: Strategy and Leadership in Service Business*. Chichester: Wiley.

Norris, P. (1998) *Elections and Voting Behaviour: New Challenges, New Perspectives*. Aldershot: Ashgate.

Nussbaum, M. (1995) 'Human capabilities, female human beings', in M. Nussbaum and J. Glover (eds) *Women, Culture and Development*. Oxford: Oxford University Press. pp. 61–104.

Nyanguru, A. (1987) 'Residential care for the destitute elderly', *Journal of Cross-Cultural Gerontology* 2(4): 345–7.

Nydegger, C. (1987) 'Family ties of the aged in cross-cultural perspective', in B.B. Hess and E.W. Markson (eds) *Growing Old in America*. New Brunswick, NJ: Transaction. pp. 71–85.

Observer (26 November 1989) 'Old people's homes go to multinationals: Charities fear big business "granny farms"'.

OECD Group on Urban Affairs (1992) *Urban Policies for Ageing Populations*. Paris: OCED.

OECD (1996) *Caring for Frail Elderly People, Social Policy Studies No. 19*. Paris: OECD.

OECD (1998) *Maintaining Prosperity in an Ageing Society*. Paris: OECD.

Olshansky S.J. (1995) 'Mortality crossovers and selective survival in human and nonhuman populations, introduction', *Gerontologist*, 35(5): 583–7.

Opie, A. (1992) *There's Nobody There: Community Care of Confused Older People*. Philadelphia: University of Pennsylvania Press.

Orme, A., McKenzie, R., Kearney, P. and Hayward, D. (1994) *Aged Care Discussion Paper 57*. Sydney: Law Reform Commission.

Ortendahl, C. (1997) 'Commentary on Mr Kobayashi's paper', in OECD, *Family, Market and Community Equity and Efficiency in Social Policy*. Paris: OECD. pp. 207–9.

Palmore, E.B. (1990) *Ageism Negative and Positive*. New York: Springer.

Pampel, F.C. (1998) *Aging, Social Inequality and Public Policy*. Thousand Oaks, CA: Pine Forge Press.

Paul, S.S. and Paul, J.A. (1995) 'World Bank, pensions, and income (in)security in the global South', *International Journal of Health Services*, 25(4): 697–725.

Peace, S., Kellaher, L. and Willcocks, D. (1997) *Re-Evaluating Residential Care*. Buckingham: Open University Press.

Pensabene, T.S. (1987) 'Multiculturalism and services for the ethnic aged: from philosophy to practice', in C. Foster and H.L. Kendig (eds) *Who Pays? Financing Services for Older People*. Canberra: Australian National University. pp. 215–33.

Pertierra, R. (ed.) (1992) *Remittances and Returnees*. Quezon City, Philippines: New Day Publishers.

Peterson, E.T. (1989) 'Elderly parents and their offspring', in S.J. Bahr and E.T. Peterson (eds) *Aging and the Family*. Lexington, MA: Lexington. pp. 175–91.

Phillipson, C. (1982) *Capitalism and the Construction of Old Age*. London: Macmillan.

Plant, R. and Barry, N. (1990) *Citizenship and Rights in Thatcher's Britain: Two Views*. London: Institute of Economic Affairs Health and Welfare Unit.

Potash, B. (ed.) (1986) *Widows in African Societies*. Stanford, CA: Stanford University Press.

Potts, L. and Grotheer, A. (1997) 'Arbeitsmigration als Frauenprojekt? Migrantinnen aus der Türkei zur retrospektiven Evaluation der Migration', in U. Loeber-Pautsch et al. (eds) *Quer zu den Disziplinen. Beiträge aus der Sozial-, Umwelt- und Wissenschaftsforschung*. Hannover: Offizin. pp. 77–101.

Pratt, H.J. (1976) *The Gray Lobby*. Chicago, IL: University of Chicago Press.

Pratt, H.J. (1993) *Gray Agendas*. Ann Arbor: University of Michigan Press.

Pritchard, J. (1992) *The Abuse of Elderly People: A Handbook for Professionals*. London: Jessica Kingsley.

Putnam, J.K. (1970) *Old Age Politics in California*. Stanford, CA: Stanford University Press.

Quadagno, J. (1993) 'Generational Equity and Politics of the Welfare State', in B.B. Hess and E.W. Markson (eds) *Growing Old in America*. New Brunswick, NJ: Transaction. pp. 342–51.

Quah, D.T. (1996) *The Invisible Hand and the Weightless Economy*, London School of Economics, Centre for Economic Performance Occasional Paper: 12. London: London School of Economics.

Qureshi, H. and Simons, K. (1987) 'Resources within families: caring for elderly people', in J. Brannen and G. Wilson (eds) *Give and Take in Families: Studies in Resource Distribution*. London: Allen and Unwin. pp. 117–35.

Qureshi, K. and Walker, A. (1989) *The Caring Relationship: Elderly People and their Families*. Basingstoke: Macmillan Education.

Richards, M. (1996) *Community Care for Older People: Rights, Remedies and Finances*. Bristol: Jordans.

Riggs, A. (1997) 'Men, Friends and Widowhood: toward Successful Ageing', *Australian Journal on Ageing* 16(4): 132–85.

Riley, M.W. (1996) 'Discussion: what does it all mean?', *Gerontologist* 36(2): 256–8.

Riley, M.W. and Riley, J.W. (1994) 'Structural lag: past and future', in M.W. Riley, R.L. Kahn and A. Foner (eds) *Age and Structural Lag*. New York: John Wiley. pp. 263–80.

Rivlin, A.M. and Wiener, J.M. (1988) *Caring for the Disabled Elderly: Who Will Pay?* Washington, DC: Brookings Institution.

Robert, N. (1992) 'Enquête sur quatre Sénégalais vieillissant en France', in *Le Vieillissement des immigrés en région Parisienne*. Paris: Fonds d'Action Sociale. pp. 405–75.

Robertson, A. (1997) 'Beyond apocalyptic demography: towards a moral economy on interdependence', *Ageing and Society* 17(4): 425–46.

Robinson, R. and Judge, K. (1987) *Public Expenditure and the NHS: Trends and Prospects*. London: King's Fund Institute.

Robinson, W.C. (1986) 'High fertility as risk insurance', *Population Studies* 40(2): 289–98.

Rondinelli, D.A. (1998) *Institutions and Market Development: Capacity Building for Economic and Social Transition*. Geneva: ILO.

Rose, R. and McAllister, I. (1990) *The Loyalties of Voters: A Lifetime Learning Model*. London: Sage.

Ross, S.G. (1996) 'Public versus private pensions: dimensions for a worldwide debate', in *Protecting Retirement Incomes: Options for Reform*. Geneva: International Social Security Association. pp. 362–87.

Rubinstein, R.L. (1990) 'Nature, culture, gender, age: a critical review', in R.L. Rubinstein (ed) *Anthropology and Aging*. Dordrecht: Kluwer. pp. 109–28.

Rwezaura, B. A. (1989) 'Changing community obligations to the elderly in contemporary Africa', in J. Eekelaar and D. Pearl (eds) *An Aging World: Dilemmas and Challenges for Law and Social Policy*. Oxford: Clarendon. pp. 113–31.

Sainsbury, S. (1993) *Normal Life: A Study of War and Industrially Injured Pensioners*. Aldershot: Avebury.

Salvage, A.V. (1991) *'Elderly People in Cold Conditions': An Annotated Bibliography Compiled from a Literature Review Undertaken for a Study of Elderly People in Cold Conditions*. London: Age Concern Institute of Gerontology.

Sawchuk, K.A. (1995) 'From gloom to boom', in M. Featherstone and A. Wernick (eds) *Images of Ageing: Cultural Representations of Later Life*. London: Routledge. pp. 173–87.

Sax, S. (1990) 'Development of public policy for the aged', in H. Kendig and J. McCallum (eds) *Grey Policy: Australian Policies for an Ageing Society*. Sydney: Allen and Unwin. pp. 23–40.

Sayad, A. (1993) *L'immigration, ou, Les paradoxes de l'altérité*. Brussels: Éditions Universitaires, De Boeck Université.

Scharf, T. (1998) *Ageing and Ageing Policy in Germany*. Oxford: Berg.

Scherer, P. (1996) 'The economics of adequacy: some observations on the debate', in *Protecting Retirement Incomes: Options for Reform*. Geneva: International Social Security Association. pp. 19–25.

Schmidt, M.G. (1990) *Negotiating a Good Old Age: Challenges of Residential Living in Late Life*. San Francisco, CA: Jossey-Bass.

Schuller, T. (1986) *Age, Capital and Democracy*. Aldershot: Gower.

Schulz, J.H. (1993) 'Economic support in old age: the role of social insurance in developing countries', in *The Implications for Social Security of Structural Adjustment Policies*. Geneva: International Social Security Association. pp. 15–82.

Scrutton, S. (1992) *Ageing, Healthy and in Control: An Alternative Approach to Maintaining the Health of Older People*. London: Chapman and Hall.

Sen, A.K. (1989) 'Women's survival as a development problem', Address to the 1700th Meeting of the American Academy of Arts and Sciences, 8 March.

Sen, A. (1993) 'Capability and well-being', in M. Nussbaum and A. Sen (eds) *The Quality of Life*. Oxford: Clarendon. pp. 30–53.

Sen, K. (1994) *Ageing: Debates on Demographic Transition and Social Policy*. London, Atlantic Highlands, NJ: Zed Books.

Sidell, M. (1995) *Health in Old Age*. Buckingham: Open University Press.

Simics, A. (1987) 'Ethnicity as a Career for the Elderly: The Serbian American Case', *Journal of Applied Gerontology* 6: 113–26.

Sinclair, I. (1988) 'Residential care: the research reviewed', in *Residential care: a Positive Choice*.

Report of the Independent Review of Residential Care, chaired by Gillian Wagner (Wagner Report). London: HMSO (on behalf of the National Institute for Social Work).

Sine, B. (1984) 'L'évolution du modèle africain' in *Mieux vivre pour bien vieillir*. Paris: Centre International de Gérontologie Sociale. pp. 315–17.

Sodei, T. (1995) 'Tradition impedes organizational empowerment in Japan', in D. Thursz, C. Nusburg and J. Prather (eds) *Empowering Older People*. London: Cassell. pp. 91–7.

Southwark (1988) *Independent Inquiry into the Running of Nye Bevan Lodge*. London: Southwark Council.

Ssenkoloto, G.M. (1984) 'Exemples de contributions des personnes âgées au développement rural africain' in *Mieux vivre pour bien vieillir*. Paris: Centre International de Gérontologie Sociale. pp. 17–32.

Stallman, J.I. and Jones, L.L. (1995) 'A typology of retirement places: a community analysis', *Journal of the Community Development Society* 26(1): 1–14.

Stearns, P. (1977) *Old Age in European Society*. London: Croom Helm.

Steinmetz, S.K. (1988) *Duty Bound: Elder Abuse and Family Care*, Newbury Park, CA: Sage.

Stevenson, O. (1989) *Age and Vulnerability: A Guide to Better Care*. London: Edward Arnold.

Stokes, E.M. (1990) 'Ethnography of a social border: the case of an American retirement community in Mexico', *Journal of Cross-Cultural Gerontology* 5(2): 169–82.

Street, D. (1998) 'Special interests or citizens' rights? "Senior Power": Social security and medicare', in C. Estes and M. Minkler (eds) *Critical gerontology: perspectives from political and moral economy*. Amtyville, NY: Baywood. pp. 109–30.

Takahashi, T. and Someya, Y. (1985) 'Japan', in J. Dixon and H.S. Kim (eds) *Social Welfare in Asia*. London: Croom Helm. pp. 133–75.

Tester, S. (1996) *Community Care for Older People: A Comparative Perspective*. Houndsmills, Basingstoke: Macmillan.

Timaeus, I. (1986) 'Families and households of the elderly population: prospects for those approaching old age', *Ageing and Society* 6(3) 271–93.

Titley, M. and Chasey, B. (1996) 'Across differences of age: young women speaking of and with old women', in S. Wilkinson and C. Kitzinger (eds) *Representing the Other*. London: Sage. pp. 147–51.

Thompson, P., Itzin, C. and Abendstern, M. (1990) *I Don't Feel Old: The Experience of Later Life*. Oxford: Oxford University Press.

Torres-Gil, F.M. (1992) *The New Aging: Politics and Change in America*. New York: Auburn House.

Tout, K. (1989) *Ageing in Developing Countries*. Oxford: Oxford University Press.

Tout, K. (ed.) (1993) *Elderly Care: A World Perspective*. London: Chapman and Hall.

Townsend, P. (1962) *The Last Refuge: A Survey of Residential Institutions and Homes for the Aged in England and Wales*. London: Routledge and Kegan Paul.

Townsend, P. (1981) 'The structured dependency of the elderly: the creation of social policy in the twentieth century', *Ageing and Society* 1(1): 5–28.

Tracy, M.B. (1991) *Social Policies for the Elderly in the Third World*. New York: Greenwood Press.

Troyansky, D.G. (1982) 'Old age in the rural family of enlightened Provence', in P. Stearns (ed.) *Old Age in Preindustrial Society*. New York: Holmes and Meier. pp. 209–31.

Twigg, J. (1996) 'Issues in informal care', in OECD *Caring for Frail Elderly People: Policies in Evolution*. Paris: OECD. pp. 81–92.

Twigg, J., (1997) 'Deconstructing the "social bath": help with bathing at home for elderly and disabled people', *Journal of Social Policy* 26(2): 211–32.

Twigg, J. and Atkin, K. (1994) *Carers Perceived: Policy and Practice in Informal Care*. Buckingham: Open University Press.

Umali-Deininger, D. and Maguire, C. (eds) (1995) *Agriculture in Liberalizing Economies: Changing Roles for Governments: Proceedings of the Fourteenth Agricultural Symposium* (14th: 1994: World Bank). Washington, DC: World Bank.

United Nations (1991) *The World Ageing Situation*. New York: Center for Social Development and Humanitarian Affairs, United Nations.

United Nations Department of International Economic and Social Affairs (1991) *Ageing and Urbanization: Proceedings of the United Nations International Conference on Ageing Populations in the Context of Urbanization*. New York: United Nations.

United Nations (1992) *Economic and Social Development Aspects of Population Ageing in Kerala, India*. New York: United Nations.

Van Den Hoonaard, K. (1994) 'Paradise lost: widowhood in a Florida retirement community', *Journal of Aging Studies* 8(2): 121–32.

Vesperi, M.D. (1985) *City of Green Benches: Growing Old in a New Downtown*. Ithaca, NY: Cornell University Press.

Victor, C. (1987) *Old Age in Modern Society*. London: Croom Helm.

Victor, C. (1991) *Health and Health Care in Later Life*. Milton Keynes: Open University Press.

Vincent, J.A. (1995) *Inequality and Old Age*. London: UCL Press.

Wagner, G. (1988) 'Residential care: a positive choice', Report of the Independent Review of Residential Care chaired by Gillian Wagner (Wagner Report). London: HMSO (on behalf of the National Institute for Social Work).

Walker, A. (1980) 'The social creation of poverty and dependency in old age', *Journal of Social Policy* 9(1): 45–75.

Walker, A. (1981) 'Towards a political economy of old age', *Ageing and Society* 1(1): 73–94.

Walker, A. (1993) *Age and Attitudes: Main Results from a Eurobarometer Survey*. Brussels: Commission of the European Communities.

Walker, A. (1999) 'Political participation and representation of older people in Europe', in A. Walker and G. Naegele (eds) *The Politics of Old Age in Europe*. Buckingham: Open University Press. pp. 7–24.

Wall, R. (1995) 'Elderly persons and members of their households in England and Wales from preindustrial time to the present', in D.I. Kertzer and P. Laslett (eds) *Aging in the Past: Demography, Society, and Old Age*. Berkeley: University of California Press. pp. 81–106.

Wall, R. (ed.) with Robin, J. and Laslett, P. (1982) *Family Forms in Historic Europe*. Cambridge: Cambridge University Press.

Wallace, S.P., Williamson, J.B., Lung, R.G. and Powell, L.A. (1991) 'A lamb in wolf's clothing? The reality of senior power and social policy', in M. Minkler and C.L. Estes (eds) *Critical Perspectives on Aging: The Political and Moral Economy of Growing Old*. Amityville: Baywood. pp. 95–116.

Weeden, J.P., Newcomer, R.J. and Byerts, T.O. (1986) 'Housing and shelter for frail and nonfrail elders: current options and future directions', in R.J. Newcomer, M.P. Lawton and T.O. Byerts (eds) *Housing an Aging Society: Issues, Alternatives, and Policy*. New York: Van Nostrand Reinhold. pp. 181–8.

Warnes, A.M. and Patterson, G. (1998) ' British retirees in Malta: components of the cross-national relationships', *International Journal of Population Geography*, 4(2): 113–33.

Wicks, M.. and Henwood, M. (1984) *The Forgotten Army: Family Care and Elderly People*. London: Family Policy Studies Centre.

Wiener, J., Illston, L.H. and Hanley, R.J. (1994) *Sharing the Burden: Strategies for Public and Private Long-Term Care Insurance*. Washington, DC: The Brookings Institution.

Whittaker, T., (1995) 'Gender and elder abuse', in S. Arber and J. Ginn (eds) *Connecting Gender and Ageing*. Buckingham: Open University Press. pp. 144–57.

Wilkinson, R.G. (1996) *Unhealthy Societies: The Afflictions of Inequality*. London: Routledge.

Wilkinson, S. and Kitzinger, C. (eds) (1996) *Representing the Other*. London: Sage.

Williams, A. (1994) *Economics, QALYS and Medical Ethics: A Health Economist's Perspective*. York: Centre for Health Economics University of York.

Williams, A.M., King, R. and Warnes, T. (1997) 'A place in the sun: international retirement migration from Northern to Southern Europe', *European Urban and Regional Studies* 4(2): 115–34.

Williamson, J.B. (1997) 'A critique of the case for privatizing Social Security', *Gerontologist* 37(5): 561–71.

Williamson, J.B., Evans, L. and Powell, L.A. (1982) *Politics of Aging*. Springfield, IL: Charles C. Thomas.

Wilson, G. (1993) 'Abuse of elderly men and women among clients of a community psychogeriatric service', *British Journal of Social Work* 42: 681–700.

Wilson, G. (1994) 'Co-production and self care: new approaches to managing community care services for older people', *Social Policy and Administration* 26(3): 236–50.

Wilson, G. (1995) 'I'm the eyes and she's the arms: changes in gender roles in advanced old age', in S. Arber and J. Ginn (eds) *Connecting Gender and Ageing*. Buckingham: Open University Press. pp. 98–113.

Wilson, G. (1997) 'Demography, economics and the study of old age: "bad science" and "ageist knowledge"', *Health Care and Illness in Later Life* 2(4): 260–70.

Wilson, G., Cylwik, H., Grotheer, A. and Potts, L. (1999) 'Age, migration, gender and empowerment: the case of older migrant women in Europe', in *Ageing in a Gendered World: Women's Issues and Identities*. Santo Domingo: UN/INSTRAW. pp. 385–91.

Wirakartakusumah, M.D., Nurdin, H. and Wongkaren, T.S. (1997) 'The role of Indonesian women in an ageing society', in K. Mehta (ed.) *Untapped Resources: Women in Ageing Societies across Asia*. Singapore: Times Academic Press.

World Bank (1994) *Averting the Old Age Crisis*. Washington, DC: World Bank.

World Bank (1996) *From Plan to Market World: World Development Report 1996*. New York: Oxford University Press for the World Bank.

World Bank (1997) *The State in a Changing World: World Development Report 1997*. New York: Oxford University Press for the World Bank.

Wright, F.D. (1995) *Opening doors: A Case Study of Multi-Purpose Residential Homes*. London: HMSO.

Wu, S.C. and Chu, C.-M. (1996) 'Public attitudes towards long-term care arrangements for the elderly in Taiwan', *Australian Journal on Ageing* 15(2): 62–8.

Yoshida, S. (ed.) (1996) *Aging in Japan*. Tokyo: Japan Aging Research Centre.

Youll, P.J. and McCourt-Perring, C. (1993) *Raising Voices: Ensuring Quality in Residential Care*. London: HMSO.

INDEX